How to Chat with Archangels

How to Chat with Archangels

Inviting Your Divine Best Friends into Your Life

DEBRA SCHILDHOUSE

Waterside Productions

ISBN-13: 978-1-960583-56-7 print edition
ISBN-13: 978-1-960583-57-4 e-book edition

Waterside Productions
2055 Oxford Ave
Cardiff, CA 92007
www.waterside.com

For Howard,
Thank you, my love, for being on this incredible journey with me.

Contents

Preface

Writing this book has been my absolute pleasure and a true labor of love. I am honored, dear readers, to introduce you to your Divine Best Friends, the Archangels, and show you how incredible it is to connect and chat with them.

Communicating with Archangels, believe it or not, is actually a natural experience for humans, although you'd never know it. It isn't something that's talked much about, let alone taught.

But I promise you, everyone can practice Angelic communication and have the kind of success they may only dream about. It becomes second nature pretty quickly; the hardest part about chatting with the Archangels is believing that you really can.

I will be introducing you to the ten Archangels who regularly come through to me during Angel chats, and to the one Archangel (often referred to as the Angel of Death) who came through a few times, and whom I'd rather didn't come back.

You'll find out who they all are and how each Archangel is suited to help humans in specific areas of life. I explain why I craved having a relationship with them in the first place, and how I first started chatting with them and receiving their side of the conversation.

You'll be amazed at the experiences I've enjoyed with each Archangel, astounded by the signs they've sent to me, and amused as those signs were showcased right before my skeptical husband's eyes.

Then I'll teach you my simple method, along with the steps that work best for me. I include ways I've discovered to fine-tune your connection—your ability to receive information from the Archangels.

There is nothing special you need to buy or know, and it doesn't matter whether you are devoutly religious or follow no religion at all. The Archangels are pure love, and their love for you runs deeper than you can imagine.

It is my dearest wish that after reading this book, you will have a better understanding of and appreciation for that love. That kind of devotion and support is bound to enhance your life, as it has mine.

And I pray that you will be ready and excited to start delighting in your own relationship with your Divine Best Friends. I know they are ready and looking forward to sharing their adoration and wisdom with you.

May you rest easy in their comfort, guidance, protection, and most of all, their love, from this day forward.

Chapter One
My Visitors Arrive

I was nervous, yet elated. My guests would be coming soon, and they weren't like any visitors I'd ever entertained. I paced the foyer of our house like a twitchy cat, stopping every few minutes to check the time on the security system keypad by the door. It was 10:26 p.m. They would arrive in four minutes.

Wearing a nightgown and slippers, I padded into the family room, where the dimmed lamps added to the subdued atmosphere. My husband slept peacefully in our bedroom down the hall.

It was no surprise to me that when I'd offered him the opportunity to meet these particular guests, Howard had declined. "Sorry hon," he smiled, "that's past my bedtime. But you're the night owl, so have a good time."

As I would have for any guests, I'd done some prep work to get ready. In fact, I had received an email six days earlier with exact instructions:

1. Prepare a small altar, and include a white flower in water, and a long-burning candle that will stay lit most of the time.
2. Place a sealed envelope containing your three hand-written and heart-felt wishes, alongside the candle and flower. Your three wishes can be about anything, such as Mother Earth, your family, or yourself.

3. Lay the sealed envelope flat. On top of it, you will place an apple that you will eat only after they leave. By then, it will have special healing energy impregnated into it.
4. Make sure your house is clean and tidy, creating a welcoming environment.

So, who were these guests with such unusual requirements? Archangels! Five of the Archangels were on their way to our home and would be staying for five days.

I had been further instructed to invite Archangel Michael, Archangel Uriel, Archangel Raphael, Archangel Metatron, and Archangel Gabriel in through my front door at 10:30 p.m. Wednesday night, February 23rd, 2011.

The Archangels had already visited a friend's house the week before. Afterward, she had asked three other friends if they'd like to host the Archangels, and I was among those who had happily accepted.

In fact, around that time in 2011, many people all over the world were receiving emails with instructions for anyone who wanted to host the Archangels.

Apparently the phenomenon began after a German medium named Imiri was visited by some Archangels. I don't know if the visit lasted five days, but it was supposedly life-changing for her.

Then after Imiri saw the movie *Pay It Forward*, she was inspired to 'pay it forward' herself by creating a way to offer people the chance to host five of the Archangels in their homes. She knew from personal experience that hosting them would bring deeper connections, love, light, and so much more to the hosts' lives.

It was 10:30. My heart thumped wildly as I flipped on the porch lights and turned the deadbolt lock. Flinging the door open, I held my breath, not knowing what to expect.

And I saw nothing. No one was there. No giant iridescent beings with glittery wings. No portal, crackling with blue lightning, opening from another dimension.

There was only our courtyard, empty and hazily illuminated by our low-wattage lights. I inhaled the cool night air, trying not to feel disappointed. I don't know what I expected, but I'd hoped there would be something happening. I stood there feeling silly.

Suddenly, a whoosh of energy smacked the middle of my chest. I'd never felt anything like it. A tingling warmth began to spread upwards toward my face and down to my feet. Hot tears sprung into my eyes as emotion swept over me. Maybe I couldn't see the Archangels, but I could sure feel their presence. They had arrived!

Keeping the door wide open, I grabbed an index card from a nearby shelf and read the requisite welcoming speech I'd copied from the email.

"Hello and welcome, Archangels, to our home. I am very grateful that you are here purifying and bringing peace to our house and to those who live here." I wiped my eyes with the back of my hand before continuing.

"I am very grateful to you for bringing harmony, joy, and serenity to us. And thank you for granting my three written wishes."

Then I stood to one side of the door, motioning the five Archangels inside. Shutting the door, I turned around, hoping I was looking at where they were standing.

"I really do appreciate your coming," I said, unsure of what to do next. "Uh, may I show you around?"

I yammered on as I led them through the house, pointing out the obvious. "And this is the kitchen, and here's the dining room, the office, and guest bedrooms." If someone had been watching me, they would have recommended a mental health evaluation.

Glancing behind, I scanned the shadows hoping to see angelic sparks of color, or any other sign that they were following me into the TV room. On a side table the altar candle flickered, softly highlighting the white rose and other items I'd gathered.

"Here is your altar, Angels. Please feel free to hang out in this room, but you are welcome to go anywhere in this house."

I sat down on one of the sofas and exaggeratedly patted the seat cushion next to me. "I'm not sure if you'd like to sit, but make yourself comfortable on either sofa."

I gave them a moment, while picturing them squeezing themselves down onto the sofa. The email had said I could just hang with the Angels, meditate with them, or I could ask them questions. It suggested I might want to sit with pen and paper to write down any answers I received.

Closing my eyes, I took some deep breaths, and forced myself to relax. I tried to concentrate on my breaths, but nothing much happened. I never was good at meditation.

After about ten minutes, I opened my eyes. Even though it was quiet and dark in the room, I couldn't hear, see, or feel anything unusual. I tried again. Another few minutes went by with the same results.

"Well," I yawned, suddenly feeling remarkably tired, "I'm going to go to sleep now. Thank you, again, for being here. I'll see you in the morning."

I blew out the candle for the night. As I headed to bed, I said under my breath, "There are Archangels in our house. How crazy is that?"

Despite my weariness, I tossed and turned, my brain afire with questions. Was I worthy of having these Angels spend time with me? Was it okay with them that I knew so little about them religiously or spiritually? Would I somehow be tested or evaluated on biblical or mystical theories?

I had grown up in a happy and loving family, but we didn't talk about Angels very often. However, hanging on the wall in my childhood bedroom, in all her exquisite glory, was a framed Angel my Grandpa Morris had painted in oils when my mom was a child. I'd adored that painting since I was a toddler.

Childlike, the Angel sits demurely in profile, naked yet modest, holding a single white daisy. Golden light radiates from her wings and her long reddish blonde hair.

Over the more than one hundred years, the background colors have darkened a bit, but the Angel still glows as she adorns the wall of our guest room, today.

I always loved when my parents would read to me from my children's bible, the book's pages edged in shiny gold leaf. There were colorful illustrations and stories of David and Goliath and King Solomon, among others.

But I was particularly mesmerized by the last two pages of the book. There, heaven was displayed in all its magnificence. God, with his long white beard and flowing robes, sat on a gilded throne atop fluffy clouds.

Small cherubs flitted above and behind him, while he spoke with several tall beings with oversized wings and brilliant halos. I fell in love with those large, strong, glorious Angels.

As I grew older, I heard the Old Testament story of how Archangel Michael had visited Sarah and told her she was going to have a baby, even at her advanced age, and how Archangel Raphael told Lot he should flee the city of Sodom before it was destroyed.

And every year during the spring celebration of Passover, I heard about the Angel of death, whom God sent to kill the firstborn sons of ancient Egyptians.

I always seemed to be drawn to the stately, serious-looking Angels whenever I saw them in paintings, drawings, sculptures, and figurines. But I learned to keep my Angel affinity to myself, after some people gave me sidelong glances or half smiles when I admitted my fascination with Angels.

Later in my life, I would mention my love of Angels to my husband and to our children, keeping the conversation light and trying not to make too big a deal about it.

In 1996, *Michael,* a movie starring John Travolta as Archangel Michael, hit the theaters. The concept of Angels loving human beings and wanting to help blew my socks off. Not only did I have to see it twice, but I bought the video and watched it at home over and over. It was the first time I really focused on the term 'Archangel' as it pertained to large, powerful Angels who were assigned specific tasks to fulfill by God.

Of course Travolta's portrayal of Archangel Michael as a human-like, crude, feisty, sugar-addicted chain smoker was pure Hollywood, and a bit hard for me to accept for a Divine being. But his mission, eventually fulfilled in a tender and loving way, made me adore the movie and the Angel.

I longed to know more about Archangels and wished I could really interact with them, like in the movie. Somehow, I just knew Archangels would be open to, and even delight in contact with humans.

That's why I jumped at the chance when my friend asked if I wanted to host Archangels in my home. Now was my opportunity to see if I could really get to know them, and maybe even be friends with them!

Chapter Two
Living With Archangels

Over the next five days, I asked the Archangels to accompany me everywhere I went. Each time I started up the engine, I imagined them piling into my car, folding their huge wings, and settling into the seats. I drove down the street with a smile, feeling proud and important chauffeuring around invisible celestial beings.

But a few times I forgot they were there, and was mortified after muttering some off-color words to other drivers. I could just envision my passengers shaking their haloed heads at me.

"Hey, the radio's playing an Angel song," I laughed one day as we stopped at a red light. It was a golden oldie by J. Geils Band with the lyrics 'My Angel is a centerfold.'

"Oops . . . I'm sorry. I guess that isn't the most appropriate song."

I had the feeling they had a sense of humor, though, and weren't offended. And it was certainly unusual how many more songs with Angel lyrics popped up on the radio over that five-day period.

Wherever the Archangels and I went, no matter how mundane the errand, people seemed glad to see me. While selecting a bag of cotton balls and some pink nail polish at the drug store, strangers—young and old alike—stopped and smiled at me. They said hello. It was like they could sense the loving Angel energy surrounding me.

I relished how it felt to have five Divine Beings by my side. So what if they weren't visible to the human eye? While they were with me, there wasn't a moment that I felt alone.

The second night of their visit, I decided to try and have a conversation with the Archangels. I waited until Howard went to bed, then settled myself on a sofa in the TV room.

Staring into the flame of the altar candle, I took some deep breaths, relaxing my muscles and allowing the day's cares to fade away. Then I asked out loud the first question that popped into my head. My voice quavered nervously.

"Dear Archangels, are you really here with me? Or is all this just my imagination in overdrive?" My eyes searched through the darkness while my ears strained to hear their answer. Nothing. I tried asking again, but the only response I heard was the furnace motor kicking on.

After trying several more questions, and struggling to use my limited human senses to see or hear something, nothing came through. Still crickets.

"Angels, this clearly isn't working. Maybe if I write down my questions like it suggested in the Archangel email?" I grabbed a well-worn spiral notebook and a pen from a desk drawer.

"Okay, if you're really here with me," I said aloud as I wrote those same words in my normal longhand, "please send me a message." I waited, listening hard.

"I'm not really sure what to ask you," I wrote and spoke. "Could you please just give me some information I wouldn't otherwise know?" Again I heard nothing.

"Well, would you tell me why I received the opportunity to learn about you at this time in my life?" I wrote furiously, while still speaking aloud. This time I kept the tip of my pen on the paper, determined to write something.

A moment later, I heard a definite voice that sounded different than my own inner thoughts ever did. It seemed to come from deep within my right ear. I scribbled the words, which for some reason came out in printed capital letters.

THE DISTANCE SHREDS ITSELF AND IT IS HAPPENING NOW. THE PIECES ARE FALLING IN LINE; LIGHT SHINING WITHIN THE CAVE. IT IS THE ORIGINAL CONCEPT BEFORE THE DECEPTION BEGAN.

SYSTEMATIC EMBLEMS RESIDE IN THE ETHER OF LIFE. ONCE THEY HAVE FALLEN AWAY, THE INNER WILL RETAIN READINESS IN HARMONY.

"I'm sorry, what?" I laughed. "I'm not following what you're telling me."

IT IS QUESTIONABLE WITHIN THE ALLEYWAYS OF HUMAN MINDS AND CAPACITY. INDEED THE OVERTURES DECIDE EACH COMING FATE WITHIN THE SPECTRUM OF READINESS.

I laid my pen down and stared at the paper. What the heck did I just write? Whatever it was, it was way over my head; these statements certainly didn't come from me. And again their words flowed out in all capitals.

"Angels, if those answers really did come from you, thank you. But I'm sorry, I'm not good at esoteric concepts. What are systematic emblems?

"Could you please speak plainly to me? Let's try this question— when you leave on Monday, may I ask you to return soon to see me again?"

YES.

"Okay! Awesome. Will I need to prepare the altar again before your next visit?"

NOT NECESSARY.

"Yes! This is great; I hear you and I understand. Thank you. So, our daughter, Jill, had an important job interview today. It lasted four hours. She would love to land this job as editor-in-chief of a travel magazine. Will she be offered it?"

YES, SHE WILL BE OFFERED THE JOB AND WILL ACCEPT THE OFFER.

These lovely answers were still coming through my right ear, but there was also a new kind of knowing exactly what I was going to hear a second before actually hearing it. It was such a unique experience, this blending of sound and knowledge coming from within.

I'd had intuition and inner-knowing experiences before in my life, but they had merely been brief whispers.

But could I really be hearing the Angels, or were these answers coming from some newfound inventiveness in my mind? I didn't know. I couldn't prove the accuracy of their answers yet, but I wanted to ask questions all night.

"Angels, will our son, David, ever settle down in the Phoenix area to live? He lives in Atlanta now."

HE WILL MAKE THE PHOENIX AREA HIS HOME.

"How about Howard and me? Will we ever move from Tucson to the Phoenix area?"

YES, IT IS GOING TO HAPPEN.

"Seriously, Angels? Wow. I can't believe it. I'd love to move there, but Howard has said over and over that he doesn't want to move to such a big city. I sure hope you're right, though."

Since Jill was already living in Phoenix, that would mean we'd all live in the same city again, which hadn't happened since we all lived in Chicago years before.

"So, Angels," I said as I wrote, "I've been concerned because there's been a lot of talk in the news lately about the lining in most cans of tomato products. They contain a resin that leaches a toxic chemical called BPA into the food. That's an endocrine disruptor that can cause the body all kinds of harm.

"I use canned tomatoes and sauces often in my spaghetti, pot roast, stew, and chicken, so is this something that I should be worried about? Will it affect our health?"

NO, IT IS NOT CONCERNING FOR YOU.

"Okay, that's good to know. But something else is worrisome—those new body scanners at the airport. I've read how harmful they are, due to the radiation they emit. Our airport here in Tucson isn't using them yet, but Sky Harbor airport in Phoenix is using them, and we fly through that airport sometimes.

"I've tried to avoid excess radiation for years, even shunning many dental x-rays. I don't know—maybe you already know that about me? Anyway, I guess this isn't really a question. But I'd hate to get cancer from a security device. I'm scared for my health and for the health of my family, Angels."

NO NEED FOR FEAR AROUND THIS. WE ARE HERE AND WE WILL PROTECT YOU AND YOUR FAMILY IF YOU MUST GO THROUGH SUCH MACHINES.

"Angels, you would do that? You would really shield us from radiation?" My tears of relief and gratitude suddenly dripped onto the paper, smearing the ink.

YES, WE WOULD. AND WE WILL.

It began to dawn on me just how powerful and loving these Archangels were. But could it really be that easy? Just ask and I'd automatically receive their help and protection?

As I tried to process the magnitude of what they said, I had to laugh through my sniffles. I realized that the Angels' responses were now given in the simplest terms—only a few words in length. They had complied with my request to dumb down their answers for me.

And I could see how their responses, printed in capital letters, provided the perfect way to differentiate my longhand questions from their answers.

Feeling more secure about life than I had in a long time, I slept like a baby that night.

The Archangels and I settled into a pleasant routine. During the day I imagined them hanging out with me as I cooked, cleaned, talked on the phone, or did laundry.

Our parrot, Monty, an intelligent and sensitive green-cheeked conure, seemed to sense the new Angelic presence. He'd suddenly stop pecking at his food to swivel his neck around, his eyes tracking something in the room I couldn't see. Then he'd puff out his feathers and bob his head up and down, excitedly squealing for no reason.

The Angels accompanied me when I took a walk around our neighborhood. There was a definite spring in my step as I pictured myself in the middle of five powerful Divine Beings, all crowding together down the narrow streets.

But it was our nightly communications that I really looked forward to. When the day's activities were done, and Howard and Monty were asleep, a deep quiet enveloped our house.

I'd sit on the sofa in the TV room, holding a pen and my spiral notebook. Staring at the candle, I'd watch the flame dance, grow still, and dance some more. Then I'd take some deep, relaxing breaths, and write down questions, saying the words out loud to the Angels as I wrote them.

Sometimes I couldn't hear their responses. So, I'd take more deep breaths and try again. If I still couldn't hear anything, I'd read or listen to music for a while before attempting it once more. At that point I would usually be able to hear answers. If not, I'd just go to bed and try again the next evening.

Some nights our conversations would flow for an hour or more. Every question or concern I had was addressed. Other nights I had to be satisfied with a couple of short messages.

But there was always a calming warmth that came over me, at some point, during our chats. It felt like being wrapped in a robe fresh from the clothes dryer.

Not all of the physical sensations were pleasant for me, though. Sometimes the Angelic energy became too much and I overheated during those conversations. Since perspiring always leads to a bumpy heat-rash breaking out on my back and abdomen, I was soon a hot mess. That itchy, miserable condition, called prickly heat, is one I've never outgrown from childhood. So, whenever I'd start scratching, I'd ask the Angels to please wait while I ran to grab an ice pack from the freezer.

What was intriguing, though, was how I still had no way to determine if I was making things up in my head or really connecting with the Archangels at that point.

And way too soon the night of Monday, February 28th arrived. How could five days have passed so quickly? My heart felt heavy as I wrote down their last messages to me.

Then it was 10:30 p.m., and I reluctantly walked Archangels Michael, Uriel, Metatron, Gabriel, and Raphael to the foyer. The email said I should express my gratitude to them. Then I was to give them the three names and addresses of their next hosts, (which I had already arranged), open the front door, and wish them Godspeed.

It also said that after the Archangels left, I was to burn the envelope containing my written wishes in order to free the energy and allow the wishes to be granted. Then I was to take the ashes and drop them in a stream of water (the kitchen sink was acceptable). I was to eat the apple which would contain lots of good nutrients and special sustenance for me. Then I was to place the flower outside on the ground of Mother Earth so that it recycled naturally.

Opening the door and saying goodbye to the Archangels was the last thing I wanted to do. I had just spent an amazing five days and nights with them. Why did they have to leave so soon? I stood in front of the still-closed door, fresh tears starting to flow.

"Oh Angels, thank you so much for everything. I know I'm supposed to open this door and say farewell to you now, but I don't want to. I've finally been able to experience you and embrace you in my life. I feel like our friendship is just beginning.

"So how can I just let you go? I know you're supposed to be at the next three hosts' homes, but I've always heard that you're omnipresent and can be in all places at the same time.

"Please, will you not go?" My chest was heaving. "I'll open that door for you, but... please don't leave me," I cried. "Won't you stay with me forever?"

I turned the knob, swinging the door wide open. I pictured them flying past me, up and away into the night. My heart fell to my feet.

But as I turned off the porch light and closed the door, a tingling sensation started in my chest, warming me like a hug. And I knew.

The Archangels didn't leave. They were still there with me. And they have been with me ever since!

Later that night when I happily chomped on the Angelic apple, I tasted the most delicious piece of fruit I'd ever eaten in my life.

And after I placed the five-day old flower (which looked as fresh as the first day) outside on the ground, I poured the remaining water from the vase, imbued with Angel essence, into a spray bottle to spritz myself whenever I felt like it. The smell was indescribably fresh.

As the Angels had foreseen, Jill was offered and accepted the job as editor-in-chief of AAA Arizona's Highroads Magazine, a position she held for three years. Howard and I moved to the Phoenix area in 2017, and David moved to the Phoenix area in 2018. I didn't know it back in 2011, but my three written wishes would be fulfilled.

So, how do I know that the Archangels have been with me ever since? Well, over time I have learned to detect their energies around me, and what that feels like.

But also, the Archangels have shown that they are with me time and time again, often with dramatic physical proof. A number of times, Howard has been an astounded witness to these incredible events. And I am delighted to share them with you in the upcoming chapters.

Chapter Three
Who Are Angels and Archangels?

According to spiritual and religious doctrines and philosophies, Angels are powerful yet loving, celestial beings who were created by God.

The Oxford Universal Dictionary defines an Angel as 'a ministering spirit or divine messenger; one of an order of spiritual beings, superior to man in power and intelligence, who are the attendants and messengers of the Deity.'

Angels are mentioned in Zoroastrianism, Buddhism, and Taoism, as well as in ancient Assyrian and Mesopotamian writings. In fact, Angels have played roles in all major religions.

According to writings attributed to Pseudo-Dionysius the Areopagite around 500 A.D. and theologian Thomas Aquinas around 1274 A.D., there are nine ranks of Angels in their hierarchy, and three spheres, including Seraphim, Cherubim, Thrones, and Dominions.

The word Archangel comes from the Greek arch, meaning chief, and angelos, meaning God's messengers. Archangels are the chief messengers of God. Their main jobs are to oversee life on earth and help humans in many ways, including with their soul growth and development. Each

Archangel has specific missions, traits, and areas of expertise, working to fulfill God's plans.

They were created to love and help all of us whether we have been brought up with religious instruction or not, pray regularly or not, or identify as devout or not. It doesn't even matter if we question God's very existence. What matters is that we're humans and we need and want their assistance.

Archangels hear our prayers and act as our advocates in delivering those prayers to God; they are extensions of God. Of course we can pray to God directly. But Archangels, vibrationally elevated beings that they are, have frequencies that are attuned lower than God's, and therefore are easier for humans to connect with.

Archangels work with us in whatever form we need in order to feel comfortable with them, whether that is in a spiritual or religious way, or simply as a loving best friend.

They know us so well—they have the ability to see and understand what's in our hearts, minds, and souls from the time we are born, and even before we take human form. They've known each of us for eons, through all our past lives. And, they love us unconditionally, just as we are, despite our failings, mistakes, poor judgements, cruel actions, stubbornness, and dark thoughts.

Think of them as trustworthy and supportive friends in all their glory, eager to help us realize, experience, and embrace the spark of God's love that resides within each of us.

Archangels help us heal on spiritual, emotional, physical, and soul levels, reminding us of how it feels to be healthy and whole. And they will assist us with making decisions, envisioning opportunities, and boosting our confidence and creativity in order to live up to our highest potential.

These Divine Best Friends are unlike any friends we've ever had, because they are without egos or ulterior motives. Archangels will never sabotage us, lie, gossip, or tell us what we want to hear just to get something from us. Totally selfless, they have our backs, one hundred percent, no matter what.

The Archangels teach us the lessons we are ready to learn by guiding us, usually in a gentle way, until we 'get it.' We'll receive their hints, nudges, or nagging feelings to hopefully ponder or act upon. And they will co-create with us to reach our goals if those goals are in alignment with our highest selves.

We still have to put in the work, though. They aren't magicians dispensing hocus pocus or genies in a bottle. There is no 'poof'—and then our wishes are granted and our problems disappear.

We can't expect the Archangels to help us find new jobs, for example, if we don't write our resumes, fill out applications, and do our homework regarding the job market.

But after doing the work, we can ask them to facilitate our success by helping us land the best job possible. They'll help us grow in many ways when we actively participate with them to fulfill our goals.

Archangels are seriously underemployed. There are many of them waiting and they want nothing more than to accomplish their missions of helping humans.

When we ask them to be in our lives, we are acknowledging their existence as well as their role as bridges between us and God. And when we ask for their help—buckle up—we are in for an extraordinary ride!

Archangels must, however, respect and obey a significant Divine decree. They must never violate humanity's free will by intervening on our behalf without our permission. We must invite them into our lives, and ask them to help us.

Is there anything to fear by inviting them in? Do we need to pray and protect ourselves religiously or spiritually? In my experience, the answer is a resounding no. I have never had a negative, scary, or disturbing experience in all the years I have communicated with Archangels.

I have been shown only their wisdom, support, protection, and unconditional love. They have been my consistent reminders that we all have the light of God within us, and that spark, so deep in our souls, is pure goodness and perfectly aligned with Divine love.

Because I have a connection to God and the Archangels in the heavenly realm, I am protected, and never have to fear evil entities or dark spirits. Those types of beings will shy away from the vibrant light of God, and seek out the shadows, elsewhere.

Can we pray for protection, anyway, when connecting with Archangels? Of course. Whatever makes us feel more at ease, safe, and receptive to the love of the Archangels is what we should do.

So, how do we invite Archangels into our lives? Again, whichever way feels comfortable and right. Our connection with the Archangels is so personal—it's as individual as we are.

It's important to find a quiet space and sit comfortably, close our eyes, and take deep breaths. If it feels right we can turn down the lights, play soft music, burn incense or candles, set up an altar, or use gemstones. Any and all of these can help us disconnect from our day-to-day lives, and focus our energy inward, especially early on in our Archangel communications.

Then we can simply say aloud or think in our minds something like this:

"Dear Archangels in heaven, please come into my life. I am giving you permission to protect, help, and guide me toward living my best life and to reach my highest potential. I welcome you, and look forward to experiencing your love. Thank you so much."

As you talk with them, whether it's this first time, or whenever you speak to them, open up your heart and soul to the experience. Be as wonder-filled as a child. This kind of connection with Divine Beings should never become routine.

What should we feel? Of course, everyone's experience will be different, but sometimes I'll feel a tingly sensation moving through me as Angel energy comes near. Other times I may feel warm waves of comfort as if a trusted friend puts their arm around me.

Occasionally I'll see flashes of color behind my closed eyelids. Since each Archangel projects a particular color or colors, we may determine which one of them is present that way. I will explain more about this beautiful phenomenon in upcoming chapters.

If you don't feel or see anything, don't be discouraged. The Archangels are definitely with you, simply because you've asked them to be. Now, just trust that they are there in front of you. It takes time and practice, as with most things, to become better able to perceive their energies. It will happen.

And the more you interact with them, the clearer your connection will be. That is certainly the case when you want to take your communications with Archangels to an even deeper level. In a later chapter I will explain how to hear their words as you write your conversations in your own Angel journal.

Once you have invited the Archangels into your life, your relationship is assured and they will be open to any and all communication. Feel free to ask for their help with any issues—serious ones, of course, but even small problems or concerns. I have found that nothing is too trivial. You can't bother them, I promise. Just be specific with what you want, even if what you want seems frivolous.

I ask them for help finding a convenient parking space as I'm driving to stores. I don't close my eyes while driving, of course, but I take a few deep breaths and make my request, silently or aloud. Most of the time a great spot will be there just waiting for me to pull into.

I also ask the Archangels to calm my nerves before going for a blood test. I hate being poked with needles at the lab, but it always goes smoothly and with minimal pain when I relax and trust the Archangels are enfolding me in their protection.

Even in social situations, I've asked for help to say the right words to relieve someone's stress or grief, or to make a positive difference in someone's day. And it works; the right words just seem to come to me.

As long as you're not asking the Archangels to hurt someone, or take advantage of somebody, which they would never do, or to bring you something that doesn't align with your life's highest path, they will be happy to assist. But as humans, we don't always know what's best for us in the long run.

I've asked the Archangels for specific things or to create certain situations that never materialized. Or they did happen, but years later and in a different context.

Although that can be disappointing, we must have faith that what they do or don't bring us, and when, is for our best interests in the bigger picture. And they always see the bigger picture. So, we must trust them because we are not privy, as they are, to God's plans.

After asking for help or guidance, it's vital to show gratitude to the Archangels. But just saying thank you isn't enough. Words can easily be spoken with little meaning behind them. We must really feel that emotion of appreciation to back up our words.

It takes practice at first. When I wasn't sure how to get that feeling of deep gratitude, I just said or thought the words 'thank you' over and over. I just kept repeating them. And soon the words expanded inside me, giving me a little kick of excitement. That method still works whenever I need to step up my devotion with emotion.

Feeling that deep, true gratitude raises us to a higher state of consciousness. Immersed in such positive energy, our frequencies are elevated, so we can meld with the Archangels as our true selves, and strengthen that all-important connection.

What if we've never communicated with Archangels before, but we find ourselves panicking in the middle of a crisis or emergency? Just think or say aloud, "Angels I need your help now!"

We have just granted them permission to assist, guide, and protect us. Permission can come in different forms, such as cries for help, prayers, or heartfelt wishes.

Archangels are there to help us, especially during hectic moments or highly emotional situations. At first, their true adoration for us can be a concept that is difficult to comprehend, trust, and even remember.

There were times, while my relationship with the Angels was still new, that I'd be worried about a health issue that someone in my family or a friend was experiencing. Or I'd drive myself crazy trying, without success, to find a solution to a problem.

Then I'd suddenly remember that I had the very best resources available to me. My Divine Best Friends, those loving, light-beings were standing by to assist.

I'd immediately ask for their help and guidance, to see things more clearly and with less panic and stress. Soon I'd feel calmer and better able to think and react more effectively. How comforting and empowering that was!

Angels and Archangels have been the subject of much interest and study throughout history. There are pages upon pages of information about them online and in books—religious as well as spiritual ones.

Experts have spent many years, and sometimes lifetimes studying the Angelic hierarchy. And, as fascinating as their findings are, I've learned that the best way to get the purest information is to go to the source.

I just ask the Archangels themselves. What better way is there to really learn about each one? I've gotten some good glimpses of their personalities over the years through our many conversations. Their own precious words are written in my journals to treasure for the rest of my life.

The Archangels wait patiently, hoping we will invite them to join us when we celebrate joyful and wonderous happenings in our lives, and to comfort us in our darkest hours of pain, fear, and sorrow. And ultimately, they love us enough to accompany our souls to heaven when it's time for us to go home to God.

Archangels certainly are God's gift to humanity, and they're also proof of His unwavering love for each and every one of us.

Chapter Four
Signs from The Archangels

*N*ow that you've invited them into your life, you can ask the Archangels for signs that they are really with you. You can say something like this:

"Dear Archangels, please show me a sign that you are here. I am open to the experience, and will be watchful for the signs you send me. Thank you."

And then, remember to look and listen, as Angelic signs can come in many different forms that will have personal meaning and significance to you. The more you open your awareness, building up your receptivity, the more frequent and amazing the messages will be.

Feathers are a common sign that the Archangels send to show they're with us. The feathers are generally white, but I have found them tinged in grey, black, blue, and brown, as well.

Are you seeing more feathers than usual? Are they in unusual places? Occasionally I find gray or white ones in drawers and other interesting places that they couldn't have gotten to on their own. The Archangels have a sense of humor, and it's delightful to see how they've hidden these loving messages for me to find.

One day a few years ago, my friend Melanie called sounding breathless and perplexed.

"Debra, I'm a little freaked out. I've got to tell you what's been going on over here. I'm sitting in our family room, and a white feather just floated down from the ceiling right in front of me. I've been seeing different sized white feathers all over lately.

"I've searched in our closets to see if one of our down comforters had fallen apart and was shedding. But nope. There is nothing that would account for this.

"There'll be a couple of feathers on the floor in our master bedroom, and then I'll find one sitting on Ray's desk in the other room. Then there are some lying along the driveway. Even when I was walking toward the office door at work the other day, white feathers were waiting for me on the sidewalk."

"That's so awesome, Melanie," I said, "and what did your hubby say?"

"He has no idea where they're coming from either. The feathers will stop showing up for a few days or a week, and I think it's over. But then they'll start up again. And this has been going on for a couple of months now! Does this make any sense to you?"

It sure did make sense to me. Melanie knew I'd been chatting with Archangels for years, and she had recently invited them into her life, too.

"Sometimes our loved ones who have passed away, will send us a white feather or two to say hello and let us know they're doing well on the other side of the veil," I said.

"But, they usually don't inundate us with feathers," I laughed. "I'm sure it's our Divine Best Friends. This sounds just like their sense of humor. They love you and are giving you some really big hellos. Enjoy it while it lasts."

"Thanks, Debra. I'm relieved to hear your interpretation. I was getting worried it might be a bad omen. I'll look at the feathers as a good thing from now on."

And sure enough, the feathers disappeared completely from Melanie's life a week or two later, and they have never returned. She still laughs with amazement looking back on her feather-filled Angel welcome.

Another sign the Archangels send to grab our attention involves number sequences. Repeating numbers are easy for us to notice and there are myriad opportunities for the Archangels to use them to say hello.

We may feel sudden urges to look at the clock or at our cell phone only to discover it's 11:11, 12:12, or 5:55, and that keeps happening over days or weeks.

Maybe our restaurant bill is $20.20 and the date is 02-20-2020. Or we're on a road trip on March 3rd, and notice mile marker 333, and then we see another car's license plates with the numbers 3333. At our destination, we register for our hotel room, and are given the keycard to room 33.

The science of numerology is based on ancient knowledge regarding the mystical relationship between events of the material world and mathematical symbols. The father of numerology, Greek mathematician Pythagoras, discovered the main law of decoding numbers by reducing them to single digits. So, numerology uses numbers 0 through 9.

Although I haven't delved deeply into the subject, there is a wealth of information out there about Angel number sequences and what certain combinations of digits represent. It is said that each Angel number or set of numbers is connected to specific vibrational frequencies that bestow meaning.

According to an online article written by an Angel numerologist, the number 444 is said to indicate that you are on the right path, whether you know it yet or not, and to keep your eye on the prize, working toward your goals.

The number 555 indicates that you need to become aware of a habit or pattern that you should change in your life, or this is a good time to change things you've been wanting to.

I notice the numbers 11, 111, or 1111 a lot in my life. So apparently I'm going through a spiritual awakening. It's a sign that my thoughts and beliefs are aligned with my true self, and I'm being encouraged to assist and inspire the human race, using my natural abilities and inner wisdom.

I bring illumination and enlightenment to others, and the Angels support me in my lightwork.

Well, how perfectly apropos is that? It's even more reason for me to keep watching for those numeric greetings from my Divine Best Friends.

There are many other signs that the Archangels use. Certain words or phrases, meaningful to us, may pop up again and again on street signs, billboards, store signs, television and radio, etc. There are also obvious symbols—iconic Angel imagery of wings, halos, trumpets, harps, swords, doves, or chalices that may catch our eye.

It becomes a very personal thing for each of us, this distinctive relationship with the Archangels, and their own unique way of connecting with us. They know how to whisper, or sometimes even shout their presence to each of us in a special way, like they did to me, with my husband and son as witnesses.

It was October of 2011, eight months after they visited me for the first time. I had been communicating with them regularly, just as I did those first nights, writing my questions and their answers in my spiral notebook, otherwise known as my Angel journal. I had been amazed and awed by their continued loving guidance. One night I wrote this message to them:

October 11, 2011 - "Dear Angels, I am so grateful that you're here and a part of my life, and I appreciate your answers to my long list of questions. I really do feel you are always with me, but I am a human, and a stubborn one at that.

"So, would you please show me a visible sign that you are really here with me? And could you make it a very obvious sign? I'd probably miss an obscure little sign—I am blonde, you know. (I had already discovered they have a sense of humor and I could joke with them.)

"Please don't plant a feather on top of a bush in the yard or sprinkle cactus thorns in the shape of a harp on my favorite outdoor chair. I probably won't notice. I need bigger. I need a sign I can't miss. Okay? Thank you, Angels!"

Two days later our son, David, who lived in Atlanta, was visiting us at our home in Tucson. David and I were talking in the kitchen when Howard decided to go outside to our backyard. He walked through the kitchen, and out the back door.

Seconds later he opened the door again, this time gesturing for us to follow him outside. He had a strange look on his face.

"Hurry. And bring my phone!" my hubby shouted.

David grabbed the phone and we ran outside to find Howard staring up at the sky, mouth agape.

"What is it? What's going on?" I asked.

He pointed upward. "What does that look like to you? You told me you asked the Angels for a sign. But this..."

Hovering above our heads was a large white Archangel! It was obviously a cloud, but it was the only cloud in the entire bright blue sky. The Cloud Angel slowly floated with outstretched wings, finally making its way over our back wall where it continued toward the mountains, growing smaller and smaller in the distance until it completely disappeared.

With wide eyes we watched the Angel, Howard taking photos until the cloud floated out of sight.

"The Angel was just hovering there over the house when I first came out," Howard explained.

"Aww, thank you dear Angels," I called out to the sky. "I asked you for a sign to let me know you're with me, and you did it. And in such a big way!"

"It couldn't have been more obvious, that's for sure," David said, shaking his head. And you wouldn't even have seen it," he added, "if Dad hadn't come out here just now."

"That's true. Honey? Why did you come outside right now?"

"I don't know," Howard shrugged, walking back toward the house. "I just felt like it."

"Well, what do you think about the Archangels now?"

Howard stopped and turned around to look at me. "I think I'm a believer."

This is one of Howard's photos of the Cloud Angel.

(You can view the color photo at www.debraschildhouse.com.)

The Archangels also use color to send us signs. That's because each Archangel has a representing color on the light spectrum that they resonate with and can project for us to see.

Have you ever noticed one or more round bubble-like emanations mysteriously floating within a photo? I've heard these referred to as orbs. Orbs have made appearances in a number of our family photos, floating high in the background, or even seemingly resting on someone's head. They are visible in all colors, their yellows, oranges, blues, greens, pinks, or luminescent whites coming through on a bright sunny day as well as at midnight.

One memorable photo of ours, taken on a cruise, shows dozens of orbs in the churning waters below, taken on a dark night beside the railing at the back of the ship. Floating up from the sea, the orbs piggy-back each other, shining like sparkly little moons.

In my experience, orbs show up and flourish in more positive, high-energy, fun, and loving settings. Yet, they aren't even visible until seen in photos. So, what are these strange colorful balls that are invisible to the naked eye?

I asked the Archangels and they explained that they are tiny gifts to be discovered, letting us know the Archangels are enjoying the occasions with us. The color of the orb indicates which Archangel is present. An emerald green one? It's Angel Raphael. And a pink or yellow orb means Angel Jophiel is sharing the fun with us. Just knowing that makes me want to take a lot more photos!

Another colorful way I enjoy connecting with Archangels happens when I close my eyes before going to sleep. I'll call upon a particular Archangel and ask them to come close to me and show me their colors.

Soon, that grainy grey landscape behind my eyelids changes to a subtle wash of colors. It's like watching an artist swirl pigments and hues for my own personal viewing pleasure. When I see vivid purples or deep blues, I know Archangel Michael has entered my space. Archangel Gabriel brings a brilliant copper.

Sometimes, with my eyes open in the dark, I'll see a creamy gold color, even if I haven't called in an Archangel. The intensity ebbs and flows, pulsating as it glows. It's a comforting 'goodnight' light from them, and a loving way to send me off to sleep.

Archangel Raziel actually projects the entire rainbow of colors. But I wasn't familiar with that particular Archangel, nor his colors, when he literally created a prism on my face, a sign that truly 'brightened' my day. And again, it happened in front of witnesses. You'll read more about that incredible experience in Archangel Raziel's chapter.

The Archangels send me loving greetings no matter where I am—at home or traveling. Howard and I love to explore new places all over the world, and in mid-October of 2016, we enjoyed the many delights of Quebec City in Canada. We spent a few days there ahead of a cruise, meeting up with our friends Louiselle and John, from Montreal.

While sightseeing in the part of the city called Old Quebec, Louiselle and John suggested that we stop at Les Trois Corbeaux Glass Studio, one of their favorites, to watch a glass blowing demonstration.

It was fascinating to observe one of the glassblowers, Jeff Ferrier, blow molten glass through a long metal pipe, pop it in and out of a large kiln, then fashion it into a specific shape with an oversized tweezer like instrument. Finally, he held a torch to the piece, the fire illuminating it brightly.

"Hey, Deb, do you see what he's making?" Louiselle asked.

"No, what is it?"

"Look closer."

"Is that…?"

"It sure is. An Angel," Louiselle said excitedly, knowing about my relationship with Archangels. "And, I've got to say, of all the times John and I have been in here, even at Christmas time, I've never seen them make an Angel. This one has to be for you!"

The next thing I knew, I was running up to the cash register to buy that gorgeous little Angel. There was not another one like it anywhere in the store.

I had to wait a few weeks until my new glass Angel was in my possession, because we were headed for a cruise and the Angel needed to cool a while before being mailed to me.

But she now graces my writing desk, her place of honor next to a framed photo of the Cloud Angel. She is less than five inches tall, her halo, arms, and wings are clear glass, and her head and body are swirled with hues of purple, white, and teal.

Curious to see if they were still selling copies of that little Angel, I checked the studio's website two years later. They were selling them as Christmas ornaments. But they had changed the angle of the Angel's arms. She was now holding them up as if she were reaching out.

But my Angel, a unique 'gift' from my Divine Best Friends, holds her arms and hands close together in front of her, as if in prayer.

The Archangels send us signs through music and song lyrics, too. I love music and listen to it daily, so it's an easy way for them to say hello to me.

I'll hear a song on the radio that catches my attention, even if the song is decades old. Either the title or lyrics contain the word Angel, or the message of the song speaks directly to me, referring to something in my past or something that's currently going on in my life. And when I hear it, I am drawn to the sound, focusing on it, even if I'm distracted or chatting with someone. It always makes me smile.

Sometimes I'll wake up in the morning with a random song in my head. Yet, if I ponder the lyrics, I may find the answer to a question I've asked the Archangels, or to a problem I've been struggling with.

I'm instantly happy whenever songs such as *Angel* by Sarah McLachlan, *Calling All Angels* by Train, or *Heaven Must Be Missing An Angel* by Tavares begin playing on the radio, especially when I'm stressed or feeling the need for an Angel energy boost.

One of the most touching ways the Archangels comforted me through music was on March 11th of 2016. I woke up feeling sad; it was the one-year anniversary of our pet parrot's death.

Our family had loved Monty for the fifteen years of his life. But he had always been 'my' bird, and I missed him and the close connection we'd shared, very much.

Over the years Monty enjoyed a variety of the music I played on the radio or the CD player. Sometimes he'd dance—really shake his little head and body to the beat. But one song in particular was his favorite. Upbeat and fun to dance to, it was an oldie from 1977 called *Turn To Stone* by the rock band Electric Light Orchestra (ELO).

I'm not sure what it was that Monty loved so much about that song, but I think it was the haunting sound of the electric violins, especially in the higher registers.

Whenever the song came on the radio (which wasn't very often) or I'd play the CD and he heard that particular track, he'd squeal and screech, while gyrating with pure delight. Sometimes I'd let him perch on my head and we'd both 'sing' and dance.

That sad morning while remembering Monty, I said to the Archangels, "Dear Angels, I miss my little bird so much. Could you please tell him I love him? Thank you."

Then it was time to start my day. I walked into the kitchen, flipping on the radio as I always did before getting the coffee started. Yep—you guessed it—out of the speakers came the unmistakable sounds of *Turn To Stone*.

All I could do was stand there and cry even though I was filled with joy, too, at this precious gift. A loving hello, not only from the Archangels, but from Monty!

Most of the signs I receive from the Archangels are clever, but much less dramatic. For instance, earlier today as I sat down at my computer to continue writing this book, I asked my Divine Best Friends to surround me with their presence and support.

"I hope I'm doing justice in describing, for my readers, the immense love you have for all of us. Could you show me if you're pleased with how I'm representing you, dear Angels?"

I clicked on my online classical radio station hoping to hear music that would help me focus. A beautiful piece was playing. Although it wasn't one I was familiar with, I could tell from the layered melodies and steady rhythm that it was from the Baroque era, one of my favorites.

As my fingers moved over the keyboard, the music transported me to a state of deep concentration. Lost in my stream of thought, I was unaware of anything else. It was bliss, until the radio announcer's voice snapped me back to reality.

"You've just heard the Academy of St Martin in the Fields, with conductor Sir Neville Marriner, playing *Concerto Grosso Number 5 in B Flat Major* by Italian composer Arcangelo Corelli."

"Arcangelo? Of all composers, huh?" I said with a wide grin. "Thank you, for your answer, dear Angels."

The Archangels often show their sense of humor when sending us signs. In the spring of 2017, Howard and I moved from Tucson to a lovely active adult community in Peoria, a suburb of Phoenix.

Inside the main clubhouse there was a nice-sized library, where volunteers regularly catalogued and shelved the books.

I decided to donate a crisp, new copy of my first book, *Bio-Touch: Healing With The Power In Our Fingertips,* to the library, handing it to an appreciative volunteer. The book is about my experiences learning and using Bio-Touch, a simple and effective touch-healing technique, and how anyone can use Bio-Touch to relieve pain, inflammation, and disease symptoms.

A few days later, I returned to the library to look for my next read. After choosing a legal thriller, I looked around, curious to see where my book had been shelved.

There wasn't a designated area for alternative healing books. In fact there were no books at all on holistic medicine, Reiki, massage, integrative touch therapies, or energy healing techniques. After a bit of searching, though, I found my book. It had been placed in the Religion and Spirituality section.

I laughed, shaking my head in amazement when I read the title of a book that had tipped over and was resting on my book, second to last on the shelf. It was called *Angels: God's Secret Agents* by Billy Graham.

The Archangels send us loving signs that can be bigger than life or quietly subtle, funny, heart-warming, eye-opening, or dramatic. And when we learn how to notice and embrace those signs, the joy awaiting us is unimaginable.

The following chapters will highlight more awe-inspiring signs, communications, and what I consider to be the best moments that I've shared with eleven of the Archangels since inviting them into my life in February of 2011.

Chapter Five
Archangel Michael
He Who is Like God

Archangel Michael is universally said to be the greatest Angel of them all. He is mentioned in the Bible in both the Old and New Testaments, in the Torah, and also in the Quran. He was the first Archangel that God created, and has been the best-known and most popular Angel throughout history.

As commander of the Angelic armies, he is often depicted in paintings and sculptures as a powerful warrior, holding up his sword of light and truth or wielding it to defend against the evil of dark spiritual forces. The scales of justice are often held in his other hand.

Archangel Michael's name comes from the Hebrew, meaning 'He Who Is Like God.' As all Archangels do, Michael projects a color or colors that represent a special frequency range in the visible light spectrum. His colors are royal purple and royal blue.

Also, as all Archangels do, Michael specializes in specific areas in order to help humanity. Protecting us is one of his greatest missions. He defends our physical bodies, our emotional health, our spiritual selves, and even our personal property, as he provides us with peace of mind and security.

"Angel Michael, please protect me and my loved ones. Keep us safe and free from harm. Thank you."

These simple words are what I always say, to myself or aloud, when I'm concerned for our safety in any situation.

Years ago, I asked Howard and our children to give their permission to the Archangels so my family could be protected without their free will being violated. I was so relieved when they each gave their okay.

But even if you don't feel comfortable making that request of your loved ones, you can still ask the Archangels to protect them. And, as long as their Divine safe-keeping aligns with their soul paths, the protection will be implemented for your family, or anyone you love or care about.

It's almost routine now, for me to ask for Archangel Michael's protection while I'm in a vehicle, no matter who's driving, especially in bad weather or crazy traffic.

In October of 2022, Howard was driving us from our home in the White Mountains to Phoenix to visit Jill for a couple of days. We had moved to that beautiful region of northeastern Arizona a year and a half before, seeking the quiet and graciousness of forested land after having lived in desert landscapes for many years. We were heading west via state route 260 through Payson. It was a sunny dry afternoon with light traffic going in both directions on the two-lane highway.

We were approaching the Forest Lakes area, both of us relaxed and enjoying our conversation. But suddenly, a car in the other lane driving eastbound pulled into our lane while attempting to pass the car in front of it.

In the blink of an eye we were in a scene from a horror movie. That passing car had badly misjudged speed, time, and space. Apparently in a hurry and inexperienced to boot, the driver was now on a collision course with our car, and running out of road.

My eyes were so wide with shock, I barely had time to call out for Angel Michael's help and protection. Meanwhile, Howard somehow managed to slow and steer our car as far to the right side of the road as possible, and still maintain control.

Then the other driver miraculously overtook the car he was passing, and swerved back into his lane at the last second, with precious few feet to spare between us.

"What the hell's the matter with that jerk?" Howard yelled. "He could have killed us all."

"I know. I thought we were goners. But Archangel Michael protected us."

"You had time to ask him?"

"Just barely," I said, choking up. "I think it's starting to become automatic now."

It took a while for us to calm down and breathe easily again. And I spent the next twenty minutes alternately thanking Angel Michael and thinking about that careless driver. I just hoped he learned something important from that stunt he pulled.

Dangers can pop up anywhere. Whenever Howard and I walk around our lovely neighborhood as the sun sets, I ask for Archangel Michael to protect us from uninvited attention from the animal kingdom—especially coyotes, bobcats, rattlesnakes, and javelina—the typical denizen in many parts of Arizona.

But uninvited attention can come from someone's pet, too. Some years ago, when we lived in the outskirts of Tucson, I was walking alone through our neighborhood on a warm, breezy afternoon. The sun was peeking in and out of fluffy clouds, creating interesting shadows around the palo verde trees.

Quail were scurrying, calling to each other as they hid among the low bushes and cacti. There were no sidewalks, so I strolled along the edge of the street. Friendly people I didn't even know waved as they drove slowly by.

It was just that kind of sweet day that always makes me feel so good about life in general. I couldn't help smiling as I ventured further from my typical route, at least a mile away from our community.

Eventually I came upon some ranch-style homes with dirt driveways that looked quite a bit older than the homes in our development. They were spaced far apart, built on large, naturally desert-scaped lots. As I passed one of those houses, I heard the whinnying of horses coming from somewhere on the fenced-in property.

Then a brown and white blur, moving fast in my direction, entered my peripheral vision. I quickened my pace. Alarming sounds of heavy panting and low growls grew closer behind me. Then barking. Lots of barking. Was I about to be pounced on?

I slowed to a stop and turned warily. My heart pounded and my mouth went dry. There stood a medium-sized, stockily built dog, who was obviously outraged at my presence. His barrel chest heaved below his bared teeth and erect ears. His dark eyes locked on mine. The handsome animal was wearing a red woven collar and I recognized his breed, from old beer commercials, as a bull terrier.

Feeling helpless with nothing but my house key to defend myself with, I remembered reading that if you were ever threatened by a dog, it was best to stand up straight, keep your arms at your sides, not show your teeth or make eye contact, and never make any sudden moves.

Doing all of the above, including averting my gaze, didn't help at all. The dog continued to rant and growl, lunging ever closer toward me. I was petrified.

I looked around to see if anyone was nearby who could help me. Not a soul.

"Angel Michael! Please help me … now!" My voice, full of fear, sounded thin and strange to my ears.

The angry snarling continued for a minute or so. Then inexplicably, the dog gave a high-pitched yelp and whipped his head around, as if startled by something behind him. Then mercifully, he ran back towards the house, disappearing through an open gate in the fence in front of the detached garage.

"Oh my God," I said weakly, catching my breath. My body went limp with relief. "That could have been very bad. Thank you so much, Angel Michael."

Walking and wiping away tears of gratitude, I continued my thanks all the way back to my house. I had been protected from possible injury, blood loss, and pain. I was safe and sound; it felt so good.

March 20, 2014 – "Please come through to chat with me tonight, Angel Michael. I need to talk about the dog incident that happened this afternoon, okay?"

ANGEL MICHAEL HERE FOR YOU NOW.

"Oh, thank you so much for coming through so quickly and for protecting me from that dog today. That was so scary. I thought I was going to get bitten for sure. Thank you for stopping him."

THE DOG JUST NEEDED SOME CORRECTING. HE WAS GIVEN ENCOURAGEMENT TO BACK AWAY FROM YOU AND RUN HOME.

"That was awesome, Angel Michael. How did you do that? Did you touch him in some way?"

HE WAS SIMPLY SHOWN WHAT WOULD BE THE RESULTING CONSEQUENCES. LIMITED OPTIONS WERE AVAILABLE TO HIM.

"Well, you sure saved my bacon. I'm so fortunate to have your protection. I love you. I love you all so much. What would I do without you?"

YOU WILL NEVER BE WITHOUT US.

Although I was no longer afraid of the dog, I didn't walk past that house again. I did drive past it a few times, though, and I noticed that the gate was still open. But inside the fencing the dog was either rolling around lazily on his back, or stretched out on his belly, head on paws, dozing. It was like he hadn't a care in the world. Who knows? Maybe his interaction with Angel Michael had given him a calmer outlook on life. I like to think so.

In the spring of 2018 shortly before midnight, there was a sudden power outage, plunging our home and community into total darkness. Howard was already asleep, the bedside battery-powered 'white noise' machine drowning out the sudden quiet.

There I was soaking in my nightly bath, when the room went black. I couldn't see my hand in front of my face. It wasn't fun fumbling around for the towel, feeling my way into the bedroom, and trying to quietly find the flashlight in the nightstand. Howard didn't stir.

Too keyed up to sleep, and worried about how hot it was going to get in the house without power for air conditioning or fans, I threw on my nightgown, grabbed my Angel journal, and sat at the kitchen table. Soon, hastily assembled candles of all sorts flickered, casting their feeble light on the pages as I wrote.

We were living in a suburb of Phoenix at that time, and it was a typically hot May. Even at midnight the temperature was in the low eighties. There was no relief when I opened the windows and sliding doors, because there wasn't the slightest breeze. Balmy air wafted inside, along with the chirps of crickets and the faraway howls of coyotes.

Moving quickly from window to window, I scanned the street and yard. The neighborhood was shrouded in deepest gray. Was that someone walking along the street? I couldn't be sure.

I flicked on the switches to all the kitchen ceiling lights so I'd know instantly when the electricity came back on.

Fanning myself with a coupon mailer envelope, I sat back down in front of my journal. With only flimsy window and door screens standing between me and whatever lurked outside, I began to feel uneasy and vulnerable. Granted, our neighborhood was as safe as one could be, but menacing looking shadows were darting around in the yard.

Although tempted to wake Howard up to keep me company, I didn't have the heart to disturb his peaceful slumber.

I picked up my cell phone to call David. At that time, he lived an hour away on the other side of Phoenix, but he was the only other one in the family who regularly stayed up late. I knew I wouldn't be waking him.

"Hey Mom, what's up?"

"Our power is out. Is yours on?"

"Yep. Everything's fine over here. How long's it been out?"

"About thirty minutes. I can't talk long. My phone is only at thirty percent power and isn't allowing me to look up the electric company's website for information."

"Yeah, that's because your modem and router need electricity. Hold on. I'm looking up your area on the APS website now. It says a major power line blew, but they expect the outage to be fixed by 2:30 a.m. Sorry, Mom. Hang in there."

I groaned as we hung up. Two more hours of this? It was so quiet, I could hear the blood pulsating through my eardrums. I looked at the silent refrigerator, picturing all the frozen meat thawing into a putrid, bloody mess.

With no other options, I returned to my journal, where I happily lost myself for a while. I had been keeping my Archangel journals for years by then, usually running out of pages in each one within a year's time.

I kept the diverse collection of notebooks and other composition-type books on a shelf, organized by year. And I always began each individual journal entry with the date, which proved invaluable when looking back, sometimes years later, to confirm what the Archangels had foreseen would happen in my life.

Suddenly, loud high-pitched yips and squeals broke out. My heart pounded to the haunting lyrics of coyote songs, so close by they could have been right outside the window.

May 15, 2018 – "Dear Angel Michael, I'd like you to come through please. I'm a little freaked out here, and I could use a boost of courage. Please protect me and Howard from any dangers out there.

"I'm being ridiculous, I know. The coyotes can't cut the screens and come in. And I'm sure there aren't any questionable people roaming the neighborhood in the dark, right? Angel Michael?"

YES, DEAR ONE, DARKNESS IN ALL ITS FORMS CAN BE VERY FRIGHTENING. THAT IS WHY WE ADVOCATE FOR THE SHINING LIGHT OF GOD. YOU ARE ALWAYS SAFE WITHIN IT.

"Thank you. Being inside the light of God sounds so good, especially right now. This darkness feels thick and heavy. I don't know … maybe it's the heat, too."

IT IS NATURALLY UNSETTLING, ESPECIALLY COMBINED WITH THE UNFAMILIAR SOUNDS. WE ARE HERE. WE ARE ALL AROUND YOUR HOME AND AREA.

"I so appreciate how you're calming me and keeping us safe, Angel Michael. I've been thinking about your sword of truth and light. Would it be possible for you to show it to me here in the dark? Please. I could really use some light about now."

Immediately I felt a calming peace spreading through me. I took a deep breath, luxuriating for a moment inside that safe feeling.

Just then the kitchen bulbs lit up the room. Loud hums from the refrigerator and air conditioner broke the eerie silence.

"Wow! Thank you so much, Angel Michael. Look at me blinking in all this brightness. Yep, this light of God sure feels better than that inky darkness. But if I knew your sword worked that fast, I'd have asked you sooner!"

Archangel Michael protects and comforts us when we're overwhelmed by our emotions, too, and are allowing sadness, jealousy, worry, confusion, or anger to rule our lives.

And if we're tired of being held back from accomplishing our goals by fears, ego, old karma, and even addictions, he will use his sword of light to cut away those physical and emotional bindings that keep us trapped. When we ask for his help, we will be able to appreciate a newfound freedom, and climb beyond our comfort zones to reach our highest potential.

Truth, justice, and integrity are also areas for Archangel Michael's expertise. We can call upon him when we have a legal issue or a court case and need the truth revealed in order to receive justice.

Archangel Michael can help us discover the truth about things we're afraid to look closely at. If, for example, we're concerned that we're in an unhealthy relationship, Archangel Michael will help us muster the courage to see past our insecurities and fears, and really examine what's happening. Once we see the truth in a new light, we can make an alternate plan that benefits us, and then follow through on it.

If we're going on a trip, whether near or far, we can ask Archangel Michael to help our travel itinerary go smoothly and on schedule. He will protect us and our possessions and luggage on a bus, train, plane, ship, kayak, hot-air balloon, bicycle, or on foot. And he will safeguard us in ways we never thought possible.

Howard and I were in Rome, Italy in early October of 2017, ahead of a Mediterranean cruise. We loved strolling around the Piazza Navona area, where we had rented an apartment for five days.

One day, the streets were unusually packed with tourists as we searched, hand in hand, for a shop we heard had the best gelato around. We quickened our pace to keep up with the crowd around us.

The iconic pavement, made of uneven and irregularly shaped basalt-block cobblestones, was hundreds of years old, and could be tricky to walk on.

Trotting alongside the crowd, Howard and I became separated, our hands letting go as people pushed between us. We rounded a sharp corner where an elderly woman was begging, rooted as if defying someone to run into her. Her raggedly clothed body was bent and wiry; her granite face weathered as the cobblestones.

I shuddered as her hostile eyes found mine and penetrated my skull. With misshapen fingers, she thrust her collection cup toward me. Unnerved, I turned my head away and quickened my pace to catch up to Howard.

Suddenly my feet were no longer under me; I was falling. It was that awful feeling when your body is flailing through the air, and you know you're going to land in a painful heap.

"Help me, Angel Michael!" Somehow, I had the presence of mind to call out to him while still in free fall.

My plunge seemed to take forever; I could actually feel myself decelerating before I finally landed on my left side on the unforgiving cobblestones. I waited for the agony to hit, but it never came.

Howard ran over to me, his face a mask of concern. Then his expression turned to shock when I quickly sprung to my feet.

"Are you okay?" he asked, taking my hand. "How can you jump up like that? I heard you smack the pavement so hard."

"Yeah, I know. But I'm okay. I just feel a little shaky and out of breath. I must have looked like such a klutz."

"It was really weird, Deb. It looked like you were falling in slow motion. I've never seen anything like it. It seemed to take forever for you to land."

"You know what? That's exactly how it felt—like time slowed down. And look, all I have are a few scrapes on my elbow," I said, inspecting myself. "No blood. Come on. Let's go find that gelato."

As we walked on, I knew it was Archangel Michael who had protected me from what could have been a serious injury. A broken hip would have certainly ruined our trip, let alone cause pain and fear with surgery and recovery in a foreign country.

And I couldn't shake the feeling that the spurned beggar had somehow contributed to my fall. The crowd had diminished, and as we walked on, slowly because of my trembling legs, I didn't dare look behind us to see if the woman was watching. But I silently thanked my Divine Best Friend over and over.

I'm convinced that Archangel Michael saved me from what's called a 'psychic' attack. A psychic attack happens when someone intentionally sends you negative energy in the form of a curse, threat, or evil wish.

That kind of attack can be caused by a stranger on the street, like in my case, or by someone you know well. Maybe you've broken off a personal or business relationship, and the other party sends you negativity via angry, vengeful thoughts.

Sometimes attacks are unintentional. Maybe you work alongside someone who is nice, but always sees the worst in any given situation. There are days when their negativity just overwhelms you. Or a needy friend who carries plenty of negative energy might unintentionally dump it on you, trying to find their own relief.

With or without evil intent, psychic attacks can absolutely lead to physical harm, depression, illness, anxiety, and 'bad luck'—definitely things that can adversely affect us.

Some people wear an 'evil eye' amulet in the form of a bracelet or necklace to ward off curses and negative energies. But luckily for us, Archangel Michael excels at protecting humans from those kinds of attacks and any other kind of evil directed at us.

He is said to be the keeper of the Psychic Protection Flame. This flame protects and repairs our spiritual immune systems. So, if you suspect you are under a psychic attack, ask Archangel Michael to shield you. And, as always, thank him from the bottom of your heart.

When I chat with the Archangels, I never know which one will be coming through to me at that particular time. I usually enjoy the anticipation, waiting to see who wants to chat, bringing messages they deem important.

But sometimes I ask for a specific Angel, hoping for that connection due to a specific issue I'm having. And often, that beckoned Angel will answer my call.

October 30, 2017 – "Hello dear Angels, who is here to chat with me tonight? Is it you, Angel Michael?"

YES. ANGEL MICHAEL, HERE FOR YOU, DEBRA,

"Thank you, Angel Michael. I'm glad you came through tonight so I can ask for your bright insight on a problem I'm having.

"My relationship with my friend Sharon is becoming more and more strained over, of all things, politics. She is starting to call attention to our differences of opinion, attitude, and outlook. She knows my political views, yet pointedly calls other people names who think the way I do. I guess she doesn't have the nerve to call me those names, at least not to my face.

"I don't care what party she belongs to, or if she's right or left wing. I don't care if her thoughts differ from mine. I believe respect is what's necessary in any of these types of discussions, though. Mutual respect.

"But she doesn't respect my opinions, and doesn't want to hear how I feel or why I feel that way, even after I've let her speak her mind. Sharon just expects me to agree with her and think like she does. I can tell she's frustrated that I don't. But I'll never see eye-to-eye or feel the way she does about these things, and I've told her that. Then I just sit there and try to change the subject to something neutral. It's tiring.

"And she isn't the only one whom I'm having this issue with. As you probably know, there are a couple of members of my extended family that take issue with my political beliefs and have felt entitled, on more than one occasion, to let me know the error of my thinking.

"Angel Michael, you stand for truth and clarity. What should I do when this happens with them or anyone else in the future?"

WE ARE PLEASED THAT YOU DO NOT ALLOW YOURSELF TO COMPLY WITH OTHERS' EXPECTATIONS OF YOU. CONTINUE TO BE BRAVE AND ACT AND SPEAK AS YOUR SOUL IS DICTATING NOW, WITHOUT RUDENESS OR RANCOR, OF COURSE.

IF OTHERS DO NOT APPRECIATE THAT, YOU MAY NEED TO DISTANCE YOURSELF IN ORDER TO HONOR YOURSELF. THAT WILL BE DETERMINED BY THEIR CONDUCT AS YOU PERSIST IN RESPECTFUL DEBATE, HONORING YOUR OWN HEART AND HOW IT SPEAKS YOUR TRUTH.

THESE KINDS OF DISAGREEMENTS AND DIFFERENCES OF OPINION DO NOTHING TO CRYSTALIZE THE REAL ISSUES OR CONTRIBUTE TO THEIR RESOLUTION.

THEY ARE SIMPLY SEGMENTATIONS AND DISTRACTIONS THAT CLOUD JUDGEMENT, SPARK THE EGO, AND PREVENT THE TRUTH FROM COMING TO LIGHT, WHICH IS SO NECESSARY FOR UNDERSTANDING AND LOVING SOLUTIONS.

November 12, 2020- "Thank you for being with me tonight, Angel Michael. As I sit here writing in this journal, I really need your protection and your words of truth. As you know, it's the height of the COVID-19 pandemic. There is so much fear and confusion about the virus, and the narratives from the government and media are constantly changing.

"I've never seen so many people this frightened about anything in my life. Talking with them is so depressing because they've lost hope for the future. What's the best way to live and not get caught up in the fear right now?"

IT IS BEST TO AVOID WORRISOME NEWS AND FRIGHTENING VIEWS. THE HEADLINES OF THE DAY ARE HANDED DOWN AMID OPINION AND SPECULATION. FACTS ARE OFTEN IGNORED FOR DRAMATICS.

DO NOT ALLOW THIS DISTRACTION TO BE EVEN A SMALL PART OF YOUR DAILY REALITY. INSTEAD, BRING YOUR FOCUS BACK TO YOUR INNER PATH AND RECOGNIZE THE LOVE, LIGHT, AND POSSIBILITIES YOU HAVE AROUND YOU. WITH YOUR CONCENTRATION THERE, YOU CAN CREATE MUCH POSITIVE, TANGIBLE CHANGE.

"Boy, that's not easy Angel Michael. I understand and appreciate your message, but how do I accomplish it for myself and help other people too?"

BECOME AN AGENT FOR YOURSELF AND OTHERS WITH A CALM, CLEAR MESSAGE OF LOVE. GOD'S LOVE ERASES FEAR. LET THAT LOVE BE SO LARGE AND SO JOYFUL, YOU CANNOT CONTAIN IT. LET IT BE YOUR TRUTH AND YOUR

ESSENCE. AS YOU SPEAK TO OTHERS. REMIND THEM OF
THE LOVE THAT GOD HAS FOR THEM.

IT MAY NOT DOUSE THEIR WORRIES IMMEDIATELY.
THEY MAY BE DUBIOUS OR DOUBT THAT YOU KNOW
THE TRUTH. BUT THE WORDS WILL BE ABSORBED ON A
DEEPER LEVEL, LIKE A BLESSING. AND THE EFFECT WILL
BE FELT IN WAYS THEY MAY NOT REALIZE UNTIL LATER.

"Angel Michael, it's always so special to me when you come through
to chat. Your amazing answers always have love as the main ingredi-
ent. It's woven throughout the truth you impart. Thank you for such
comforting and important reminders. And thank you for all the love and
protection you give to me and my family. You make my heart rest so
much easier."

OUR LOVE WILL BE WAITING FOR YOU, WHENEVER
NEEDED. JUST LISTEN…WITHIN YOUR STILLNESS…AND
WE WILL BE THERE, ALWAYS.

Chapter Six
Archangel Uriel
Light of God

Archangel Uriel's name means 'Light of God' or 'Fire of God.' He projects the colors amber, ruby red, and gold as he brings us the shining light of knowledge, wisdom, and critical thinking from God.

He is considered to be the wisest and most intellectual Archangel, who illuminates situations for us during our darkest and most confusing times. In a crisis, Archangel Uriel guides us to find the best solutions to our problems.

As we face deep adversity, he helps us overcome uncertainty and deception. And he encourages us to control our emotions, safely release our angers, and put our fears and anxieties into perspective.

Archangel Uriel is also the Angel of Weather, overseeing rain, lightning, thunder, hail, snowstorms, earthquakes, hurricanes, tornadoes, floods, etc.

If we are concerned, he can allay our weather-related fears, rein in the power of a severe thunderstorm, bring needed rains to our parched earth, ease the strength of howling winds, and/or bring an end to an overabundant snowfall.

Another special area of Archangel Uriel's is helping writers, teachers, students, and anyone teaching or seeking higher learning of any kind. He enjoys energizing us so we can gain more insight and clarity with regard to information we are receiving. He also brings focus and motivation to us, encouraging our minds to be open to new ideas and 'aha' moments.

When asked, Angel Uriel will stir our creative juices and sharpen our acuity for intellectual endeavors, such as studying, test taking, interviewing for a job, contributing usefully during meetings, organizing thoughts, comprehending what is being taught, and retaining knowledge.

When I began writing my first book in 2011, I asked Angel Uriel to join and support me at every writing session. As I typed away, I'd occasionally look over at a small photo of him that I kept next to my computer.

There were many images of him online, but this one was my favorite. It depicted him wearing red and gold robes, and holding a large book to his chest as his wings erupted in flames. Whenever I imagined it was my own book he was holding, I received some powerful motivation to keep on working.

During the three and a half years it took to complete that manuscript, his energy encouraged me whenever I sat, frustrated with writer's block or the temporary inability to find the correct words or phrases—typical issues for writers.

I'd simply close my eyes and imagine Archangel Uriel standing in front of me with his hands reaching for mine. Seeing his reassuring smile would, more often than not, send a sudden zing through me, a warm tingling that immediately reinvigorated my brain. The words or ideas I'd been searching for would then become apparent, and flow more easily into coherent sentences.

August 21, 2013 – "Dear Angel Uriel, I'm glad you came through tonight. I know you're interested in helping writers. I was told something disturbing by several speakers at a writers workshop, and I want you to tell me if it's true.

"They said that as a new and unknown writer, I'll never be fortunate enough, in this day and age, to have a literary agent show interest in my manuscript. They said since I'll never attract a literary agent, I should only consider self-publishing my book. That was so discouraging, Angel

Uriel. All the other new writers I spoke to afterward felt dejected too. Is it true?"

OH NO, NOT TRUE IN YOUR CASE. YOU WILL HAVE A LITERARY AGENT AND A PUBLISHER, TOO.

"Really? Oh wow! That is such a relief. I was so stressed having to figure out how to get my book out to people who need it, and trying to do it on my own."

DERIVE PEACE AND PLEASURE KNOWING THAT YOUR BOOK HAS ITS PLACE, AT THIS TIME, AS IT COMES ALIVE ON ITS PATH.

"That is so exciting, I can hardly stand it! But it sounds almost too good to be true, Angel Uriel. I don't mean to sound like I'm doubting you, but could you please tell me…what is the name of the literary agency that is going to sign me?"

WOOD. BURN.

"Woodburn? That's the name of the literary agency? Please speak louder. I don't think I'm hearing you clearly."

WOOD. SIDE.

"Now I'm hearing Woodside. I'm really straining to hear you. Have I got it right? Woodside?"

WOODSIDE.

"Angel Uriel, I think I hear Woodside, but I'm just not sure. Thank you very much anyway. I guess I'm going to have to wait and see if I really am hearing you correctly."

A year later, when I'd finished my manuscript, I felt so excited, grateful, and very blessed as I signed a contract with an awesome literary agency.

And what was the name of the agency? Well, it wasn't quite the one I thought I heard…Woodside. But it was close. My new literary agent was Bill Gladstone of Waterside Productions.

The fact is, we can't always hear the Archangels perfectly. We're vibrating at our human frequency, after all, and trying to meld and communicate with Divine Beings at their elevated frequency. So it's not like chatting on the phone. But, although the connection isn't always crystal clear, many times it's close enough.

October 18, 2014 – "Hi Angel Uriel. Thank you for being here for me tonight. I need your wise words to give me clarity and comfort.

"I'm struggling to keep my friendship going with Vicky. She has changed so much over the last year or so. I know she hasn't personally suffered any tragedies, nor has her family. But she has become so negative, sarcastic, and cynical about people and life in general.

"We rarely get together for lunch anymore, and we used to enjoy those dates once a month or so. It was always fun trying out and critiquing new Tucson restaurants with her.

"It was such a downer talking to her on the phone today, I made an excuse to hang up quickly. I just want to avoid her calls, now. But then she'll leave a message and I'll have to return the call out of a sense of duty.

"What is going on with her? And why can't she just lighten up and have fun anymore? I'm happy to talk about some dark, serious subjects, of course, but just not all the time. She rarely has anything pleasant or interesting to share these days. But she'll recount the unfairness of her daily life down to the smallest detail.

"I can't even relax and enjoy her rare, funny quips. I automatically tense up waiting for her to say something mean about people we know or people we don't.

"When I try to change the subject to a great new novel I'm reading, cute kitten videos to watch, interesting health articles, or new recipes to try, she seems bored. She only wants to gossip. Should I keep trying to stay friends for old time's sake?"

YOU ARE CORRECT. THERE IS SOMETHING THAT HAS CHANGED YOUR FRIEND, AND IT HAS RUINED HER DAILY OUTLOOK. SHE IS OVERWHELMED NOW AND IT SEEPS FROM HER LIKE AN UNPLEASANT SCENT.

OF COURSE YOU ARE AWARE OF THE INJUSTICES IN THIS LIFE, AND HOW THEY CAN HAPPEN TO PEOPLE QUICK AND LOUDLY, OR SNEAK UP AT A QUIET, BARELY PERCEPTIBLE PACE.

PLEASE TRY NOT TO ADD TO HER PLIGHT BY BEING UNAVAILABLE TO HER NOW. INSTEAD, BE EVEN MORE POLITE. PRACTICE KINDNESS; ASK IF SHE NEEDS ANYTHING.

SHE MAY NOT REALIZE WHAT IS BEFALLING HER. SHE MAY BE TRYING TO MAKE HER WAY THROUGH HER NEW ANXIETY AND DARK FEARS BY JUDGING OTHERS AND USING ANGER AND A HARD SHELL FOR PROTECTION.

BUT YOU ARE IN A POSITION TO HELP HER. BE ALIVE WITH THAT KNOWLEDGE. BE PATIENT AND ACT SO WONDER-FILLED, JOYOUS, AND LIGHT ABOUT LIFE, THAT SHE HAS NO CHOICE BUT TO PAUSE IN HER DRAMATIZATIONS.

WITH ENOUGH CONSISTENT CARING, SHE MAY EVEN SEE HER WAY BACK TO BEING THAT PERSON YOU RECOGNIZE AND ENJOYED SO MUCH BEFORE.

"Thank you, I'll try. I doubt it'll help, but if you say so, I believe it."

I took Archangel Uriel's wise words to heart. It wasn't easy, but I forced myself to be consistently cheerful around Vicky, and have patience when she spewed negativity.

She never really told me what was eating at her, but I learned to take control and insist that she meet me for lunch instead of just talking on the phone.

When we were face to face, Vicky was less apt to give endless cynical speeches. I'd listen to her views for a while, then tactfully steer our talk to a positive story that I had at the ready. Usually she'd let me finish without interruption.

Getting up and walking around a few stores after lunch, instead of sitting too long in conversation, helped too. She even made me laugh sometimes, like old times.

Things weren't quite the same in our friendship as before, but now I could see the benefit of trying. And it felt good to think I might be helping my friend as she struggled with something she couldn't or wouldn't acknowledge.

November 30, 2017 – "Hi Angel Uriel. This question is for humanity as a whole. Why do more and more people seem unsatisfied in their lives? It's so much more obvious, lately, in what people say and in the articles I'm reading, and on the news, of course. What's going on? What's missing for them?"

THE PRIME REASON FOR UNHAPPINESS AND DISSATISFACTION IN LIFE IS THAT PEOPLE WANT MUCH MORE THAN THEY NEED. THEY SPEND MANY PRECIOUS YEARS YEARNING, CHASING, ACQUIRING. THEIR UNHAPPINESS REMAINS, BUT THEY OFTEN DON'T COME TO SEE THE TRUTH UNTIL THEY ARE AT THE END OF THEIR TIME HERE.

"What is the truth? What do they really need, Angel Uriel?"

THE TRUTH IS, THE ANSWER IS ALWAYS LOVE. THAT MAY SOUND AS SIMPLE OR DIFFICULT AS THESE CHOICES WILL BE.

"Thank you for the reminder. That's a good lesson to learn early and often."

August 6, 2019 – "Good evening, Angel Uriel. May I ask you about something I've been thinking about for some time?"

YES ABSOLUTELY, DEBRA.

"How can I do a better job of knowing what I'm supposed to be accomplishing in my life? I'm proud of what I have achieved so far. But I know there's more to do yet. Some folks I know seem to be hard at work achieving all their goals. It's like they know their path without question, or they're trying to create their path, always running to the next important thing on their schedules.

"I feel like I may be failing to do something I am here to do—something very important that I promised someone, somewhere, at some time."

THERE IS NO FAILING FROM YOU. YOU ARE NOT BREAKING ANY PROMISES. PLEASE DO NOT BE FOOLED BY THE BUSY-NESS OF THE PEOPLE YOU KNOW. YES, THEY SEEM TO BE DOING IMPORTANT THINGS IN YOUR EYES. BUT IF YOU LOOKED DEEPER, WOULD YOU SEE THEIR ACTIONS AS FULFILLING THEIR SOULS' PURPOSES? MAYBE AND MAYBE NOT.

YOUR FOCUS SHOULD BE LOOKING DEEPER INTO YOUR OWN HEART AND DISCOVERING THE LARGE AMOUNT OF LOVE THAT RESIDES THERE.

THAT'S WHAT REFLECTS ALL OF YOUR TRUE BEING AND WILL CONTINUE TO GROW TO ACCOMMODATE ALL THAT IS NECESSARY IN YOUR EXISTENCE AT PRESENT AND IN YOUR FUTURE FOLLOW-THROUGH.

THAT LOVE IS AN IDEAL AMOUNT AND REFLECTS, ALSO, THE PERSON YOU ARE—A CHERISHED SOUL WHO NEEDS TO LOVE HERSELF MORE, AND NOT FEEL INFERIOR TO OTHERS.

YOUR HEART SPEAKS VOLUMES. AND THAT IS YOUR PROMISE FULFILLED.

"You make me feel worthy. Thank you so much for that wonderful feeling, Angel Uriel."

October 9, 2019 – "There seems to be so many ways to look at life, Angel Uriel…so many different versions of truth and points of view. The mainstream media says one thing. The alternative news says another. People are divided. There are warnings about the battles of evil versus good on this planet.

"What is really going on here, and how do I ever find the truth? And if I did find the truth, could I handle it?"

ARRANGE TO PARTICIPATE IN LIFE'S TOURNAMENT BY PREPARING YOUR OWN WAY TO GO WITHIN YOURSELF TO DECIPHER AND DISCERN THE TRUTH.

WHEN YOU HAVE THE TRUTH APPEAR BEFORE YOU, DRINK IT IN WITH THE KNOWLEDGE THAT YOU CAN FEEL IT, HAVING DISCOVERED WHAT TRUTH FEELS LIKE, KNOWING THEN THAT IT IS TRUSTWORTHY.

YOU SEEK THIS ABILITY NOW AND YOU WILL HAVE THIS ADDRESSED AS YOU PRACTICE IT. AS YOU ASK FOR HELP WITH DISCERNMENT, YOU SHALL RECEIVE IT IN FAITH. BE UNAFRAID OF TRUTH, NO MATTER HOW HARD IT IS TO HANDLE. CLARITY ALLOWS FOR GROWTH.

YOU ARE SURROUNDED BY US AND OUR LOVE FOR YOU. WADE IN THE RIVER OF UNDERSTANDING AND FLOAT ATOP ALL THE SURGING BENEATH. IT CLEARS FOR

YOU, AND THE DARKNESS DEPARTS AHEAD OF THE TIME OF KNOWING.

October 14, 2019 – "I'm sorry I have so many questions tonight, Angel Uriel. I have at least ten. That's more than I usually have.

"Am I coming across as too demanding or annoying? You know, by now, how important it is for me to learn as many details as possible about what's coming up for me and my family. But I don't want to overstep my bounds with you and the other Angels."

DEAR ONE, YOU ARE NOT ANNOYING OR DEMANDING. WE UNDERSTAND YOUR NEED TO KNOW, AND TO TRY AND PREPARE WHERE AND WHEN YOU CAN, FOR THE UNEXPECTED.

BUT PLEASE RESPECT THE FACT THAT IT ISN'T NECESSARY OR EVEN POSSIBLE FOR YOU TO BE TOLD EVERYTHING YOU WANT TO KNOW, RIGHT NOW OR ANYTIME.

AWAITING THE OUTCOME IS PART OF THE LIVING OF LIFE. THINGS WILL HAPPEN IN THE WAY THEY ARE SUPPOSED TO, REST ASSURED.

WE WILL GIVE YOU THE ANSWERS WHEN WE CAN ABOUT THE THINGS WE CAN, AND IN THE MEANTIME, FIRE UP YOUR FAITH AND PATIENCE. LET YOURSELF RELAX IN YOUR LIFE'S FLOWING.

March 4, 2020 – "I read so much about the importance of finding our pure paths and fulfilling our soul contracts. That sounds like a lot of inner spiritual work. And truthfully, it sounds so serious and over-whelming. Aren't we also supposed to be having some fun down here on this earth plane, Angel Uriel?"

OH YES YOU ARE, DEAR ONE. FUN IS NECESSARY FOR SPIRITUAL GROWTH TOO. ONE OF THE PURPOSES HERE IS TO EMBRACE YOUR LABORS OF LOVE. THOSE ARE LIFE'S WORKS THAT BRING YOU SUCH JOY THAT YOU DO NOT MIND THE EFFORT OR STRUGGLE ATTACHED TO THEM. THE FUN GENERATED FROM SUCH ENDEAVORS REACHES DOWN TO INVIGORATE THE SOUL.

THESE JOYFUL ENTERPRISES CAN COVER A SPAN OF MANY YEARS OR JUST A SHORT TIME. THEY WILL ALL BE UNDERSTOOD IN THE DEEPEST LEVELS AND FOUND SATISFYING.

IT IS ALSO AN IMPORTANT FULFILLMENT IN LIFE TO FIND ENJOYMENT IN PLAYTIME. PLAY RELEASES CREATIVITY, WHICH PROMOTES JOY. JOY INVITES LOVE. LOVE IS THE ULTIMATE SPIRITUAL WORK.

"That's good to hear. Playtime and fun…they sound so freeing. But let's talk more about labors of love, which I know we've spoken about before.

"You know of course, Angel Uriel, that one of my true labors of love is writing. I am starting to organize all my Angel journals so I can write my next book about you—teaching my readers how to communicate with Archangels.

"As you also know, back when I lived in Tucson, I taught a few separate groups of people how to chat with you in their own journals. That was in-person, at my friend Madeline's house, and it went well. Most of them were able to write down messages they received from various Archangels that night.

"But this will be in book form. I'm going to have to organize my thoughts, experiences, and instructions differently. I'll need to use the right verbiage, sentences, and phrases instead of how I simply spoke the information to my audience. Can I really pull this off?"

ABSOLUTELY YES, OUR DEAR ONE. IT WILL WORK WELL IN BOOK FORM. BUT IT IS IMPORTANT FOR YOU TO CREATE, USING YOUR CHOSEN WRITTEN WORDS, A MOST LOVING ATMOSPHERE WITHIN ITS PAGES. IT IS IMPORTANT TO SHOW EVERYONE WHO SEEKS CONNECTION WITH US THAT WE ARE ALREADY HERE FOR THEM.

AS YOU SHARE YOUR OWN EXPERIENCES WITH AN OPEN HEART, YOUR READERS WILL FEEL OUR DEEP LOVE THROUGH YOUR WORDS, EVEN BEFORE THEY TRULY EXPERIENCE IT FOR THEMSELVES.

April 19, 2020 – "Oh, Angel Uriel. Why am I not hearing you very well tonight? I know you're here, as I heard you say your name. But now I hear only silence when I ask my questions.

"I'm sure you know I'm pretty stressed out over this COVID-19 pandemic we're all unfortunately dealing with, here and all over the world. Please help me hear your answers clearly now.

"I'm worried about keeping our family's good health, and about the health of our friends, too. If this virus is as bad as they're saying on the news, it could really sicken a lot of people we care about. Could you please share your insights with me about this?

"Hello? I'm still not hearing you. And I really need your comforting answers and encouragement. I want to hear that it'll all be alright. Could you please speak louder?

"Still nothing? Well, maybe I'd better put my journal away and try again tomorrow. Sometimes that works when I can't hear you. But I feel like time is of the essence. I really need you tonight."

YOU WILL HEAR. CALM YOURSELF. REST EASIER, FOR NOW.

"Okay, I'm taking a big breath, Angel Uriel. I'm forcing myself to relax. My neck and shoulders are unwinding. My arms are sagging now. I'm taking more slow breaths now. I'll sit quietly like this for a few minutes.

"Okay. Alright. I am much more relaxed."

ALWAYS, THE BEST WAY TO INTENSIFY YOUR EXPERIENCE WITH US IS TO WAIT UNTIL YOU ARE WITHOUT ANXIETY, ANGER, OR FEAR. THEN LET THE CALM IN YOUR HEART LEAD YOU TO HEAR US AND FEEL US, ALLOWING YOU TO WRITE THE GIVE-AND-TAKE OF OUR DIALOGUE WITH YOU.

"Yes, thank you! I can definitely hear you now."

EMOTIONAL UPSETS WILL PREVENT THE TRANSFER OF UNDERSTANDING BETWEEN US. IT WILL HINDER THE MELDING OF OUR VIBRATIONS AND THOUGHTS TOGETHER.

TRANQUILITY, THEREFORE, EQUALS TRUE COMMUNICATION.

"But who can remain cool and calm in the face of worry and mayhem? That's a huge challenge for me, and I'm sure for many other people.

"Of course, it does make sense that humans will connect better and hear your important messages when we're not freaking out."

WE UNDERSTAND THE DIFFICULTY OF MASTERING HUMAN EMOTIONS. THAT CAN BE AN IMPOSSIBLE TASK. BUT YOU MUST REACH A STATE OF CALM FOCUS. MORE AND MORE DEEP BREATHS AND IMAGINING US SURROUNDING YOU WILL HELP IN THAT EFFORT.

WAIT UNTIL YOU FEEL OUR LOVE AND SUPPORT. YOU WILL KNOW. DO NOT TRY TO RUSH IT. WE WILL ALWAYS BE AVAILABLE FOR THE RIGHT TIMING OF OUR INTERBLENDING.

"Thank you, Angel Uriel. You and the other Archangels always make me feel so much better. You illuminate so many dark, confusing, and worrisome situations for me."

And speaking of brightening a dark and scary situation for me, Howard and Jill had gone to Alaska on September 2nd, 2022, for a twelve-day father/daughter adventure. They enjoyed seeing moose, orca, sled dogs, and even the aurora borealis when they spent the night in a modern igloo at Borealis Basecamp near Fairbanks.

But they both came home sick with sore throats, coughs, and upper respiratory symptoms. Howard recovered fairly rapidly, but Jill continued to feel worse and worse.

She began having fevers and tightness in her chest and breathing became more and more difficult. Because she works from home, her fiancé, Ryan, who also works from home, made sure she had plenty of tea and soups and whatever else she needed.

Unfortunately, Jill got to the point where she couldn't lie down in bed because it caused her breathing to be more labored and her coughing to be even more severe. So she began sleeping poorly, a couple of hours at a time, sitting propped up on the couch.

Suspecting that she might have pneumonia, she went to see her primary care physician. Sure enough x-rays and blood tests revealed that she had bi-lateral bacterial pneumonia. She was given antibiotics and enough albuterol for four nebulizer breathing treatments a day at home.

But she wasn't improving. She was still sleeping upright, still coughing severely, and still having trouble breathing.

The doctor put her on a different antibiotic after the first one had run its course and we all began worrying about her recovery.

Howard and I were booked on an upcoming flight to visit our son, David, who now lived in Charlotte, North Carolina. We planned to spend nine days visiting him. We hadn't seen him for a year and we would be celebrating his birthday, too. Jill was supposed to join us on the trip, but she was obviously too sick to go.

On Monday October 3rd, the day before our flight, Howard and I packed our bags and drove three hours down the mountain from our home to Phoenix. We checked into a hotel close to the airport, convenient for our flight the next morning.

We knew Jill had another follow up appointment with her doctor at four o'clock that day. Ryan drove her because she was too weak and breathless to drive herself.

Howard and I decided to kill some time meanwhile, so we headed to a Kohl's store to snoop around.

As we drove we noticed how weird the sky looked. Huge muddy-colored clouds of reddish brown and greyish purple were spreading out, overtaking the clear bright blue.

"Do you think that's a haboob coming this way?" I asked, alarmed.

"I don't know. Maybe it's just a regular storm rolling in."

"I've never seen clouds quite that color. Look how murky the sky is. It looks like doomsday's coming."

A haboob is a violent dust storm caused by strong winds flowing downward and outward from a thunderstorm. They can lead to near-zero visibility, causing dangerous road conditions. The Phoenix area can experience them a few times a year.

We hurried into the store to get out of the winds that were starting to pick up. Strolling the aisles, we hadn't walked far when Jill called.

"Mom, I'm in trouble here," she said softly. "I'd cry, but it's too hard to breathe."

"What's going on, honey? You never cry." I steeled myself and grabbed Howard's arm for support.

"The doctor says I'm really sick but he's going to try his best to keep me out of the hospital. My right lung has improved, but my left lung is still filled with fluid. He says he's sorry, but I have to have a procedure to drain the fluid.

"He said the antibiotics should have gotten rid of the fluid, but that just hasn't happened. So he put me on a third antibiotic to keep me from possibly getting sepsis while we wait for the procedure."

"When will that be?"

"He wrote an order for it. It's called a thoracentesis and it'll be done as an out-patient at the hospital.

"They have to put a long needle into my lung…it sounds so awful. And he said there's a twenty-five percent chance that my lung could collapse during the procedure. If that happens, I will have to lie flat until it re-inflates, maybe eight hours later. And during the procedure they'll have to take precautions due to my Factor V."

Jill and I both have Factor V Leiden, a genetic mutation of our blood that makes us more susceptible to clots.

"Oh Jilly, I'm so sorry. When will they do this?"

"It depends on my insurance and when they can schedule it, but maybe in the next few days."

"Oh no, we're flying out tomorrow morning."

"I know, Mom," she said softly, obviously holding back tears. "I can't believe how bad this timing is."

"Are you still at the doctor's office?"

"No, we're in the car driving home in this haboob."

"Do you want us to come over?"

"No, I'm just so exhausted."

"Are you going to tell me what's going on?" Howard asked with concern.

"Jill, you just go home and relax. Dad and I are going to find someplace to have dinner and talk. We'll call you a little later."

While we walked toward the front doors of the store, I briefly filled Howard in on everything Jill had told me. But before he could say anything we stopped in our tracks and watched how people were lining up in front of the store's large windows. They stood peering out at the storm.

Thick brown dust now swirled in angry eddies around the cars in the parking lot. The wind howled through the outer sets of doors, blowing puffs of dirt inside. And now the mucky, leaden clouds had fully blotted out the sun.

I immediately thought of Archangel Uriel. As the Angel of Weather, he rules over the wind, rain, and any kind of storm, including this weird haboob.

He is also one of the wisest and most intellectual Archangels, illuminating whatever is going on during our darkest and most confusing times. In a crisis, Archangel Uriel guides us and helps us find the best solutions to our problems.

"We should head out before this storm gets worse," Howard said. "We'll find someplace to eat close by and ride it out."

"Okay, but stick to the surface roads, please. The freeways are notoriously dangerous during haboobs."

We ran to our car, shielding ourselves from the gritty gusts as best we could. As we pulled onto the main street, traffic was backed up and barely moving. An ambulance, siren blaring, did its best to maneuver around us and the other stopped cars.

The noise and the ominous sky added to our stress as we slowly headed deeper into our surreal surroundings.

I quietly asked Archangel Uriel to keep us safe driving in this storm, and to lessen the severity of it as well.

"Please Angel Uriel. There's so much weird and frightening stuff going on. This storm looks apocalyptic and Jill is so terribly sick. She has to have a scary procedure to drain her lung. I'm so worried I can't think straight right now.

"And we're supposed to fly out to see David tomorrow morning. It's just too much. I need your help big time on this one. Please surround me and my family with your love, support, and wisdom, and with God's light. Also, please give us strength now. Thank you."

"Do you want to go to Cracker Barrel?" Howard asked. "It's right over there, nice and close. And we can get out of this storm."

"Not really," I muttered.

Howard loves Cracker Barrel. As a family, we'd enjoyed plenty of meals at many Cracker Barrel restaurants over the years, throughout Arizona.

For me, the restaurant was synonymous with good times, happy gatherings, and laughter. Exactly the opposite of how I was feeling right then.

"We really should eat there, Deb. The sooner we can pull over the better."

"I'd rather not. I'm just not in the mood."

As we drove on for another minute I realized Howard was right. Driving around in this dusty soup was ridiculous.

"Okay honey," I said. "Maybe we should go to Cracker Barrel."

Howard nodded and made several left turns, then a right, detouring back to the restaurant entrance. It was a relief to park the car in the nearly empty lot. Scurrying to the front door, we were rudely pushed around by the dirty winds.

We were seated promptly, as this usually crowded restaurant had plenty of seats available. I looked out the window as the storm raged.

"Well, we're having a fun day," Howard said ruefully, shaking his head.

The server, a pretty brunette, came over to ask if we were ready to order. I was still looking over the menu, so Howard gave her his order.

When I raised my head to speak to her, I was immediately struck by something in her eyes. They were dark brown with an unusual depth and shine to them. I couldn't fathom why, but I suddenly felt like this young woman was someone I could share all my burdens with.

I dismissed the odd feeling, and simply told her what I wanted to eat, although I wasn't very hungry.

After she left the table, Howard looked at me uneasily. "So, what are we going to do about Jill? Are we going on this trip tomorrow?"

I burst into tears. Howard watched helplessly as I tried to muffle the intensity of my ugly crying by mopping my mouth and eyes, over and over, with every paper napkin on the table.

Hot tears streamed down my face, and I just couldn't stop them. Pent up fear and worry poured out of me. Although the release felt good, I was embarrassed; a woman was staring at me from another table. Not one for public displays of drama, I had never cried while sitting in a restaurant in my life.

Suddenly the server was back at our table addressing me.

"I just have a quick question about your order," she began. "Did you say you wanted the soup or … oh my goodness … are you alright? Is there anything I can do?"

"I'm sorry, I don't usually … " I broke off the sentence with a sniffle, still mopping at my mascara-ruined eyes.

I looked up into her face. Her expression was so full of concern, it made me feel, again, like I could tell her, a perfect stranger, everything. I looked at her nametag.

"Our daughter is very sick, Claudia. We're a little shell-shocked right now because we just found out that the antibiotics aren't working and she needs a procedure for her pneumonia that sounds barbaric. The doctors need to drain her lung with a long needle."

"Oh, she needs to have a thoracentesis?" she asked.

Howard and I looked at each other, surprised that our server knew about the procedure, let alone the correct medical term for it.

"Yes, that's the word," I said. "I couldn't remember it."

"Well, it's not the most pleasant procedure, but your daughter will feel immediate relief and be able to take good full breaths right away."

"But she has a blood clotting disorder, and that can complicate things," I said, apparently not wanting to have my horror diminished yet.

"Oh, she has Factor V Leiden?"

Shocked, Howard and I stared at Claudia.

"Yes she does," I said, feeling a tingle run up my spine.

"Well, as long as the doctors know that ahead of time, there shouldn't be any problems. It'll be okay."

"Claudia, how do you know all this?" Howard asked.

"Well," she smiled, "I'm an oncology nurse and many of my patients have needed to have a thoracentesis. They all do well with it and feel better immediately afterward. Your daughter will be fine. She might actually need a second one done, maybe a week later. But don't worry if that happens. It isn't unusual."

"You're…a nurse?" I asked trying to wrap my head around that information.

"Yes," she laughed. "This is my side job, being a server here. I do this a few hours a week because I love the happy energy of healthy people here in the restaurant. It's a good balance to the different kind of energy from my main job."

Claudia put her arm around me. "What is your daughter's name?"

"Jill."

"If it's okay with you, I'm going to pray for Jill's recovery tonight. But don't you worry, she's going to be just fine. Now, you wanted the soup, right? I'll be right back."

Howard was grinning ear to ear. "Now aren't you glad we came to Cracker Barrel? Where else could we have gone where our server would also be a nurse who just happened to know about this procedure?"

"Absolutely nowhere else," I said, suddenly feeling calm and relaxed.

Through the window I could see that the haboob had slowed down in intensity and the sky looked less ominous. There were cars pulling into the parking lot and people heading inside for supper.

My tears had dried by the time Claudia brought our food. She checked back with us every so often to see that I was eating some soup. Her attentiveness felt so warm and inviting, like an extra blanket on a cold night.

Howard and I decided to cancel our trip. We couldn't fly across the country now, especially not knowing when Jill's procedure would take place. We wanted to be there with her. And we knew David would understand and would want us to be there for his sister during her health crisis.

When dinner was done, we thanked Claudia profusely for helping calm us down and making us feel so much better about Jill.

"It was my pleasure," she said. "And if you need me, you know where I am."

I squelched the urge to ask for her cell number, although she probably would have cheerfully given it to me. I hugged her tightly, not wanting to leave her loving presence. "You'll never know what you've done for us today, Claudia."

"Let's head back to the hotel," Howard said putting his arm around me. "We'll call David on the way and then we'll call Jill and let her know we're not leaving as planned."

Once back in the car, all I could do was silently thank Archangel Uriel over and over. He had settled down the haboob, at least in the area we were driving in. And more importantly, he had shone a loving light into our darkness and fear by arranging the scenario we'd just experienced. Seriously, what are the odds that our server at Cracker Barrel would also be an experienced nurse?

And the icing on that Angel cake? Jill began to rapidly heal on her own after that day. The fluid in her lung disappeared well before her thoracentesis appointment. So the procedure was cancelled.

Thank you Archangel Uriel! And thank you for your prayers, Claudia.

When I told my friend Melanie about Claudia a few days later, Melanie said, "Wow! The most incredible things happen to you. But this is an amazing story, even for you. I'm sure oncology nurses don't moonlight as servers at family restaurants very often. Do you think Claudia was an Angel sent to help you?"

"I don't know. She sure seemed like one."

"Deb, you have to call up that Cracker Barrel. You have to see if she's a real person; if she really works there. If they've never heard of her, you'll know."

I called immediately and spoke to the manager. At first he was rather guarded when I asked if Claudia was an employee. But when I explained how she had helped us, his voice grew warmer and he confirmed that Claudia was, indeed, an employee, and that she was also in the medical field.

"Please would you give her a message? Tell her that our daughter is healing and feeling much better. And thank her for her prayers and her compassion. We'll never forget her, and will always think of her as an Angel sent from above."

"Thank you, ma'am, for letting me know. I'm going to give her your message and I'm going to let our general manager know about her kindness as well."

October 11, 2022 – "Dear Angel Uriel, how can I ever thank you enough for Jill's ongoing recovery?"

WE KNOW HOW MUCH YOU WERE DEALING WITH AND ARE SORRY FOR SUCH A PAINFUL TIME FOR ALL. BUT THINGS WERE BEING WORKED ON FOR A GOOD OUTCOME.

"Yes, I know now how true that is. And that's why I'm so grateful to you. You calmed the haboob and arranged for us to meet Claudia, didn't you?"

YES. THERE WAS ALWAYS A LIGHT TO BE FOUND TO HELP YOU REALIZE ALL WOULD TURN OUT WELL.

"It was all perfectly done. Maybe a bit dramatic with the haboob though!

"But really, Angel Uriel, thank you so much. We were in such dark despair. And then we really felt your caring and support through Claudia. I'm just amazed at the way you work through lovely souls like her to help other people. Thank you for that incredible experience.

"You and the other Archangels have shared your love and compassion with me time and time again since I asked you to come into my life. How and why did I ever live so many years without this knowledge and understanding of you?"

BECAUSE, DEAR ONE, FOR ALL THOSE MANY YEARS, IT WAS ENOUGH THAT WE HAD KNOWLEDGE AND UNDERSTANDING OF YOU.

Chapter Seven
Archangel Metatron
Serves Behind God's Throne

Archangel Metatron's name, unlike that of most other Archangels, doesn't end in 'el' which means 'Of God' because instead of being created as an Archangel by God, he was once a human being who lived on earth. In fact he was the prophet Enoch of the bible. He led such a pious life that when he died, he ascended, via God's reward, to become a Divine being.

One other human of the bible, prophet Elijah, was blessed with the same experience, eventually becoming Archangel Sandalphon. That's why Archangels Metatron and Sandalphon are sometimes referred to as the twin Angels. And because they experienced what it's like to be human, they can more easily relate to our everyday problems, worries, fears, and insecurities.

Archangel Metatron's name is said to mean either One Who Serves Behind God's Throne or One Who Guards. He projects the colors iridescent violet, dark green, and bright silver/white.

Also known as the Angel of Life, Archangel Metatron is the guardian of the Tree of Life. He sends creative energy downward from the crown of the tree toward all of creation.

Archangel Metatron also oversees the flow of energy inside a brightly lit, mystical structure called Metatron's Cube. This Cube of sacred geometry is made up of every geometric shape in God's creation, exhibiting the building blocks of all physical matter found in nature from crystals to human DNA.

It is said that Archangel Metatron employs the Cube to help people release what no longer serves them physically, emotionally, energetically, and spiritually, ridding them of low, negative vibrations.

The Cube spins clockwise causing the unwanted energies to be pushed away by centrifugal force. And with those low energies dispatched, we humans can break free of our limited thinking patterns. Instead of automatically falling back to our usual customs, we're free to experience new ways of looking at our issues, problems, blessings, and everything else in our lives.

Also referred to as The Divine Record Keeper, Archangel Metatron is often depicted sitting next to God's throne, writing down every aspect of humanity, every little detail, which is then stored in the Akashic records. These records are called the Book of Life, the great archive of the Universe, where everything that has ever happened or will ever happen—all of humanity's thoughts, feelings, actions, and deeds over many lifetimes—is recorded.

With a soft spot for human record keepers, Archangel Metatron is happy to assist bookkeepers, accountants, historians, human resource managers, court reporters, and anyone else who needs help with accuracy and clarity in their records.

Archangel Metatron also helps and protects all children, while being particularly attentive to children who are more sensitive or spiritual than others. He helps comfort their nightmares, anxiety, illnesses, and fears. He also soothes sensitive adults, especially those having trouble adjusting to new situations at home, work, school, or healing from experiences with violence, crime, or emotional traumas.

And finally, as if he doesn't have enough important work to do, Archangel Metatron is also the Angel of Ascension. What is ascension?

According to my research, the explanation varies from source to source. But, basically it means to become enlightened, holy, and to achieve full comprehension, true revelation, and deep insight into the how and why of all things. It means reaching our highest vibrational frequency leading to an understanding of the mind of God, and perceiving everything in an interconnected unity. It is the highest state that humanity can achieve—being one with everything that is and has ever been.

Ascension sounds like a tall order to me. Apparently it requires the ability to rein in our low frequency human egos, angers, jealousies, fears, judgements, and resentments, while living consciously, in gratitude, joy, and compassion.

It is the shifting from our lower physical earth plane of existence to a higher plane or frequency, through our attention and awareness. We can then finally achieve the goal of living in the light, aligning with the Divine, and returning to the true oneness of God's love.

Not surprising, many people will not be able to achieve this lofty goal in this particular lifetime, which is only one of many we've lived. Everyone is on their own unique journey and progression rate. But there are always people who are ascending. They aren't disappearing visually, so to speak, but their reality is changing. They are doing their spiritual homework and expanding to their higher purpose, having learned their lessons on this earth plane, and graduated into living in the true light.

When we call upon him for help in this area, Archangel Metatron guides us in our ascension process. He may lead us to read the right articles or books for inspiration. He may send us signs, messages, and reminders to look at our daily experiences with a new attitude of gratitude, find more patience when dealing with difficult people, or catch ourselves before we judge others.

A Facebook friend of mine had posted a mean-spirited message for all her friends to see. It was divisive in how it called out an entire group of people for blame and shame. I became instantly irritated with her, even though such nastiness didn't seem like her typical character.

I wasn't about to post a reply and dignify her message with a response. But I couldn't help growling at her through my computer screen. I'm sure my nice high frequencies immediately plunged to match her low negative ones as I unleashed a stinging retort that she would never hear.

But with a sudden jolt, I realized that I was judging her for being judgmental of others! And that was exactly what Archangel Metatron had warned me about when I had recently asked for his help with my path to ascension.

He had explained how I needed to catch myself when I was triggered. I needed to take a step back, remove myself from ego-filled condemnations of others, and simply become an observer.

So, taking a few deep breaths, I forced myself to smile (okay, maybe I was gritting my teeth) and I became a casual observer only, with no opinion of the situation. The only thing I allowed myself to say was, "How interesting."

And just like that, I took myself, my critical thoughts, and my heated emotions out of the equation. I became a non-player in the no-win judgement game.

I was then able to click off her post, unfazed, and move on with my day. The best part? Those heavy feelings of annoyance and righteous scorn quickly dissolved, leaving me feeling calm and peaceful. My frequencies must have been soaring back up. I hadn't realized how assessing her actions had been such a burden on me.

But it takes lots of practice to become a casual observer. Meanwhile, 'fake it 'til you make it' as they say. When things that people say or do get your blood boiling and you're in danger of judging them, or being pulled down by their negative frequencies, simply force your lips into a smile, fake or not, observe, and say to yourself, "How interesting."

October 31, 2014 – "Thank you for coming through to chat with me, Angel Metatron. I hope I can finally get some sleep tonight. Why am I so restless lately? I can't seem to sleep through the night anymore. I wake up and toss and turn for hours. What is my problem?"

THE REASON YOU ARE AWAKE MANY NIGHTS AT THREE OR FOUR O'CLOCK AM IS BECAUSE YOU ARE ON AN ANSWER-SEEKING QUEST.

THAT IS A GOOD THING. HOWEVER THOSE ANSWERS, WHEN GIVEN TO YOU, CAN CAUSE MORE CONFUSION AND TAKE SOME TIME AND DIFFERENT INNER ROUTES TO PROCESS COMPLETELY FOR YOUR COMFORT AND UNDERSTANDING.

IT IS NOT UNUSUAL FOR THIS TO DISRUPT SLEEP CYCLES TEMPORARILY. TRY TO OPEN YOURSELF UP TO MORE OF OUR HELP AT THIS TIME, LISTEN, AND BELIEVE.

ALSO, SOAK YOURSELF IN QUIET. WITHIN YOURSELF ARE ALL THE PATHWAYS TO TRUE UNDERSTANDING. IT'S WHERE OUTSIDE INFLUENCES CANNOT GO. INNER KNOWLEDGE SAYS ALL IS WELL. BELIEVE IT. BELIEF IS THE KEY; IT IS THE ALL.

FAITH AND BELIEF
WILL GIVE YOUR HEART RELIEF
FROM DEEP QUESTIONS AND PAIN
YOU CANNOT ASCERTAIN
AND WE MAY NOT YET EXPLAIN.

"Wow, you wrote me a poem! It's so awesome. Thank you Angel Metatron."

November 18, 2014 – "Hi Angel Metatron. I'm glad you're here with me tonight. Many years before I began to communicate with you and the other Archangels, back when I was thirty-nine years old, I attempted to play the violin. I took lessons for a year before admitting defeat.

"I had no illusions of grandeur, but I had always adored classical music, especially the violin, and had been in awe of violinist Itzhak Perlman for years. Even disabled by polio, he was able to play the instrument in a way few have achieved. I've watched the video of him playing Beethoven's Violin Concerto countless times.

"When I was in my fifties, I tried to play the flute. It only took six months to realize I couldn't play that, either. Not enough breath and no talent whatsoever. I knew better than to even attempt the harp, another instrument I'd love to play. Were you aware of any of this?"

YES OF COURSE. WE KNOW OF YOUR DESIRE TO PLAY THOSE INSTRUMENTS.

"Angel Metatron, there are so many gifted and talented people in this world—people who write amazing novels or create gorgeous works of art. But the musicians! They're my favorites. Especially an incredible musician and composer like Ludwig van Beethoven. His music always reaches down deep, thrilling my soul, and has done so since I was a little girl.

"Why do I have the capacity to adore music to such a degree, yet I don't have the talent to play it? And my singing voice? It hurts my own ears. My children used to ask me to please stop singing them lullabies when they were young.

"So, I thought I'd ask you these questions since you keep the Akashic records. Could you please look into my personal records and see why musical talent isn't in the cards for me?"

OH, BUT TALENT IS SOMETHING THAT EVERY HUMAN SOUL POSSESSES. ALL TRUE INNATE HUMAN TALENT COMES FROM A PLACE OF LOVING CREATION WITHIN THE SOUL. IT EVOLVED FROM THE BEGINNING TO HOLD AND PRESERVE IT IN SUCH A WAY AS TO PASS IT ALONG FOREVER.

IT MAY NOT ALWAYS PRESENT ITSELF IN AN OBVIOUS WAY, YET IT IMPROVES AND EVOLVES AS IT DEEPENS, RADIATING FROM THE HEART OUTWARD.

THAT KIND OF TALENT CAN BE ARTISTIC, CREATIVE, OR MUSICAL, OF COURSE, BUT IT CAN ALSO BE A SPECIAL GIFT ONE HAS FOR LISTENING, LEARNING, TEACHING, AND HELPING OTHERS IN MANY DIFFERENT WAYS.

YOU ALREADY KNOW THE TALENTS YOU POSSESS, YET MAKING MUSIC MAY NOT BE ONE OF THEM IN THIS LIFETIME.

HOWEVER, YOUR ABILITY TO DERIVE A GREAT DEAL OF PLEASURE FROM THE INTERPLAY OF THE NOTES, AND YOUR GIFT FOR HEARING THE PITCH AND RECOGNIZING THE QUALITY OF THE SOUND IS TALENT IN ITSELF. AS IS YOUR ABILITY TO COMMIT LARGE PIECES OF MUSIC TO MEMORY.

"Oh yeah, I have memorized seven of Beethoven's nine symphonies and his violin concerto. Not the written notes, of course; I'm not good at reading musical scores. But the sound of those entire works, in all its glory, is in my memory. I couldn't forget it if I wanted to. And I can recall it, really hear it all in my mind, whenever I want to. Thank you. I guess I do have musical talent. It's just … hidden inside of my own head."

WHAT A PERFECT PLACE FOR YOU TO ENJOY IT

December 29, 2014 – "Good evening, Angel Metatron. Tonight I'm feeling sorry for humanity, past and present, as I contemplate 'man's inhumanity to man.'

"There seems to be so many angry people disrespecting each other and disharmony of all kinds all over the world. It's reflected all day in the alarming narrative of the news media.

"Why does this world have to be so negative? We hear much more about life's miseries and people's failures than about the good people doing remarkable things. Could we please experience a little heaven on earth for a change? How will any of us ever ascend? Or is it supposed to be like this? You're here to help us with all of this, right?"

WE ARE HERE TO SERVE AS YOUR ANCHORS TO THE REAL WORLD. WHICH WORLD IS THE REAL ONE? YOUR EARTHLY WORLD IS TRULY THE ILLUSION. IT SEEMS SO REAL WHILE YOU'RE THERE, WE KNOW, BECAUSE IT'S SUPPOSED TO BE THAT WAY. IT FOSTERS THE LESSONS, ALWAYS MORE LESSONS, FOR YOU TO LEARN.

BUT TRY NOT TO GET CAUGHT UP IN THE DECEPTIVE DARKNESS AND NEGATIVITY WHICH CAUSES FEAR AND LOWERS YOUR VIBRATION. MOST OF WHAT YOU ARE PRESENTED WITH ARE STORIES FILLED WITH EXAGGERATION AND FABRICATION.

CONSIDER SUCH DISCOURSE AS UNTRUSTWORTHY, AND AS TEMPORARY AS SAND THROUGH YOUR FINGERS.

ALWAYS PROTECT THE FLEDGLING FIRE OF HOPE AND JOY IN YOUR HEART FOR THE GOODNESS TO COME. AND COME IT WILL. THE DIVINE LIVES IN YOU—THAT SPARK IS THE TRUE REALITY THAT WILL BRING SOME MORE HEAVEN TO YOUR EARTHLY EXPERIENCE, AS YOU KNOW IT HAS BEFORE.

April 14, 2020 – "Dear Angel Metatron, we are in the throes of the COVID-19 pandemic, and there is so much fear and worry all over the world right now, let alone in our country, state, and community. What can you tell me about this situation we're all in?"

THERE CERTAINLY HAVE BEEN MORE CURTAINS OF DARKNESS FALLING AROUND HUMANITY OF LATE, AND BRAZEN MECHANICS ON THE PART OF THOSE WHO LIVE FOR TROUBLE AND STRIFE.

THOSE CURTAINS ARE NOW BEING PULLED SLOWLY BACK TO ALLOW MORE OF GOD'S LIGHT TO PENETRATE. THERE WILL BE A LIFTING OF THE HEAVINESS YOU'VE BEEN FEELING.

REGAIN YOUR SHINING BRILLIANCE FROM THAT LOVING LIGHT, DEBRA. WE MISS YOUR USUAL GLOW.

"Aww, really? Thank you. I do miss feeling breezy and positive about things. This heaviness in my heart isn't fun."

FEAR NOT THIS PRESENT TIDE OF HOPELESSNESS. IT IS INEVITABLE THAT SOME WILL FEEL THE PAIN, BUT OTHERS WILL CONTINUE TO FLOURISH AND GROW.

BE NOT AFRAID, CHILD, AS THY MAKER SEES THE BIG PICTURE, ALWAYS. GOOD THINGS CAN GROW ONLY WITHIN A GARDEN YOU HAVE FEARLESSLY AND LOVINGLY PLANTED. CREATE THAT GARDEN NOW. AND PLEASE TREAT YOURSELF AS IF YOU LOVED YOURSELF MORE THAN YOU DO—AS MUCH AS WE LOVE YOU.

"Oh, now don't make me cry like you all do so often, okay? That all sounds so good, Angel Metatron, but how do I quit being afraid for the future for my family and myself? I've been trying to find things to stay positive about, but the worries usually win out."

YES, THE PAIN AND WORRY OF THE WORLD CAN BE OVERWHELMING, WE KNOW, SO GIVE US YOUR WORRIES, FEARS, AND CONCERNS. WE ARE HERE TO RECEIVE THEM FROM YOU.

JUST ASK US TO UNBURDEN YOU AND THEN PICTURE YOURSELF PHYSICALLY REACHING UP AND HANDING ALL OF IT TO US. EVERY LITTLE WORRY.

WE LOVE BEING ABLE TO HELP IN THIS WAY, FOR YOU DESERVE THE LIFE YOU ENVISION FOR YOURSELF, TO CREATE YOUR JOY AND PASSION, AND TO BE FREE OF

THE WORLD'S HEAVY BURDENS. YOUR BACK ISN'T BROAD ENOUGH TO CARRY ALL OF THAT. NOR SHOULD IT BE.

July 11, 2020 – "Okay, Angel Metatron. I've got to admit…this has been so awesome. I've been handing you all my worries, fears, and concerns for a few months now and it's really helping me.

"Whenever I read about some new world-wide gloom and doom, and start feeling the first flutters of fear, I just remind myself that I have no worries anymore.

"Then I reach up with my heavy hands and give the new burden to you. I instantly feel lighter, breathe deeper, and feel more peaceful and optimistic. It is such a relief to share these things with you.

"Of course, I was skeptical at first, I'm sorry to say, but now I know I can quickly relieve those first stirrings of dread, and just be left with gratitude.

"Thank you so much for helping me and other humans in this way. In this tough game of life, I know that you and the other Archangels truly have my back."

And speaking of Archangel Metatron having my back, in August of 2021, our son drove from his home in the Phoenix area to our home in the White Mountains for a three-day visit. Our elevation, above six thousand feet, always provided a cool reprieve from the desert heat, which David appreciated.

In the evenings after dinner David, Howard, and I would sit out on the back deck enjoying the sounds of the breezes whooshing through the tall pines. We could hear the last of the bird calls and the first strains of the night's cricket symphony.

David and I are both night owls, so one evening after Howard had gone to bed, we stayed out on the deck talking until after one a.m. I lit some candles and brought out warm throws for us to cozy up with. It was perfect until David broached a subject that made me feel ill.

"Mom, I can't stop thinking about moving to Charlotte, North Carolina. As you know, I have a lot of friends in that area, many who work in NASCAR."

"Yes, I do know that," I said warily.

"They say I could probably get back working in NASCAR again, but obviously I'd have to be living there to do that."

David had worked for a NASCAR truck team a decade before when he lived in Atlanta. He had been a mechanic as well as a spotter—the guy who wears a headset and talks directly to the driver during a race, providing vital information and warnings about real time happenings on the track. Exciting stuff.

"Well, I know how much you loved that life. Heck, you've loved everything NASCAR since you were eleven years old. But things are different now. You've gone back to college and earned your accounting degree. You have a life in Phoenix and a good job as an accountant. You have Jill close by and we're only three hours away."

"I know, and that would be the hardest part…leaving my family. But I still have that dream that has never gone away.

"And you're right, Mom. Things are different now. I'm ten years older. I'm not a kid anymore, and maybe this dream isn't even possible. I've been away from it for so long. But I feel like I have to try. And now I'm in a better position career wise. I can take an accounting job in Charlotte while I investigate the NASCAR possibilities."

"Oh, David. I had a feeling this would happen someday, that you'd get that itch again." I sighed deeply. "I just don't want you to move away."

"Well," David said with a smile, "you and Dad moved away from us recently, didn't you?"

"Yes, we did," I admitted. "But we didn't want to move away from you and Jill. We just needed a break from the desert and it's only three hours…not way across the country."

"I know. And we understood. Now I hope you'll understand why I need to pursue this before it's too late."

We sat in hushed stillness, as my heart filled with dread knowing how much I'd miss my son. Then, knowing I needed help, I silently appealed to Archangel Metatron.

I asked him to please do his spinning thing with his sacred Cube, giving me strength and cutting away my old, automatic, negative thinking process. It was crucial for me to break out of that thought prison of my own making.

And despite my resistance to our family living so far apart, and the sorrow I was already feeling, I knew my son wanted my support and encouragement in trying for his long-held dream.

"Well, then you should plan a trip to Charlotte soon," I said, shocked to hear those words coming out of my mouth. "Call your friends and contacts there, stay for a week or two, and see if it's a viable option. It's the only way to know for sure."

David's face lit up. "That's exactly what I was thinking of doing."

"Well, make it happen. You don't want to wait another ten years. Go after your dream now." I stood up and walked over to my son for a hug. "I'm going to bed. Sleep well, honey. See you in the morning."

What had I just done? Had I really given David the green light to move two thousand miles away? Mixed feelings flooded through me as I stepped into the house. On the one hand I was surprised and proud of myself for so gracefully putting my feelings aside for David's benefit. And on the other hand, I wanted to tear out my traitorous tongue.

"Thank you, Angel Metatron, I think. No, really, I mean it," I whispered as I walked through the darkened family room. "I know you intervened on that one for me. You knew I didn't want to act negative and selfish; I only want his happiness. But that one was tough. I know I have to accept his moving away again. More growth for my soul, right? I'm sorry, but I'm tired of growth always being so painful.

"Sure, I'll be shedding tears, but if David is meant to live in Charlotte and it's for his best life, I'll be thrilled for him. And I know Howard will feel the same way when we tell him tomorrow. Thank you again, Angel Metatron."

A month later, after he had visited the area, David moved to Charlotte, rented a lovely three-bedroom home in a nice neighborhood, found a great accounting job, and enjoyed spending time with his friends. Ten months later, he was offered, and accepted, a management role with Alpha Prime Racing, a NASCAR Xfinity Series team.

Yes, Archangel Metatron helped me to be the person and the mother I wanted to be, and he does so whenever I ask for his assistance. His Cube reminds me to keep my ego in check and gives me a new way to look at things in a more positive light. It becomes easier for me to say the things I should, and to be a better person, even if I don't get exactly what I want. Even if I would rather have a pity party for myself.

March 5, 2022 – "Good evening Angel Metatron. Thank you for coming through to me this evening. I'm hearing so much about ascension these days. Lots of people online seem to be talking about our goal, as humans, to move from the third dimension to the fifth dimension, apparently a better plane of existence for us all to live in. What should I know about it? How can I better control my human ego so I can ascend quicker?"

ASCENDING IS A NATURAL OCCURRENCE WHEN HUMAN SOULS ARE READY. IT IS AN ELEMENTAL PROCESS. TIMING IS WHAT IS IMPORTANT FOR EACH SOUL.

IT IS NOT NECESSARY TO BE A SAINTED OR PERFECT SOUL. A SOUL IS READY WHEN IT HAS RIPENED AND MATURED, EVEN LITTLE BY LITTLE IN WAYS THAT ARE OBVIOUS TO THEMSELVES AND TO US. THE PROGRESSION IS NOTED AND APPRECIATED. AGAIN, DIVINE TIMING WILL TAKE CARE OF ASCENSION FOR EVERY SINGLE SOUL.

AS OPPOSED TO WHAT YOU'VE READ AND HEARD, ASCENSION IS ACTUALLY A NEW RICHNESS OF IMMERSION INTO THE LIGHT—A SENSE OF WELL-BEING AND RELIEF, AND A LIGHTER LOAD TO CARRY. IT IS A RETURN TO A TIME YOU WILL REMEMBER WITH GREAT FONDNESS, ONCE YOU ARRIVE.

YOU WILL NATURALLY BECOME HIGHER IN YOUR VIBRATORY RATE AND IN YOUR SPIRIT BODY, AS YOU SHED THE NON-IMPORTANT.

DEBRA, WE NOTE HOW YOU ARE MAINTAINING A BETTER UNDERSTANDING OF THIS AS YOU ASPIRE TO BE KINDER AND MORE COMPASSIONATE WITH REGARDS TO THE PAIN, FEAR, AND UNCERTAINTY IN OTHERS.

YOU ARE TRYING TO BE MORE PATIENT AND LESS JUDGMENTAL, AND LESS LIKELY TO HOLD A GRUDGE

AGAINST THOSE WHO WOUND YOU, YOU ARE MORE FORGIVING OF THOSE WHO WRONG YOU NOW AND IN THE PAST.

WE KNOW HOW YOU ARE TRYING TO REALIZE ALL THE DIFFERENT WAYS PEOPLE INTERPRET AND ACT ON THINGS BORNE OUT OF THEIR OWN EXPERIENCES AND POINTS OF VIEW.

WE SEE YOUR EFFORTS AND YOUR PROGRESS, WHICH WILL ENSURE YOUR SOUL'S LIGHTENING AND LIFTING, FILLING EVERY CELL WITH BUOYANCY FROM GOD'S LIGHT. YOU WILL BE ABLE TO PERCEIVE A DIFFERENT WORLD, ONE OF SO MUCH MORE BEAUTY AND POSITIVITY.

YES, THE HUMAN EGO IS HARD TO TAME. BUT DO NOT DESPAIR THE EGO, AS IT IS DESIGNED TO PROVIDE LESSONS. PAINFUL LESSONS NEED TO BE LEARNED AND SURVIVED IN ORDER TO FILL THE TRUE EXPANSION OF YOUR ESSENCE.

AS YOU BECOME MORE ALIGNED WITH HOW YOU WOULD RATHER FEEL, SAY, DO, AND REACT IN ANY GIVEN SITUATION, YOU WILL ENJOY MORE CONTROL AND TAP INTO YOUR CREATIVE CAPACITY AND INNER KNOWLEDGE. THIS IS THE PROCESS YOU WILL WANT TO CONTINUE AS YOU ASCEND. THEN YOU ARE ON YOUR WAY TO GLORY.

"Thank you for that important information, Angel Metatron. So what should I be doing to make sure my family and I don't miss the boat when it's our time?"

CREATE YOURSELF ALREADY THERE. INSIDE YOUR IMAGINATION, WRITE YOUR OWN SCENES. DESIGN SOMETHING THAT CALMS AND PLEASES YOUR HEART. IT IS ALL YOU NEED TO DO.

IMAGINE A NEW REALITY FOR YOURSELF. PICTURE IT IN DETAILS; THE BLUES AND PINKS OF LIFE, THE SIGHTS AND SOUNDS AND SMELLS, AS WELL AS THE DUST MOTES FLOATING THROUGH THE SUNBEAMS.

SEE YOURSELF IN JOY THERE. SEE YOUR FAMILY AND FRIENDS THERE WITH YOU. REALIZE THAT YOU HAVE THE POWER TO CREATE THE LIFE YOU DESIRE.

IMAGINE YOUR OWN MOVIE AS ON A LARGE SCREEN. SEE YOURSELF REACTING TO LIFE IN A LIGHTER, EASIER WAY, FILLED WITH COMPASSION AND GRATEFULNESS. SEE HOW YOU FLOW INSIDE THIS WORLD WITH NEW CONNECTIONS TO ALL TRUTH, ALL LOVE.

CREATE THE ENVIRONMENT FOR YOURSELF IN WHICHEVER WAY YOU DELIGHT TO DO. PLAY YOUR MOVIE OFTEN AND YOU WILL FEEL THE LIFT IN YOUR HEART WITH EACH SHOWING.

REMAIN STRONG IN FAITH AND BELIEVE THIS: IF YOU DON'T CONSCIOUSLY CREATE YOUR OWN REALITY, YOU WILL CREATE IT UNCONSCIOUSLY.

"Wow. That sounds amazing. I'm going to try it right now because I sure don't want to create my reality unconsciously. That could be a disaster."

I closed my eyes and took some deep breaths. Imagining a gigantic white movie screen, I saw myself, in technicolor, walking. Hmmm ... do I want to be in my sixties for eternity? I erased that image and made myself into a younger version, despite the fact that vanity was definitely a low vibration.

So now I looked younger, and immediately I was joined by Howard, also looking younger, and Jill and David, both looking like they do in the present.

Foothills, covered in green grass, gently rose around us. Lush bushes dotted the landscape. Weeping willow trees swayed in the breeze above Texas bluebonnets and daffodils, my favorite flowers. Sparkling turquoise ponds appeared with ducks and swans swimming peacefully.

Friends were riding bikes, and family members strolled by smiling and waving at us. Other friends played with their grandchildren, enjoying a picnic by the water's edge. Everyone looked truly relaxed and happy, and I could feel the love from them and for them.

Tall graceful beings with shimmering wings, our Divine Best Friends, smiled at us in welcome. One of them waved for us to join them under a pink and white flowering tree. As I ran to hug each of them, I could hear Beethoven's Fifth Piano Concerto reaching a crescendo in the background. It was glorious!

I have played this movie in my mind often since then, usually before nodding off to sleep. Sometimes I add more details or different scenarios. Not only is it fun, but just as Angel Metatron said, I get a lift in my heart each time.

It seems too easy, though. What's the catch? Usually soul growth is tough and can be painful. Maybe I'm not consciously creating effectively enough to boost toward ascension. But I'll keep practicing as Angel Metatron suggested. After all, if this is one of the main pathways to glory, I'm in.

Chapter Eight
Archangel Gabriel
Strength of God

Archangel Gabriel's name means 'Strength of God.' She helps humanity with understanding dreams and their interpretations. She is also involved with communications and messages of all kinds, and assists with any and all child and family matters.

Even though Archangels don't have true gender identities, they do have distinctly male or female energies that some humans can differentiate during communications.

Throughout history, artists have painted Archangel Gabriel with a feminine face and figure, long wavy hair, and a flowing gown around her. She is often shown carrying her musical horn to symbolize how she trumpets messages from God. Her horn is made of copper, and that is the color she projects.

In the Old Testament's Book of Daniel, Archangel Gabriel appeared to Daniel to help him understand his dreams and visions of the future.

Archangel Gabriel will help us interpret our dreams too, especially when they are puzzling, scary, or repetitive. When we ask, she'll send us ideas, signs, or messages to help us understand the symbolism, warnings, or lessons found in our weirdest nightmares or our sweetest dreams.

Because Archangel Gabriel is known as The Divine Messenger, communications are her specialty. Her key role is delivering loving and powerful messages to people, full of wise counsel and clarity, regardless of their personal beliefs or religious affiliations.

In the New Testament's Gospels, Archangel Gabriel appears in the Book of Luke with a message announcing the forthcoming births of John the Baptist and Jesus.

Archangel Gabriel will deliver important messages to us as well, and will even help us deliver the right messages to others. Call upon her for guidance in choosing the appropriate words, spoken or written, to de-fuse arguments, or to uplift our family members, friends, and even strangers, leading to understanding and connectiveness.

Archangel Gabriel is always ready to help people who deliver significant messages, such as writers, lyricists, composers, journalists, teachers, life coaches, and communicators of all kinds. She guides those who aspire to reach others in creative, loving, or healing ways. She can even help with clarifying ideas and concepts in business plans, marketing strategies, publishing, etc.

Another important role for Archangel Gabriel is assisting parents and their children during conception, pregnancy, childbirth, and parenting. She can be called upon to help a much-anticipated adoption go smoothly. She is interested and involved in all areas of child-care and family issues.

Archangel Gabriel can reduce the stress when trying to conceive a baby. She helps us when we are worrying about a child's health, or feeling overwhelmed by the demands of parenthood. She calms us so we, in turn, can soothe a fussy toddler or meet the needs of a sensitive teenager. And she guides us when our adult children need our wise counsel, too. It doesn't matter if our children are four or forty-four. She is delighted to help.

September 26, 2012 – "Hi Angel Gabriel. I know you are the Divine Messenger, and so what message do you bring for me tonight?"

BE OPEN AND CHILDLIKE IN YOUR DISCOVERIES OF LIFE'S SECRETS. THERE IS MUCH TO UNCOVER, EVEN IN YOUR ADULTHOOD, AND TO BE IN AWE OF. IT REQUIRES

A SENSE OF WONDER FOR SUCH FULFILLMENT TO OCCUR.

LIVE SIMPLY AND ENJOY YOUR SPACE AND TIME HERE. STAY INSIDE THAT KNOWLEDGE, ABOVE ALL.

YOUR LIFE EVOLVES TOWARD A GLORIOUS SUMMATION OF VIBRANT ELEMENTS WOVEN TOGETHER IN A PLEASING WAY.

AS ANOTHER DAY DAWNS, KNOW YOU ARE EXPERIENCING LIFE AS YOU ARE SUPPOSED TO—YOU ARE REACHING TOWARD YOUR POTENTIAL NOW—AND ARE READY TO EXPERIENCE THE TOTALITY OF THAT. IT IS A JOYOUS INTERVAL FOR YOU. TAKE THE TIME TO ENJOY IT. BE BURSTING WITH POSITIVITY.

"Thank you. I promise, I will. That's a lovely message, Angel Gabriel."

November 11, 2012 – "I can tell, Angel Gabriel, that when I write to you and the other Archangels in my journals, you hear me. I know by your answers that I am getting through to you. But do you also hear me when I pray silently to God or speak silently to you and the other Archangels without using my journal? I can't always tell without your immediate feedback on paper."

WHENEVER YOU PRAY YOU SEND A LOVING LIGHT MESSAGE TO THE DIVINE. SO PRAY AND RECEIVE A BLESSING. WE HEAR YOU, YES. WE LISTEN AND KNOW HOW YOU HUNGER FOR ANSWERS TO YOUR MANY QUESTIONS.

WE WANT YOU TO KNOW THAT WE ALSO SEND ANSWERS IN OTHER WAYS—NOT JUST IN YOUR JOURNAL WRITING. ENDEAVOR TO BE OBSERVANT AFTER PRAYING, SO YOU MAY RECEIVE.

WE SEND LOVE TO YOUR ADORING SOUL. WE WANT TO THANK YOU FOR BEING ONE WHO SENSES US AND NOTICES THE LOVE WE POUR FORTH. IT'S FOR YOU; IT'S FOR ALL HUMAN SOULS WHEN THEY ARE READY TO RECEIVE.

May 6, 2014 — "Archangel Gabriel, thank you for coming through for me tonight. I'm looking forward to receiving your newest message, as always."

NEVER GIVE UP TRYING TO BE YOUR OWN BEST FRIEND, FIRST. GIVE YOURSELF THE LOVE, RESPECT, AND APPRECIATION YOU DESERVE.

SPEAK AND THINK KINDLY TO AND ABOUT YOU. IT IS NECESSARY TO FORGIVE YOURSELF FOR THINGS YOU MAY HAVE DONE IN THE PAST, EVEN WHEN YOU MAY NOT FEEL PROUD OF SUCH CHOICES OR ACTIONS. YOU ARE BEING REMINDED OF THIS FOR YOU ARE A CHILD OF GOD'S GLORY. AND GOD'S LOVE FOR YOU IS OF THE HIGHEST IMPORTANCE.

ALSO, IT IS WISE TO SPEND SOME TIME RELEGATING OLD PROBLEMS TO THE GARBAGE HEAP. THEY SERVE YOU NOT. BE RID OF THEM. PUSH THEM INTO NON-RELEVANCE, SO AS TO APPROACH LIFE IN A FRESHLY BETTER WAY.

ESTABLISH A SENSE OF CALM AND PEACE AROUND LIFE'S CHALLENGES AND PETTY ISSUES. THEY ARE BUT LESSONS TO LEARN FROM. IT IS NOT EASY, WE ACKNOWLEDGE, BUT ALL WILL WORK OUT AS ORDAINED.

FLOAT ABOVE THE FRAY. EVEN WHEN ALL SEEMS UNSETTLED AROUND YOU, IT IS TRULY GOING WELL BEYOND YOUR NORMAL SENSES AND THOUGHTS.

YOUR UPCOMING YEARS WILL BE FILLED WITH TRANSFORMATION. YOU WILL BE UPLIFTED. REJOICE.

"Wow. Thank you for making me feel so good about things tonight."

So I must admit, dear readers, I have strong opinions on things. And I don't always wait until I'm asked to share those opinions, especially with Howard, Jill, and David. By now, my family often knows what I'll say about things before I even open my mouth.

Jill was offered an interesting and lucrative employment position with a new company, and she was considering taking the offer. However she would have to re-locate from Phoenix to Dallas.

August 28, 2014 – "Dear Angel Gabriel, because you assist parents, I need to receive a message from you, please, before I have a chance to give Jill my un-asked for thoughts on this subject. Of course I'm happy and excited for her job offer. It sounds like it could provide her with a great opportunity.

"But Howard and I would worry a lot about our little girl moving there. She doesn't even know anyone in Dallas. Would she be safe alone? Has she even considered the dangers? I haven't said any of this to her yet, but I'm sure she knows what I'm thinking."

TAKE CARE NOT TO PROJECT YOUR FEARS AND FEELINGS ONTO OTHERS, INCLUDING YOUR FAMILY MEMBERS. LET THEM FEEL THEIR OWN FEELINGS AND SEE THINGS FROM THEIR OWN EXPERIENCE. SUPPORT THEM, INSTEAD OF TELLING THEM HOW TO FEEL AND WHY TO FEEL IT.

RESIST THE URGE TO TRESPASS SO FREELY UPON THE GROUND OF THE LIVES OF YOUR LOVED ONES. YES, YOU ENJOY A SPECIAL BOND WITH THEM. THEY KNOW AND CAN FEEL THAT AS WELL. BUT IT MUST NOT HAMPER THEM.

HAVE FAITH THAT THEY WILL SEEK AND FIND THEIR TRUE DIRECTION, EVEN IF IT IS DIFFERENT THAN WHAT YOU WOULD PREFER FOR THEM. THEY WILL BE PUT INTO THE RIGHT PLACE AND TIME FOR THEIR DESTINIES.

It was sage advice, of course, from Archangel Gabriel. So I embraced her counsel. I reined in what my heart wanted me to say to Jill, and all the guilt I wanted to lay on her which was, "It's just too dangerous for you, Jill, all alone in a big, strange city. And besides, we'll miss you so very much. You just can't move away."

Instead, I listened to her whenever she spoke about it, and only offered ideas or comments when she asked for them. It was quite a challenge, keeping my mouth shut. But I kept replaying Archangel Gabriel's words in my head for motivation. Jill seemed a bit suspicious of my new-found impassivity, but it was obvious that she appreciated the no-pressure approach.

In the end, Jill turned down that offer and accepted an even better position with a company in Phoenix. I was giddy with relief.

But Archangel Gabriel had provided me with invaluable direction on how to be the best parent possible in that situation—listen more and keep my fear-based thoughts to myself. It wasn't easy, but it was worth it.

A few years later when Howard and I moved into the active adult community outside of Phoenix, we were happy to be meeting and getting to know new people. Most of the folks were friendly and fun and we were enjoying a busy social life.

As is usually the case, though, there were a few residents who seemed stand-offish or unapproachable. That was to be expected in such a large community. So we just concentrated our time and energy on the friendly ones.

One night, there were twenty-four women, including me, chatting and milling around the card tables in a small room at the clubhouse. We were getting ready to play a dice game called Bunco. I had enjoyed playing with those ladies every Wednesday night for nearly six months.

It was a balmy evening, especially for November, and although the air-conditioner was running, the room soon felt warm and stuffy with all the body heat.

Like I always did when it was too warm, I walked over to the wall thermostat and turned it one degree cooler. As the motor clicked on, several ladies thanked me while fanning their sweaty faces.

Bunco requires players to rotate around to different tables throughout the game, playing with a variety of people. I liked making new friends, so I chose to start the game at a table where a woman was sitting alone. I had never seen her before.

I sat down, and with a big smile said, "Hello. I'm Debra. I haven't seen you playing here before. What's your name?"

She frowned and her body stiffened. Pulling a heavy white cardigan tightly around her, she looked at me with hostile grey eyes, magnified by large glasses.

"My name is Dawn, and if you touch that thermostat again, I'll smack you."

My jaw dropped; she wasn't joking. Her eyes didn't twinkle, nor did a smile play on her lips. I just stared at her. She wouldn't really smack me, would she? Maybe. She looked pretty sturdy.

I glanced around to see if my friend Mariann or anyone else had heard her threat. Nope, everyone was chatting and totally unaware.

Regaining my senses, I said, "Well, Dawn, I'm glad you have that winter sweater to keep you warm. But I can't exactly strip my shirt off to cool down. You see, if I get too sweaty, I break out in an awful, itchy rash."

With a roll of her eyes, she turned her whole body away from me.

"I should probably not be living in the desert, huh?"

She didn't answer. She obviously didn't care to make conversation or to let me off the hook. I spent the rest of the evening feeling stung, avoiding her table whenever possible.

My pathetic attempts to get her to lighten up angered me, later, as I related the incident to Howard.

"Why was I trying so hard to be nice to her when she was so nasty? Someone told me later that she's just a sourpuss and rarely plays Bunco anyway."

"You were just trying to be friendly in an awkward situation … you couldn't have known she'd be such a jerk. No one else ever cared whether the thermostat was turned down. So of course you weren't prepared for her overreaction. Just forget about it, Deb, and be the bigger person. Sounds like she has some problems in her life."

Of course Howard was right. I should have felt sorry for her. I should have prayed for her. But instead, tossing and turning in bed that night, I thought up brilliant things I should have said back to her. Too bad they were seven hours too late.

Believe it or not, this wasn't the first time I had gotten into trouble by turning down the thermostat on an air-conditioner. Several years earlier the scenario had involved a hot, airless room inside the Bio-Touch Center. That was a building in Tucson where I was a certified practitioner of the touch-healing technique, and a volunteer, giving people Bio-Touch sessions to help them de-stress and feel better. Also involved was an old, inefficient cooling unit, and Paul Bucky, the Bio-Touch director, and my friend and mentor.

While I was giving a Bio-Touch session to a woman in one of the small treatment rooms, she and I began to feel like we were in a hotbox. I could feel myself getting sweaty. I instantly worried that my customary heat rash would pop out all over my back and torso, driving me nuts with itching.

I excused myself, hurrying out to the hallway thermostat to turn the dial down one degree. The loud compressor kicked on immediately as cool air began to flow.

But my relief was short-lived. Soon I was sweating in that small sauna-like room again. I didn't know for sure, but I suspected that Paul had turned the dial back up one degree. Again I went to turn down the thermostat. This covert game continued for a few minutes, until Paul finally taped a small sign over the thermostat that read 'Leave Alone.'

Scratching at the rash sprouting over my stomach, I ignored his sign and re-dialed down one degree.

That didn't go over well, and soon Paul and I were in the midst of an intense exchange of words, out of earshot, in the parking lot.

Paul irritably pointed out that he and others in the various rooms were too chilly when the cool air blew. He said I was being selfish. And he couldn't believe I'd ignored his sign.

I explained, rather sharply, that the person I was working on and I were sweating and I didn't think that one lousy degree was going to freeze anybody out and become such a big deal.

Seeing how miserable my rash was making me, especially outside in the one-hundred-degree heat, Paul suggested we go inside for a compromise.

He moved me to a different room to work in—one that received a little more air-flow. Then he plugged in two small fans, directing them to where I stood beside the massage table. The circulating air helped a bit, drying the sweat on my skin, but I longed to feel the difference that one little degree of air conditioning would have made.

After that day, I took to bringing personal ice packs to the Center. And although Paul and I still laugh about it years later, that incident did bruise our friendship for a while.

November 14, 2017 - "Angel Gabriel? Have I lost the ability to communicate well with people? Why are some of my words and/or actions coming out so wrong? I need your help de-fusing some 'heated' situations. Am I suffering from thermostat-incitement syndrome? I can't believe it happened again. But this time I wasn't even acquainted with the woman I ticked off tonight at Bunco. She was really triggered.

"And her reaction really unnerved me. Of course, you know how I'm feeling—I can't ever hide anything from you, dear Angels—I'd love nothing more than to frighten her back. I want to get in her face and tell her to just try and smack me, and it'll be the last thing she ever does."

YES, WE KNOW YOU, DOWN TO YOUR SOUL. WE KNOW HOW YOU THINK AND WHAT YOUR HEART FEELS. YOUR HEART HAS AMPLE LOVE AND IS PERFECT WITH WHAT YOU ALREADY POSSESS.

TRY TO FOCUS CALMLY ON YOUR OWN SPECIAL QUALITIES WHEN SOMEONE TREATS YOU UNKINDLY. WE KNOW YOU DID NOT TRY TO TRIGGER ANYONE; YOU DID TRY TO GET RELIEF FROM THE HEAT. SOMETIMES IT IS AS SIMPLE AS THAT.

BUT, AS YOU HAVE SEEN BY NOW, PEOPLE WILL USUALLY NOT ALTER THEIR DESIRES OR NEEDS IN ORDER TO ACCOMMODATE YOUR SPECIFIC COMFORTS. THIS IS A LIFE LESSON.

ALSO WHEN THESE KINDS OF THINGS HAPPEN, THE OTHER PERSONS MAY JUST NEED MESSAGES FROM YOU WITH SOME COMPASSIONATE, UNDERSTANDING WORDS. MAYBE THEY SUFFER WITH AN UNSEEN ISSUE THAT OVERWHELMS THEM.

OR MAYBE THEY HARBOR ILL-WILL TOWARD THEMSELVES AND IT'S TOO HARD FOR THEM TO LOOK WITHIN, TO FIX WHERE THEY ARE OUT OF SYNC WITH THEIR HIGHER SELVES.

OR MAYBE THEY CONSIDER YOUR ATTEMPTS AT CHANGING THE WAY THINGS ARE WITHIN THEIR ENVIRONMENT AS IMPUDENT.

IT DOESN'T MATTER WHY THEY REACT A CERTAIN WAY. BUT YOUR REACTION TO THEM DOES MATTER. WE APPRECIATE YOUR RESTRAINT. AND, THE ANSWER IS—WHEN A THERMOSTAT IS NOT YOUR OWN, ASK PERMISSION, IF POSSIBLE, TO TURN IT DOWN.

SO, REMEMBER THE BIGGER PICTURE ALWAYS, REGARDING WHOM YOU REALLY ARE, DEBRA. YOU ARE A BEING OF LIGHT WITH A DIVINE SPARK. GOD'S LIGHT OF LOVE. DON'T ALLOW A TRIVIAL DISAGREEMENT WITH ANOTHER PERSON TO EVER DULL THIS LIGHT, FOR EVEN ONE MOMENT.

"Thank you for putting it all into perspective for me, Angel Gabriel. Of course you're so amazing at communication. Your words help me so much."

June 1, 2018- "Angel Gabriel, since you are the Angel of dreams and interpretations, what are dreams, anyway? They don't seem to make much sense."

WHEN YOU SLEEP, YOU'RE DOWNLOADING VITAL INFORMATION INTO YOUR BEING. IT IS TELEGRAPHED AND MATCHED WITH RELEVANCE THROUGH A SERIES OF FREQUENCY BURSTS. AS THE INFORMATION COMES THROUGH, IT CREATES A MOVING COMPILATION OF IMAGES YOU CAN BE INTERACTIVE WITH.

DREAMS CAN BE SIMPLE REFLECTIONS OF THE MESSAGES BEING DELIVERED, OR THEY CAN BE THE MESSAGE UNTO THEMSELVES. SOMETIMES THEY ARE VIVID REMINDERS OR FLEETING HINTS OF THE PAST, PRESENT, OR FUTURE IN REGARD TO POSSIBLE ACTIONS OR OUTCOMES. MOREOVER, DREAMS SERVE AS WAYS FOR US TO REACH YOU WITH LESSONS, PORTENTS, GUIDANCE, AND ANSWERS.

"Could you please come into my dreams tonight so I can see you? Or maybe you could materialize right now so I could see what you look like with my own eyes? I've read that some people have actually seen Angels.

"Of course, I'm always thrilled whenever I feel that you're near me ... there's that slight shiver around my forehead, and when you lightly touch my shoulder or arm or ear, almost like a slight breeze, there's a definite tingling. But I'd really like to see you and experience your love that way. Would that be possible tonight?

"Hello? Are you still here? Well, I'm not hearing you right now. But that's okay. I'm suddenly so sleepy. Thank you Angel Gabriel. Goodnight."

Falling into a deep sleep as soon as my head hit the pillow (a rare occurrence), I dreamed I was in the lobby of a hotel. It appeared to be in a foreign country. I really wanted to pay my bill and check out of the place, and I was frustrated because I couldn't find the desk clerk.

Suddenly three rough-looking men wearing military style boots and uniforms walked in, speaking a language I didn't understand. Their voices grew louder as they pointed in my direction. Fear gripped me. I couldn't understand what they were saying, but I knew I was in danger. Were they going to arrest or shoot me? What did I do wrong?

I noticed a staircase and was getting ready to make a run for it when the desk clerk materialized behind the check-out counter. At first I was relieved; she would save me.

But she looked as helpless as I felt. She was elderly with a hunched posture, her silver-white hair spilling out of a messy bun. Her long gold-colored dress seemed too large for her.

Noticing the growing agitation from the men, she slowly made her way out from behind the desk to speak to them. After some animated conversation in their foreign tongue, the men abruptly turned and walked out the door, letting it slam behind them.

Then the clerk turned her head to look at me. Her sapphire eyes sparkled and her sweet smile filled me with such warmth, my heart bubbled like a pot of hot cocoa. I knew she had protected me from those nasty-looking guys.

As I stared at her, she slowly grew taller, straighter, and younger, her hair now fluid waves of silver and gold.

My hand reached out. With an irresistible urge to touch her, I moved closer. As soon as my fingers made contact with her shoulder, deep sensations of joy consumed me, spreading throughout my body, my being, and my soul. I was vibrating!

It felt so incredible, I wanted more. I reached out again, now resting both of my hands on her shoulders. It was like holding onto an electrified fence shooting me through, again and again, with a loving current.

All the while, she was transforming into a luminous figure of glowing white intensity. I couldn't hold on anymore.

I woke up breathing hard. Tears blurred my eyes as I realized I was no longer with her. I just wanted to dive back into that dream.

In the morning I grabbed my journal.

June 2, 2018 – "Angel Gabriel, that was you in my dream last night, wasn't it? You finally showed yourself to me. It was incredible! I really felt your love. Thank you. But what did it all mean?"

YES, DEBRA, WE ARE ALWAYS WITH YOU WHETHER OR NOT YOU CAN RECOGNIZE US WITH YOUR OUTWARD EYES. FOR IT TAKES INWARD VISION AND FAITH TO SEE THROUGH ANY LOOMING, DARK BRANCHES OF THIS LIFE, AND VENTURE TOWARD THE BRIGHT LIGHT OF THE CLEARING.

REMEMBER THAT IN TIMES OF FEAR AND MISCOMMUNICATIONS, OR MISUNDERSTANDINGS WITH OTHERS, REACH INSIDE YOURSELF TO FIND YOUR OWN CLARITY AND RECAPTURE YOUR CALM. INSIDE IS WHERE YOU'LL SEE THE WORLD THROUGH MORE DISCERNING EYES.

LISTEN, ALWAYS, TO YOUR OWN TRUTH AND TRUST THE FLOWING RHYTHMS WITHIN YOURSELF. CONTINUE YOUR QUEST TO DEVELOP DEEPER CONNECTIONS WITH THE DIVINE REALMS.

GOD'S LOVE IS ALL-ENCOMPASSING. HE IS ALWAYS HERE FOR YOU. WE ARE ALL HERE TO HELP YOU FURTHER YOUR PATH WHILE YOU LEARN TO UNDERSTAND ITS IMPLICATIONS.

"You're so beautiful, Angel Gabriel. Thank you for allowing me to see you, if only in my dreams."

A few years later, a different kind of dream, a terrible one, tore me from sleep. I'd never experienced such a nightmare before. It left me in a cold sweat, with a pounding heart and a choking sensation squeezing my throat.

Four gray shadowy-looking creatures with cruel smirks and black eyes had appeared. They began darting around and closing in on me. Although the creatures seemed to know me, I didn't know who they were or what they wanted. Their expressions made it obvious, though; they meant to harm me.

Clawed hands struck out, slashing my upper body and neck. They took turns inflicting their stinging cruelty. Then I fell onto my back and they climbed on top of me to continue their assault. I gasped, trying to grab a few ragged breaths. My skin was slippery with blood. I tried to fight back but I was no match for their strength.

Somehow I realized that I was asleep and dreaming. Yet, I also knew I was in trouble.

"Angels, please help me now…I need you!"

Immediately the creatures vanished, and along with them, their suffocating weight. Relief flooded through me; I knew I was safe. Although my heart was still thudding and my throat felt strange, I was able to open my eyes, catch my breath, and calm down.

My terrors hadn't awakened Howard, still gently snoring beside me. But he could sleep through a thunderstorm, so I wasn't surprised.

I slipped out of our bedroom, grabbed my journal, and filled the teakettle for a much-needed cup of chamomile.

February 27, 2021 – "Angels, please come through to explain the meaning of that awful dream," I wrote, settling myself at the kitchen table.

"I'm still shaking. What was that? I know it wasn't just the cold slice of pizza I ate before bed.

IT IS ANGEL GABRIEL HERE NOW.

"Oh Angel Gabriel. Thank you for being with me."

YES, WE ARE HERE WITH YOU DEBRA, DEAR CHILD. YOU WERE BEING SET UPON IN A DEMONIC WAY. WE KNEW IT HAD NEVER HAPPENED TO YOU BEFORE. FOUR OF US SURROUNDED YOU—ONE OF US TO STAND IN EACH DIRECTION ARMED WITH GOD'S LIGHT OF SUPREME LOVE.

"You saved me," I said, tears already dripping down my cheeks. "Thank you so much, my Divine Best Friends. I don't even know how to give you the proper thanks.

"But I'm so glad I had the presence of mind to call on you for help. That dream felt too real. I think I could have been physically hurt. Maybe a heart attack. I don't know. Should I be worried that they'll come back again? What should I do?"

THERE WAS CAUSE TO BE ALARMED AT FIRST. BUT YOU MUST NOW UNBURDEN YOURSELF. YOU ARE, AND WILL BE SAFE.

BE AT PEACE. FEEL IT INSIDE YOUR HEART AND SOUL. KNOW DEEP DOWN IT WILL ALL BE OKAY.

GEAR UP, BUT DO NOT FREEZE UP. JUST KEEP THAT ALL POWERFUL, WHITE-HOT LIGHT OF GOD PULSATING THROUGH YOU.

FEEL US NOW AROUND YOU AND KNOW THAT WE ARE ALWAYS HERE. REACH OUT TO US AND KNOW OUR LOVE PROTECTS YOU AGAINST THE TURNING TIDES OF THE DARKEST WATERS. YOU ARE BATHING IN GOD'S BLESSINGS.

"Thank you so much, all of you. I'm not afraid to go back to sleep now."

And I'm relieved to say I haven't had another nightmare like that since. But if I do, I know who to call upon for instant deliverance.

Naturally, since Archangel Gabriel loves to help writers in their endeavors, I haven't been shy about asking her guidance and support while writing this book about the Archangels, themselves.

March 30, 2021 – "Angel Gabriel, I feel so compelled to write this book. I'd love to share what I've learned about you. I know it'll give people hope and information about how your love can change their lives.

"But even though I've been communicating with you for ten years, am I really the one to write this book? I'm not a certified expert on Angels or the Angelic realm. So, how can I hope to adequately and accurately represent you? You are Divine Beings. Am I overstepping my bounds here?"

YOU SAY YOU FEEL COMPELLED. COMPULSION FOR AN HONORABLE ENDEAVOR IS A FEELING TO BE HONORED. DID YOU NOT FEEL IT WHILE WRITING YOUR FIRST BOOK?

"Oh, you know I did."

AND SO IT IS, AGAIN. AND YOU WILL DERIVE A GOOD SENSE OF SELF-APPRECIATION BY EMBRACING TRUTHS YOU HAVE LEARNED, AND SHARING THEM WITH OTHERS. YOU WILL BE DOING SO LOVINGLY, EVEN IN SUCH A QUIET WAY AS THIS, THROUGH PLANTING A SEED THAT CAN GROW AT A LATER TIME.

YOU MUST PURSUE THIS, AS WRITING IS YOUR HIGHEST TALENT. YOU HAVE ADVANCED COMMUNICATION SKILLS, VERBALLY AS WELL AS WITH THE WRITTEN WORD.

YOU ARE NOT A CERTIFIED ANGEL EXPERT, AS YOU SAY. BUT HOW DOES ONE VALIDATE OR AUTHORIZE THAT KIND OF CERTIFICATION? YOU ARE AN ARCHANGEL EXPERT AS FAR AS YOUR OWN EXPERIENCES WITH US, ARE YOU NOT?

YOU ALSO EXCEL AT WANTING TO COMFORT PEOPLE, AND HELP THEM FEEL BETTER ABOUT THINGS IN THEIR LIVES.

THOSE SKILLS WILL HELP YOUR READERS OPEN TO THE IMMENSE POSSIBILITIES THAT CAN AWAIT THEM AS THEY EXPERIENCE NEW-FOUND HOPE AND OUR PROFOUND LOVE FOR THEM.

YOU ARE STRIVING TOWARD AND GETTING CLOSER TO BECOMING SOMEONE WHO THRIVES, EVEN WHILE MANAGING LIFE'S COMPLEXITIES. YOU HAVE THE ABILITY TO MAKE A DIFFERENCE. NOW IS THE TIME TO FULFILL YOUR SOUL'S OBLIGATION TO IMPART THIS WISDOM TO OTHERS.

"Wow, I'm overwhelmed. Thank you. I was hoping you'd say something like that. But do I also have what it takes to teach others to communicate with you and the other Archangels in book form for a larger audience?"

YES. THE READERS NEED ONLY TO HAVE A DEEP DESIRE FOR SUCH COMMUNICATION, AND TO BE OPEN TO IT. YOU WILL EXPLAIN TO THEM TO LET OUR WORDS REACH THEM AS GENTLE, OUTSTRETCHED HANDS, MELDING INTO THEIR OWN KNOWING.

AND AS SOON AS YOU FEEL IT IS THE RIGHT TIME TO PROCEED WITH YOUR WRITING, DO NOT HESITATE OR FALTER. IT WILL BE THE RIGHT TIME TO GO FULL STEAM AHEAD. TRUST THIS.

"That's so awesome, thank you!"

As I've mentioned earlier, dear readers, whenever I sit down with my current Angel journal and a pen, I ask which Archangel is there to chat with me, and I ask what messages they have. After hearing their messages, I begin asking questions.

But some nights I have an urgent question, or ten, and I forget to ask if they have any messages for me. Other nights they don't have a message and are just happy to take my questions.

One night Archangel Gabriel came through, and before I could ask her anything, she immediately launched into a message she wanted to share with me.

May 18, 2021 – "Hello Angels. Who is here to chat tonight?"

THE MESSAGE FOR YOU TONIGHT IS ABOUT KALEIDOSCOPES.

"Oh that's cool, but who am I speaking with, please?"

THIS COMES FROM ANGEL GABRIEL.

"Thank you Angel Gabriel. Kaleidoscopes? Why?"

BECAUSE THEY EXEMPLIFY LIFE.

"You mean because they are colorful and ever-changing?"

YES, BUT ALSO BECAUSE THE PIECES THAT MAKE UP THE WHOLE PICTURE FILTER DOWN AND FIT AND THEN RE-FIT, EVOLVING INTO PARTICULAR DESIGNS. THOSE ARE THE PATTERNS OF LIFE.

"Is this message because there's something or some things I should change in my life right now? Is there a particular pattern I should be striving for, Angel Gabriel?"

YOU ARE LIVING LIFE IN A FAMILIAR AND COMFORTABLE PATTERN. THAT IS SATISFYING TO YOU AT THIS TIME.

"Are you saying that my life will be changing, even if I don't want it to?"

THAT IS CORRECT, BECAUSE AS WITH THE KALEIDOSCOPE, CHANGE IS INEVITABLE.

"Well, I'll admit that I'm comfortable in my life, and I don't really like change, Angel Gabriel. It isn't always positive. Change can bring uncertainty, fear, discomfort, worries, and a lot of work."

YES, IT CAN DO JUST THAT. IT CAN ALSO BRING RESTORATIVE ATTITUDES, NOVEL PERSPECTIVES, AND JOY AS ONE ADAPTS AND GAINS INSIGHT.

"Uh oh. When can I expect these changes? I know your timelines don't always match ours down here, but can you give me a rough estimate? In a year? A month? How can I prepare?"

JUST KNOW THAT THE REPOSITIONING OF YOUR KALEIDOSCOPE'S PIECES WILL PROVIDE POSITIVE EXPANSION FOR YOU.

"Thank you. That sounds ominous, although good in the end, I guess. But please don't leave me hanging like this. Can you tell me if the changes involve just me, or me and Howard together, or just our kids?"

THE LARGER CONCEPT IS IMPORTANT AT THIS TIME. AS YOU HAVE ALREADY HEARD FROM US MANY TIMES OVER THE YEARS, YOU DO NOT NEED TO KNOW THE ANSWERS TO ALL YOUR QUESTIONS.

"Oh, okay. Thank you, Angel Gabriel. I'm sorry for always pushing for more, but I can't help wanting to know all the answers. Life would be so much easier if I knew it all, saw all the changes coming, and glimpsed all the obstacles on the road ahead. But, that would be too easy, I guess. Okay, I'll try harder to accept and understand. It has to be this way."

JUST REMEMBER HOW MUCH YOU ARE LOVED EVERY DAY AND LET THAT COMFORT YOU THROUGH ANY AND ALL OF LIFE'S CHANGES.

Chapter Nine
Archangel Raphael
Healing Power of God

Archangel Raphael's name means 'Healing Power of God' because he is the Angel with the very important job of helping humans heal in body, mind, and spirit.

Archangel Raphael is known in the bible as 'The Divine Physician' for healing Abraham after his circumcision, and for healing Jacob's dislocated hip. He helped Noah build the ark, giving the man a medical book before the flood started.

In artwork, Archangel Raphael appears holding a fish. The bible says it is the fish that Tobias caught when he was traveling to Media with Archangel Raphael. Tobias had no idea that he was traveling with an Archangel, who taught him how to use the gall bladder of a fish to restore the eyesight of his father.

Archangel Raphael understands that many of us here on the earth plane suffer with disease, bouts of pain, physical ailments, mental issues, emotional traumas, and spiritual loss of faith.

When we ask for his help, he is there, surrounding and nurturing us vibrationally with vivid emerald green, which is the healing color and the light he projects.

Along with his assistance in the healing process, he inspires us with ideas, suggestions, and thoughts, providing hope and the right information to help with whatever healing we need.

Sometimes he even gives us a warning about things that can harm us. That warning can sound like an urgent whisper or a loud command to get your immediate attention. Later you might say that 'something' told you not to do something. That was Archangel Raphael.

When we ask for relief from pain, he calms our fear and anxiety, helping us to relax so the pain can lessen and the healing can progress. He will guide us to the best doctor or therapist for whatever ails us, and he will accompany us to a dentist appointment, or into surgery, giving us confidence and peace.

Sometimes our illness or pain is a pre-determined part of our learning journey—it's the divine plan and timing for us. And when it's our time to die, Archangel Raphael cannot change that outcome. However, he will be there as a loving and comforting presence, doing all he can to help us until our passing.

When asked, Archangel Raphael will give aid, support, and motivation to human healers of all kinds, whispering inspiration and new ideas into the ears of doctors, specialists, surgeons, nurses, body workers, therapists, caregivers, and even scientists working on medical cures. Veterinarians can also benefit from his support to relax and heal their furry or feathered patients.

There are other situations where Archangel Raphael can be called upon to foster healing. These include rocky relationships, turbulent marriages, family disharmony, addictions, anger, stressful lifestyles, deep-seated fears, depression, loss, and grief.

I have called upon Archangel Raphael's healing powers many times over the years. Sometimes for a minor issue—a sore throat, a dizzy spell, or a muscle sprain. And, those things, and many others, healed up quickly and easily.

And I have called upon him, actually cried out in fear and pain and pleaded with him, several times, when things weren't so minor.

One night, cleaning the kitchen after dinner, I wiped down several of our vinyl woven placemats. As I grabbed them to throw into the

drawer, one of their pointed corners flipped up toward my face, slicing across my eyeball. The sharpness of the pain was shocking, and enough to let me know it wasn't a simple scrape.

When Howard drove me to the urgent care center minutes later, tests showed a corneal abrasion. The doctor gave me antibiotic drops and warned me that I'd be feeling pain for some time.

She said I was lucky—it could have been worse. But I wouldn't be able to wear eye makeup (I never leave the house without it), I'd have to protect my eye from the harsh Tucson sunlight, and I'd most likely have a lot of tears dripping down from that eye for weeks.

October 6, 2014 - "Angel Raphael, it's been a month since I injured my eye. The pain has finally lessened, and thank you so much for that, but my eye is still bothering me so much. It's still so sensitive, I have to stay inside most of the time to hide from the glaring sun, and I spend so much time dabbing and mopping up under my eye with tissues. It's difficult to read or write, too.

"I am so grateful that I didn't do more damage to my eye, but would you please speed up the healing process for me?"

HEALING OF THE HUMAN MIND OR BODY IS A PROCESS, DEAR ONE. HEALING HAS TO BE COMPLETED WITHIN THE TIMELINE NEEDED, EVEN IF THAT TIMELINE DOESN'T PLEASE THE SUFFERING PERSON, AND IT RARELY DOES.

THIS ISSUE FOR YOU WILL BE A DIM MEMORY SOON, NOW. THE TIMELINE IS NEARLY COMPLETE. REACH UPWARD WITH YOUR HANDS TO THE HEAVENS AS WE CAST A LOVING LIGHT ONTO YOUR HEAD. GOD'S RESTORATIVE BRILLIANCE WILL POUR INTO YOU. RECEIVE IT WITH A WARM HEART.

"Thank you, thank you so much. That sounds wonderful, Angel Raphael."

I looked up, reaching my arms above me. Then I imagined a nurturing emerald green hue bathing me in its light. Pretty soon I felt a tingling sensation warming up my face. It flooded my head, engulfed my eye area, and traveled down my neck.

It felt glorious, basking in that heat for a few minutes. It felt like everything, all that had happened before and all that would happen in the future, and even life itself, was and would be alright. It was such a comfort. Of course I couldn't sleep that night, though, with all that energy swirling and vibrating through me.

Three days later, my eye was completely back to normal. Totally healed. And thank heaven it's never given me trouble since. But unfortunately, eye issues were not yet over for my family.

December 8, 2017 - "Angel Raphael, a few days ago on the fourth of this month, Howard enjoyed a strenuous sixty-mile bike ride with the other members of his cycling club. It was the longest and most arduous ride of his life. The weather that day was cool, sunny, and dry, which was perfect for such a long ride.

"As you know, my husband is in excellent physical shape, active and healthy, and although he was understandably tired from the ride, he felt great.

"But the next morning he awoke to discover his right eye wasn't normal. Though he had no pain, he felt something was off, and figured he had a stye forming in the inner corner, or that he had gotten grit in his eye from the road dust.

"The primary care doctor examined his eye the next day and couldn't find anything wrong. But the prescribed eyedrops did nothing to relieve the weird sensations Howard was experiencing.

"Today, in the late afternoon, Howard finally realized and expressed to me that his right eye had actually lost vision. He looked at me from across the room and, to my shock, he said, 'When I close my left eye, I can only see the top half of you. The rest is just a gray mist.'

"Angel Raphael, I know you heard my prayers, as I ran and called eye doctors in a panic trying to find one who would see Howard at dinnertime on a Friday. The only one available, an optometrist who was nice enough to stay late for us, was gentle and kind after his examination, but only told us that there was a problem with the optic nerve—some inflammation—and that we needed to see an ophthalmologist as soon as possible. I will begin calling ophthalmologists tomorrow morning, but we're both a bit freaked out tonight. What is going on with Howard's eye?"

HOWARD IS BEING SHOWN THINGS ASSOCIATED WITH LOOKING INWARD, AND LOVING AND APPRECIATING ONE'S BODY.

"Oh, okay. But I'm really worried. I won't let him drive, of course, and I can tell he doesn't have full vision, even just around the house. He describes how the gray mist in his eye lifts occasionally, and flashes of color take over. It's so distracting for him."

THE EYE IMPAIRMENT WILL AFFECT HIM AND HIS LIFE ONLY TEMPORARILY.

"Thank you so much, Angel Raphael."

December 11, 2017 – "Angel Raphael, today was Howard's first ophthalmologist appointment. He was put through a lot of different examinations and blood tests, as they're testing for many possible diseases that could be causing the inflammation of his optic nerve. He will also undergo a sleep study to see if he has sleep apnea, which could have contributed to his issue. This is so sudden and frightening for both of us."

THIS IS A DIFFICULT TIME, BUT REMEMBER THAT HOWARD WILL OVERCOME THIS IN THE END. STEROIDS ARE NEEDED TO EASE THE SWELLING AND INFLAMMATION. WE ARE WITH YOU BOTH.

December 22, 2017 – "Angel Raphael, as you know, Howard and I have been on this overwhelming medical journey to a diagnosis, that has taken time, many eye doctor appointments with different doctors, examinations, confusion, worry, frustration, and fear.

"And now we have the diagnosis. But no answers. And it's terrible. It's called NAAION. Non-Arteritic Anterior Ischemic Optic Neuropathy. One of the doctors had looked quite solemn when she spoke all those words. But in the end all she could say was how sorry she was; there was no effective treatment and little understanding in the medical community of this rare eye disorder.

"Apparently, all they know is that most of the people who develop NAAION, which is always painless and usually discovered upon waking from sleep, are generally over the age of fifty, and suffer from sleep apnea, diabetes, obesity, and/or high blood pressure.

"She said that because Howard was fit and healthy, didn't have sleep apnea or any of the other risk factors, except being over fifty, it was one of the more heartbreaking cases. She used the word 'idiopathic'—relating to disease for which there is no known cause.

"Her best guess was that Howard had gotten overly dehydrated on his long bike ride—he just hadn't taken in enough water, even though he wasn't feeling thirsty.

"During the night while asleep, his blood pressure had plummeted, causing disruption of the circulation of blood to the optic nerve. Without the normal blood flow, his optic nerve became damaged. That optic nerve had now atrophied to the point that he had lost at least seventy percent of the vision in that eye.

"Permanently atrophied, Angel Raphael. Dear God and Archangels in heaven, how can this be? Didn't I hear you right? I thought I heard you say that he needed steroids. But no he doesn't… the doctor said no. She insisted that there is no effective treatment at all. None."

YOUR HOWARD IS READY FOR HIS TIME OF HEALING. BE A PART OF IT WITH HIM. HE WILL LEARN TO ADJUST TO HIS NEW WAY; HE WILL BECOME AT EASE WITH IT.

"But before you said it would only affect his life temporarily. This is not temporary. And why did this have to happen to him in the first place? He doesn't deserve this. And will it happen to him again in his other eye? This is like a bomb suddenly exploding inside a healthy person, and the fallout affects him and his family and friends. Everyone is shocked. It's too cruel."

THIS IS DIFFICULT TO MAKE SENSE OF NOW AND ACCEPT, BUT AS HE BEGINS TO TRULY SEE WITHIN, HE WILL UNDERSTAND HOW HIS VISION FLOWS TWO DISTINCT WAYS. INWARD AND OUTWARD. EACH WAY IS IMPORTANT, BUT INWARD VISION MAKES FOR ENLIGHTENMENT AND LESSONS LEARNED. AS HE GROWS IN A STRONGER KNOWING, HIS FAITH WILL GROW TOO. HE WILL SEE BETTER THAN NOW, OR EVER BEFORE, IN SOME WAYS.

"That sounds very important, Angel Raphael, but will this happen to him again?"

THERE IS NO INDICATION OF THAT HAPPENING, NOR ANY REASON TO BELIEVE SO. IT IS NOT SLATED TO OCCUR.

"Oh, thank you dear Lord God and Angels for that, but I don't know how we're going to handle this in the meantime."

YOU MUST REACH OUT TO CLAIM MORE INFORMATION ABOUT HIS CONDITION. LEARN ALL YOU CAN.

"Okay, I will."

And that's exactly what I did. I began researching and reading everything online that I could find on NAAION. There were detailed articles about what some researchers had discovered, but there were also plenty of articles debating those findings.

Simply put, there weren't enough patients waking up with this disorder to warrant much research money to study it. It was still considered rare, although more and more people, healthy like Howard, and younger than fifty, were being struck down with it.

Frustration is one of the most universal feelings with NAAION for the patients, their families, and the doctors. There are so many more questions than answers. And apparently, no surgeries, therapies, or medicinal protocols were available to help bring back viability of the optic nerve. No hope was offered.

But then, about three months later, I happened upon a Facebook group page called *Non-Arteritic Anterior Ischemic Optic Neuropathy-NAAION*. Although it was a private group, I could read some of the discussions and posts. I requested to join the group immediately and read through everything, including their files and studies on NAAION treatment.

With my heart pounding and hot tears streaming down my face, I read something I hadn't seen anywhere else in my months of research.

It was a pharmaceutical protocol created, studied, tested, and then written about by the late professor and doctor Sohan S. Hayreh MD at the University of Iowa.

Apparently, his protocol doesn't work for every patient, but it is the only documented therapy that has ever worked on any NAAION patients, to bring down the optic disc swelling and inflammation, and stop further vision loss due to deterioration of the optic nerve using…oral steroids.

STEROIDS! Just as Archangel Raphael had said. But instead of having faith in his answer, and trusting that I had heard him correctly, I believed and trusted human doctors who admitted they had no answers and no treatment options!

Dr. Hayreh's protocol is to treat with oral steroids, if the patient can tolerate the high initial dosage (which then tapers off gradually) within the first ten to fourteen days after occurrence of the NAAION episode. That's because eighty percent of optic nerve fibers and retinal ganglion cells die off within that period. So, the earlier the better. The oral steroids work by accelerating the resolution of the optic disc swelling.

However, there is only a fourteen-day window in which to treat with this protocol, after which it will not be effective. And sadly, we were well past that window now.

What if we had learned about this earlier and then found a doctor willing to prescribe the steroid protocol? (I found out later that many doctors aren't comfortable putting their patients on such a high initial dose of steroids, worried about side effects.)

Would some of Howard's precious eyesight have been preserved? That's the big question. And we'll never know the answer. He would have gladly risked some steroid side effects for a shot at holding on to more eyesight. But he wasn't given the choice. His doctors never even mentioned the steroid protocol, even though it is well known in the ophthalmology world.

What a bitter and painful lesson. Because I had dismissed what the Archangels told me, some uninformed doctors were able to take away any hope and options that our Divine Best Friends had offered us.

June 9, 2018 – "Dear Angel Raphael, I am distraught—struggling with how to help my husband. It's amazing how hard he's trying to adapt to his vision loss and keep a good attitude. He puts on a brave face and downplays it whenever people ask how he's getting along.

"But I know how difficult it is for him to be constantly reminded of what he's lost. He has no peripheral vision in his right eye. When I walk next to him, he can't see that I'm there. And all the things he loves to do long walks, hiking in the desert, taking photos, writing, reading are tough challenges now. And riding his racing bike? He continued riding with the bike club, but after a nasty fall he gave that up.

"He drives short distances now, and sometimes I accompany him. He's so careful, constantly moving his head around to better see from all angles with his good eye, but I'm nervous the whole time.

"I feel so bad for him. He says he isn't, but I know he's depressed. It's been six months already. How could he not be? On the NAAION Facebook page, patients talk about how they are taking medication for depression, anxiety, and sleeplessness, and how they struggle to keep up hope for a good quality of life. Some of them have had both eyes affected. They call themselves bi-lateral NAAION patients.

"I just want to make things better for him. What can I do with my own feelings of fear and resentment when my husband, who's never been vulnerable like this in our forty-four years of marriage, shuts me out or covers up his fear and pain with sarcasm and false bravado?

"He says he doesn't need to talk to a therapist, but he won't talk to me about his feelings, either. Howard had always been so physically and emotionally strong and healthy. He's always been my rock. This new paradigm is throwing us both for a loop. But how could it not? Without warning, to be robbed of vision? How can anyone accept that?

"Please fill me with your insight and guidance. What should I do for him? How can we get past this hurdle and feel close in our loving marriage again?"

CHILD, YOU ARE THE LOVE AND LIGHT OF GOD. BE REMINDED OF THIS NOW. BREATHE, BREATHE, BREATHE, AND FEEL THAT FLOWING THROUGH YOU TO CALM YOU. HOWARD IS HURTING DEEPLY AS HE TRIES TO LIVE NORMALLY. HIS REACTIONS ARE NORMAL FOR WHAT HAS BEFALLEN HIM AND HE TRIES TO ADJUST, BUT HIS FEELINGS OVERWHELM HIM NOW.

"Should I insist he go talk to a therapist? Would that help him?"

IT IS DOUBTFUL HE WOULD AGREE TO THAT PRESENTLY. JUST BE A FRIEND TO HIM. THAT'S WHAT HE NEEDS AS ONLY YOU KNOW HOW TO BE. YOU CAN DO THIS NOW THE

RIGHT WAY AND BE ALL THE THERAPY HE NEEDS. DERIVE COMFORT FROM THIS THOUGHT: ONCE YOU DECIDE TO DO SOMETHING YOU KNOW YOU ARE UNSTOPPABLE.

"Yes, I am! Okay, I can do that. I've always been his best friend, as he has been mine. I'm happy to just be that friend for him now. But will he ever go back to being my hero…being the man he's always been?"

OH YES, YOU WILL SEE HIM AS YOUR HERO AGAIN.

Well, another painful lesson learned, dear readers. Be careful what you ask for! Twenty-seven days later, on Howard's birthday, I suffered a severe back injury. I lifted a too-heavy glass table leaf, twice, trying to maneuver it into place to extend the dining room table before our guests arrived for the birthday party.

I'd never even had the slightest backache before, but suddenly I heard and felt a ripping pain. I didn't know it then, but I had just herniated a disc at (lumbar) L2-L3 of my spinal vertebrae. And soon it would be painfully obvious that I now also had pinched-nerve involvement that sent electric-like shocks of misery down the front and side of my left thigh like I'd never experienced.

During Howard's party, I lay on our bedroom floor on a quilt, with an ice pack, trying to find a comfortable place to put my body. Because it felt like an alligator was gnawing on my thigh, the bed seemed like too much trouble to navigate. Friends and family regularly checked on me, sorry that I was missing out on all the fun, food, and cake.

The next morning, getting out of bed and trying to walk was terribly painful, so I only did so to use the bathroom. And that was how I spent the next three weeks. Basically bedridden. Luckily, I discovered certain positions in bed that gave me temporary relief.

I only left the house when Howard drove me to the doctor and the x-ray offices, and then a few days later, to the emergency room for two big shots of pain killers in my rear end, so I could then go to the imaging center and tolerate lying on the hard table for my MRI. The anti-inflammatories and opioids I had been prescribed were barely cutting the pain.

Then the physical therapy appointments began. Thank the Lord and Angels, my therapist understood how serious the nerve pain was down my leg, and she never pushed me to work through that pain, which was worse than my back pain.

The physical therapy appointments, two to three times per week, would last for five long months. I was disabled, and in a wheelchair for the first time in my life. I couldn't leave our bedroom, except for those appointments, for ninety-six days.

And although friends and family helped and were wonderful, who do you think was taking total and complete care of me? You guessed it—my hero, Howard. Lovingly and without complaint, he woke many times during those awful nights to give me pills and hot and cold packs, and to comfort me in my pain and fear.

One night early on, my agony was so great I was loudly wailing. I'll never forget the look of fear and worry on Howard's face as he rushed to my side. He had never heard me cry out in pain before, not even during my long labors during the births of our children.

"I wish it were me going through this instead of you," he whispered solemnly. There were tears in his eyes, and I knew he really meant it.

In our new routine, he gave me sponge baths in bed, changed my bedsheets (he was sleeping in the guest room to give me the whole bed), did the laundry, cooked, brought me meals (I could only lie on my back or left side and I had to eat like that), cleaned the house, and drove me to all my appointments.

He even sat next to me during each physical therapy session, encouraging my progress as I shakily graduated from wheelchair to walker to cane. He cheered me on as I struggled with my exercises, totally dedicated to my recovery.

I couldn't help but notice that Howard was now maneuvering his body, driving the car, reading, and doing everything else with more ease and confidence. His personality and sense of humor were returning as he focused on my needs.

I had read how the brains of many NAAION patients eventually and miraculously compensated for the missing eyesight and I was thrilled and grateful to see it happening for my husband.

August 3, 2018 – "Oh Angel Raphael, I can hardly read what I'm writing here in my journal, because I'm lying flat in bed. I have begged and begged you to please hurry my healing. You know how hard it's been for me to endure this awful pain and to be bedbound, tortured just having to get up and use the toilet.

"Haven't I learned whatever lessons are necessary for me so I can now heal and move on please? I need to put this agony behind me. I've never felt like this before. It's been nearly a month. If the rest of my life were to be like this, I'd rather end it. And you know my heart. You know I'm not just being dramatic here."

DEAR CHILD, THERE IS MUCH WISDOM THAT COMES FROM SUFFERING. IT CONNECTS YOU TO MORE SPECIFIC AREAS THAT YOU ARE HERE TO EXPERIENCE AND LEARN ABOUT. IT IS NOT MEANT TO BE EASY, YET IT IS SO NECESSARY. AND MOST IMPORTANTLY, IT IS CRUCIAL AS IT WILL BE BENEFICIAL LATER ON AS YOUR SOUL EXPANDS.

WE CANNOT RUSH THE HEALING OR INTERFERE WITH THE PROCESS OF GROWTH ALONG YOUR SPIRITUAL PATH. WE'VE SPOKEN BEFORE WITH YOU ABOUT THE HEALING TIMELINE.

WE DO NOT WANT YOU TO SUFFER, AND WE KNOW HOW MUCH YOU HAVE. BUT IT IS IN THAT SUFFERING THAT THE CHANGE HAPPENS—THE CHANGE THAT IS NECESSARY TO ALTER AN IMPORTANT ASPECT OF YOURSELF. WE WILL REMAIN HERE WITH YOU. WE LOVE YOU. YOUR HEART OF LOVE FILLS US EVEN NOW.

"I'm angry and disappointed in your response. Haven't I cried enough tears already? Can't you just help relieve the pain a little? The pills do nothing, and I don't want to stay on them.

"I'm trying to trust your big-picture viewpoint, but it's hard to do and it's hard for me to care right now. My heart is cold."

LIFE WILL RETURN TO NORMALCY FOR YOU... TO THE POINT WHERE YOU WILL, AT TIMES, BE ABLE TO FORGET THIS ENTIRE TRYING EPISODE OF YOUR LIFE.

"That's hard to believe. Where are you Angel Raphael? I need you."

I ALIGHT.

"What does that mean?"

IT MEANS TO DESCEND, MAKE A LANDING, COME TO REST. I AM SITTING HERE WITH YOU.

"Here? On my bed?"

YES. BELIEVE IT. ALIGHT ALSO MEANS BURNING, FIERY, ABLAZE, AGLOW. AND NOW YOU MUST RE-LIGHT YOUR HEART AND YOUR INNER SPARK AND BE LUCENT AGAIN. FOR YOUR CRISIS WILL PASS.

NOT A DAY GOES BY THAT WE DON'T SEE HOW HAPPY THOSE BECOME WHEN THEY REALIZE THEY CAN COMMUNICATE WITH GOD. AND THEY REALLY ALWAYS CAN. PRAYERS ARE ALWAYS HEARD, ALWAYS. AND THEY NOT ONLY HAVE A POSITIVE EFFECT ON THE PERSON PRAYING, BUT THERE IS A SWEET RIPPLE OF CHANGE THAT HAPPENS IN THE HEAVENLY REALMS TOO.

TRY TO REMEMBER THAT PAIN CAN PROMOTE GROWTH AS A CRACK IN AN EGGSHELL PROMOTES NEW LIFE IN THE HATCHING.

ALSO, AS YOU USED YOUR OWN HANDS TO HELP THE SOOTHING OF HOWARD'S EYE, HE CAN USE HIS HANDS TO HELP YOU NOW.

"You mean with Bio-Touch?"

YES.

During the initial phase of Howard's NAAION journey, I would regularly use the touch-healing technique called Bio-Touch on him, lightly touching specific points around his eyes.

I had seen how well Bio-Touch helped a lot of people with pain and other symptoms when I volunteered at the Bio-Touch Center, which is why I had written my first book about it.

"Well, I'm sure Bio-Touch would help, but with everything else Howard is doing for me, I didn't want to ask him to do that too. But I know he'll be happy to work on my back and leg.

"Thank you for being here, Angel Raphael. I'm feeling bet-ter...calmer...warmer...and the pain has subsided some. I love know-ing you're sitting here with me right now."

December 14, 2018 – "Good evening Angel Raphael. It's been five months since my back injury. I am so grateful for how far I've come and that I've finished physical therapy, finally. The pain is manageable now with a little aspirin and I no longer need a walker or a cane. Pretty soon I'll be able to drive again.

"Now my problems are more about getting back to my normal life and self. I feel like a fearful ninety-six-year-old, too afraid of my frailty to enjoy life. I miss the carefree way I always moved my body, and how it felt to plop down in a chair without thinking about my spine. I'm afraid of so many things that could happen to reinjure my back."

YOU MUST NOT EMBRACE THIS APPREHENSION OF LIFE. PLEASE TRY TO RELEASE THE FEAR; IT STOPS YOUR PROGRESS TO WHOLENESS. REJOICE, AS WE DO, WITH WHERE AND HOW YOU HAVE JOURNEYED.

"Okay, I will try harder to not be scared. Just keep hanging around beside me."

December 21, 2018 - "Dear Angel Raphael, our Jill was in California wine country on a business trip last month. She was enjoying a winery tour when, as you know, she twisted around to look out the window at the beautiful scenery. Apparently her knee hadn't twisted along with her because as she turned back, she heard a sickening popping sound and then shooting pains wracked her left knee.

"Some people on the tour called 911 and helped her hobble over to a chair, and as she lifted up her leg, her knee popped back into place.

"The next thing she knew, three paramedics had her in a portable chair and were carrying her down three flights of stairs because there was no elevator. An ambulance whisked her to the emergency room.

"She didn't need surgery, thank you all very much, but she is in pain, with a brace, crutches, and is looking at months of physical therapy for her dislocated kneecap.

"This whole thing happened right before she was scheduled to take a ten-mile bike ride through the streets of wine country to visit several more wineries.

"Why would something so strange happen like that? It wasn't like she was doing anything strenuous—she simply twisted her body. She had been feeling a bit apprehensive about taking that bike ride, though, as she hadn't been on a bicycle since she was a kid.

"As you know, I had asked you to protect her as she left for her trip, as I always do when she travels. And I know she asked for your help with healing when the incident happened. Jill's injury could have been so much worse. She's grateful to you and she's healing quickly, too.

"My question is, was there a reason her injury happened?"

THE ANSWER TO YOUR QUESTION IS THAT INDEED, JILL NEEDED TO BE STOPPED FROM TAKING THAT BIKE RIDE. IT WOULD HAVE PROVEN TO BE PERILOUS FOR HER AND WOULD HAVE AFFECTED OTHERS AS WELL.

"Wow. You just gave me the chills. So, something really bad would have happened on that bike ride?"

YES.

"Worse than having her knee dislocated?"

YES. WORSE THAN THAT.

"Oh my God. Thank you so much, Angel Raphael. Look at the tears dripping on me. I need a bib when I'm talking with you. I can't help it … I'm always crying, it seems, because I'm so touched.

"How can I begin to thank you enough for intervening and protecting Jill, and for all the times you've watched over me and my family all these years? I am very, very grateful.

"And I have to mention my deep appreciation to you and God, Angel Raphael, because I have almost completely recovered from my back injury without needing surgery. I feel almost normal again.

"And Howard is feeling almost normal again, too. He's adjusting beautifully to seeing the world through vision in only one eye.

"It's just like you said, Angel Raphael. I have my hero back in all his glory. And I know we will continue on our healing journeys together."

YOUR HEALING CONTINUES TO COMPLETION. YOU ARE SO LOVED FROM HERE.

Chapter Ten
Archangel Sandalphon
Co-brother of Metatron

Archangel Sandalphon's name, like Archangel Metatron's, doesn't end in 'el' which means 'Of God' because instead of being created by God as an Archangel, he was once a human being who lived on earth.

He was the prophet Elijah of the Old Testament, and he led such a pious life that when he ascended, God rewarded him, just as he did the prophet Enoch (Archangel Metatron), with the honor of becoming a Divine being.

That's why, as I mentioned in Angel Metatron's chapter, Archangels Metatron and Sandalphon are sometimes referred to as the twin Angels. And because they have experienced what it's like to be human, they can more easily relate to the everyday problems, worries, fears, and insecurities of all of us.

Archangel Sandalphon's name actually means 'co-brother' or 'brothers together' reflecting his being the spiritual brother of Archangel Metatron. And, as Archangel Metatron presides over the entrance to the Tree of Life, Archangel Sandalphon presides over its exit.

Archangel Sandalphon projects the color turquoise. He is sometimes portrayed wearing turquoise and white robes, holding a glowing golden harp. Thought to be one of the tallest Angels, it's said that his height allows him to reach up to heaven while his feet are still on the earth. It is also said that Moses, in a vision, saw Archangel Sandalphon in heaven, and referred to him as 'The Tall One.'

Archangel Sandalphon is the Archangel of Prayer. As a former human, he understands the importance, the hope, and the occasional desperation in our prayers, and how much it means to receive answers to those prayers. In his role as powerful connector between us and the Divine, he receives and delivers our prayers to God so that they can be clearly heard and answered.

He is also the Archangel of Music in heaven and on earth. As such, he works with other Angels to create sacred music in heaven, singing praises to glorify God. On earth he encourages musical composition and joyous singing through choirs, in houses of worship, as well as by individuals and small gatherings of people in prayer. Many worshippers find that music is a powerful and emotionally uplifting way to communicate with God.

When called upon, Archangel Sandalphon assists musicians, composers, and singers, helping inspire them in their quests to create their own fulfilling forms of music.

I had been regularly chatting with the Archangels for about five years, when Angel Sandalphon first came through to me. I wasn't familiar with him and hadn't even heard his name before. This is how our first meeting went:

February 5, 2016 – "Good evening Angels. Who is here to speak with me tonight?"

HERE WITH YOU NOW, DEAR DEBRA.

"Who are you?"

ANGEL SAND DOLPHIN.

"I'm sorry, what did you say?"

ANGEL SAND DOLPHIN.

"Sand dolphin? Is that right? Sand dolphin?"

YES.

"Really? I can't be hearing you clearly. Sand dolphin… like a dolphin in the sand?"

YES.

"Okay, that's an interesting name. Are you an Archangel?"

YES.

"I'm sorry, but I've never heard of an Archangel Sand Dolphin," I wrote, giggling to myself. "Okay…what message do you have for me tonight, Angel Sand Dolphin?"

THERE IS SOMETHING WE WANT TO TELL YOU. YOU ARE TO BE CONGRATULATED.

"Oh? Thank you, but for what?"

FOR TAKING THE TIME TO BE KIND IN MANY RECENT SITUATIONS THAT WE KNOW TRIED YOUR PATIENCE WITH PEOPLE. WE CAN FEEL YOUR LOVE AND JOY. KEEP ON LIVING IN IT. WE BELIEVE IN YOU, DEBRA.

WE KNOW YOUR HEART. YOU ARE A GOODNESS-FILLED SOUL. THE GOODNESS INSIDE YOUR HEART RADIATED WARMTH UP AND OUTWARD. YOU REALLY HELPED THOSE PEOPLE, AND THEY FELT THE LOVING CONNECTION YOU HAD FOR THEM.

"I'm so glad. Thank you for letting me know."

NOW YOU MUST ABSOLUTELY RECOGNIZE YOUR TRUE GIFTS TOWARD OTHERS—THEY LIVE INSIDE YOU.

"Please, what are they exactly?"

THEY ARE COMPASSION AND UNDERSTANDING. WITH THOSE, YOU ARE MAKING PEOPLE FEEL BETTER. ALSO, YOU EXCEL IN COMMUNICATION—WRITTEN AND ORAL. USE THESE GIFTS ON BEHALF OF THOSE WHO NEED THEM.

"Wow. Thank you so much. I'd like to be even kinder and be so more often. I know I need to keep working on that. This is always so special and surprising; I never know what to expect when I talk to you Archangels. Anything else you want to tell me tonight?"

YOUR LIFE AND ITS TIMINGS ARE WELL IN HAND, SO FEEL THE RELIEF AND RELAX WITH IT ALL. GOD LOVES YOU AND LOVE IS THE TRUEST THING.

"Thank you so much for coming through with these beautiful messages for me, Angel Sand Dolphin. Goodnight."

Upon closing my journal, I grabbed my phone to check out this Sand Dolphin. In a search engine I typed: Archangel Sand…

Immediately the name Archangel Sandalphon popped up, with lots of information about this well-known Archangel.

He had been trying to tell me his name, over and over, and I kept mishearing it. But, I was close! And that was good enough for him. With a laugh, I sat back and simply basked in the loving feelings he had left me with.

April 26, 2016 – "Oh Angel Sandalphon, nice to have you come through again. May I ask you this question? I have over-committed, again, on my calendar. Why can't I ever just say no to people when I know I should? They aren't life and death things, just social engagements, but I never want to disappoint. Then I end up feeling pressured and resentful. What's the best solution?"

WHEN YOU ARE ASKED, BUT STRUGGLE TO ACKNOWLEDGE YOUR TRUE FEELINGS, AND PRETEND IT'LL WORK OUT, NO ONE WILL BENEFIT FROM THE UPCOMING ENCOUNTER.

DISMISS THE GUILT OF SAYING NO. JUST USE YOUR HEART AS YOUR GUIDE AND RESPECT YOUR TRUE FEELINGS. IT'S THE WAY THAT WORKS BEST FOR YOU AND ALL OTHERS INVOLVED IN THESE SITUATIONS.

July 14, 2016 – "Angel Sandalphon, as I'm sure you know, I'm seriously considering writing my next book. It'll be my Archangel book. I confided that to a few friends at lunch today, and told them about my relationship and connection to you and the other Archangels. They were surprised (or maybe freaked out?) but then they seemed excited about it, and told me to hurry up and get going on the book.

"Was it okay to tell them prematurely? Should I tell others? Or should I keep quiet about the book until I'm much further along in the process? And, although it shouldn't concern me, it does…will people think I'm a nutcase who talks to Angels?"

IT IS ABSOLUTELY OKAY TO SHARE NOT ONLY YOUR INTENTION TO WRITE THE BOOK, BUT ALSO ABOUT THE ETERNAL CONNECTION WE SHARE. AND THEY CAN

SHARE THAT WITH US AS WELL. IT'S NOT JUST SUPPORTIVE, BUT IMPERATIVE FOR PEOPLE TO DISCOVER THAT THEY ARE NEVER REALLY ALONE. WE ARE BUT A WISP AWAY. IF THEY WANT US, WE ARE ALREADY NEARBY.

"And, the nutcase part?"

SOME MAY, INDEED, BELIEVE YOUR MIND IS IN AN ABNORMAL STATE. OTHERS WILL NATURALLY BE SKEPTICAL OF YOUR CLAIMS.

SOME ARE NOT READY TO HEAR YOUR MESSAGE. OTHERS WILL FOLLOW THEIR CURIOSITY TOWARD THIS NEW WAY FOR THEIR LIVES. ALL OF THAT IS ACCEPTABLE AND EXPECTED.

BUT THOSE WHO FEEL THE INNER PUSH TO DISCOVER THESE TRUTHS FOR THEMSELVES, WILL RECOGNIZE AND EMBRACE THIS OPPORTUNITY.

"Good to know, Angel Sandalphon, that only some folks will think I'm crazy. Now, I'm sure I already know the answer to this next question, but I'm asking anyway.

"I need to know, before I start writing the book, will everyone truly have the ability to communicate with you as I do, and receive your love, support, information, and guidance? I'm not some special kind of Angelic message-receiver, right? All humans can do this?"

YES. EVERY HUMAN SOUL CAN RECEIVE THESE THINGS AND MORE IF THEY JUST KEEP TRYING, AS MORE COMMUNICATION LEADS TO BETTER CONNECTION.

"Will everyone be able to hear you or receive a knowing like I do when you answer them?"

EVERYONE WILL RECEIVE ANSWERS IN ONE WAY OR ANOTHER... IF NOT THROUGH HEARING, THEN THROUGH KNOWING, FEELING, SEEING, TOUCHING, DREAMING, SIGNS, OR VISIONS. THE MESSAGES WILL GET THROUGH.

"Good, I thought so, and that will be the premise of my book. Any soul can communicate with you. I guess I'd better start figuring out how I'll present the information in book form. How's the best way to get my message across? Where do I even begin? Any suggestions?"

CONTEMPLATION, COMPASSION, CONNECTION
COMPILE, COMPRISE, COMPLETE.

January 2, 2017 – "Good evening Angel Sandalphon. I'm so glad you're here. My main question tonight is, why do you and the other Archangels never give up on me? You are patient and devoted all the time, no matter my repetitive questions or my fears, worries, or anger. You're always there for me with support and advice. Even on the nights when I can't hear you clearly, I know you're trying to get through to me. Why?"

WE COULD NEVER GIVE UP ON HUMAN SOULS BECAUSE WE SEE THE TRUTH IN YOUR EXISTENCE. WE SEE PAST EVERYTHING ELSE. YOU ALL POSSESS THE LUMINOSITY FROM GOD, THE SHINING SHARDS OF THE DIVINE DEEP WITHIN, WHICH MESH SO BEAUTIFULLY WITH THE FABRIC OF CREATION AS A WHOLE. AS DESIGNED.

"Wow. That's amazing. You make us limited humans sound like precious beings. It's so nice to know that's how you think of us. Thank you."

January 9, 2017 – "Angel Sandalphon, here's something fun and very different tonight. As we were eating dinner, I asked Howard if he had any questions for the Archangels for a change. He thought about it for a moment, then his eyes twinkled. So here are his two questions, and they're on the subject of time. He's always been crazy about clocks, watches, and timepieces in general:

1. *How do Archangels keep time?*
2. *Will I need a watch up in heaven? I really enjoy wearing them.*

TO HOWARD – OUR ANSWERS ARE THESE:
WE REFLECT THE GLORY OF GOD, AND AS SUCH, WE REPLACE TIME WITH PURPOSE. TIME IS AN EARTHLY MEASUREMENT, LINEAR IN SCOPE, WHICH HOLDS NO BEARING HERE.

WHEN YOUR DAYS ON EARTH HAVE ENDED, YOUR NEED TO ENGAGE IN TIME INCREMENTS WILL ALSO END.

YOU WON'T MISS YOUR WATCHS' PRESENCE HERE, WE ASSURE YOU.

May 18, 2017 – "Angel Sandalphon, true love is such a game changer for humans. I'm grateful for all the love I have in my life. But what is your take on love?"

MANY PEOPLE LONG FOR A SPECIAL FORM OF LOVE THAT WILL FULFILL AND HEAL EVERY CORNER OF THEIR EXISTENCE, AND WILL SHINE LIGHT IN ALL THE DARKNESS OF THEIR BEING.

THAT KIND OF TRUE LOVE IS FOUND—SO DEEP DOWN INSIDE, LIKE A DEPTHLESS WELL BRINGS UP THE PRECIOUS WATER OF LIFE—IN A CONNECTIVENESS WITH THE MAIN SOURCE OF ALL TRUE LIGHT AND LOVE. THAT IS GOD. THAT IS THE LOVE THAT FULFILLS AND HEALS ALL DARK CORNERS AND BEYOND FOR US ALL. AND YOU ALREADY HAVE GOD'S LOVE. EVERY HUMAN SOUL DOES. NEVER FORGET THAT IT'S THERE FOR YOU ALWAYS.

May 28, 2017 – "Angel Sandalphon, before I ask my questions, do you have a message for me tonight?"

LOOK TO SEE WHAT IS IN FRONT OF YOU AND WHAT IS COMING DOWN THE ROAD NOW. THE REAR VIEW MIRROR IS NOT ABLE TO GIVE YOU ACCESS TO YOUR DREAMS.

IT'S OKAY TO GLANCE BACK AT LESSONS LEARNED THROUGHOUT YOUR PAST, BUT KEEP FOCUSED ON NEW OPPORTUNITIES AND EXPERIENCES. THEY ARE TO BE WELCOMED; NOT THINGS TO FEAR. THE LIGHTS ARE NOW GREEN, FOR MOVING FORWARD TO THE PLACES YOU WISH TO GO.

July 22, 2017 – "Good evening, Angels! Thank you for coming through tonight, Angel Sandalphon. I would love to be better at recognizing truth when I read or hear it, and also better at recognizing baloney. Some information 'experts' seem to so easily spout lies and distortions. How can I know what is really the truth?"

TRUTHS SHOULD RING OUT CLEARLY AND SHINE BRIGHTLY IN YOUR OWN KNOWING, WITHOUT BENEFIT OF MASSAGE TO BUFF IT UP. LISTEN WITH AN INQUISITIVE HEART AND AN AWARENESS OF HOW THE WORDS FEEL INSIDE OF YOURSELF. PAY ATTENTION TO EVEN THE SMALLEST PINGING DEEP WITHIN, REALIZING THAT EVEN A FLUTTER OF DOUBT CAN BE A VITAL ALERT. THIS IS WHERE DISCERNMENT COMES FROM.

November 11, 2017 – "Dear Angel Sandalphon, As I'm obsessing more and more about writing my Angel book, and thinking about it almost all the time, I can't help but wonder what different things it will be able to offer people who may have read many other articles and books about Angels and Archangels. How will my book really help people? Is the time right for my book?"

YOUR BOOK WILL BE UNIQUELY YOUR OWN STORY, WHICH IS ALWAYS VALUABLE. YOU WILL LOVINGLY OFFER YOUR EXPERIENCES TO SHARE WITH OTHERS IN TRUTH. MANY PEOPLE KNOW SOMETHING IS MISSING IN THEIR LIVES, BUT DON'T KNOW WHAT THAT IS. THIS BOOK WILL HELP THEM REALIZE HOW TO FILL THAT VOID.

YOU WILL ALSO OFFER THEM ACCESS TO OUR LOVE AND SUPPORT IN A STRAIGHTFORWARD MANNER, THAT IS EASY TO UNDERSTAND FOR MOST. CONCEPTS THAT ARE TOO DEEP TO DECIPHER WOULD ONLY MUDDY THE WATERS. YOUR CLARITY IS SO VALUABLE NOW.

THERE ARE READERS WHO WILL BE FILLED WITH HOPE WHEN THEY DISCOVER THEY CAN COMMUNICATE WITH US. GIVING THEM THIS MESSAGE, YOUR OWN WAY, WILL BE A GIFT OF JOY TO THEM. IT IS YOUR RIGHTFUL ROLE.

SOON THE TIME WILL BE HERE — THE TIME TO SHARE THIS VISION FROM YOUR SOUL. YOU WILL FIND AN AVENUE FOR HEALING FOR YOURSELF IN YOUR WRITING, TOO. AND SHARING YOUR KNOWLEDGE ABOUT US,

USING YOUR WORDS AND OURS, WILL BE AS YOUR OWN SOOTHING BALM.

INDEED, WE WILL SURROUND YOU WITH ENERGY FOR CLEAR EXPRESSION AS YOU LOVINGLY FILL YOUR READERS' NEEDS. DEBRA, YOU WILL BE IGNITING A SPARK FOR HUMANITY'S SOUL AS YOU STOKE THIS FLAME.

"I am just overwhelmed and crying, of course, Angel Sandalphon. I'm absolutely blown away by your answer. Thank you so very much."

February 23, 2018 – "Do you have a message for me this fine night, Angel Sandalphon?"

TAKE THE TIME NECESSARY TO FORM A BOND WITH YOUR HIGHER SELF TO TRUST YOUR OWN COUNSEL AND YOUR OWN KNOWING MORE AND MORE AS TIME GOES ON.

"How should I go about doing that? I know I doubt and second guess my own wisdom too often."

DO AWAY WITH THE FALSE IDEA THAT OTHER PEOPLE KNOW MORE THAN YOU DO ON SO MANY LEVELS. YOU ALREADY RESIDE IN HEAVEN. SO, ABSORB THE LIGHT OF GOD'S LOVE; PICTURE ITS BRILLIANCE AROUND YOU AS YOU DRINK IN YOUR TRUE KNOWING.

"Wait, what? What do you mean I reside in heaven? I do? While I'm still in this body?"

ABSOLUTELY. EVERY PERSON MAINTAINS AN ESSENCE OF THEIR SOUL IN THE HEAVENLY REALMS AT ALL TIMES— THEIR HIGHER SELF. PRACTICE SEEING YOURSELF AS A RESIDENT OF THAT DIMENSION AND YOU WILL BEGIN TO TRUST YOUR INNER WISDOM.

May 10, 2018 – "I haven't felt well the last few days. I've been sneezy, headachy, and fatigued. I've tried to talk with you, but I couldn't hear you at all.

"So, I'm trying again tonight, now that I'm feeling much better. I'm able to hear you now, but not easily. Could you speak louder please? Hello? Am I still connected to you, dear Angel Sandalphon?"

YOU ARE VERY MUCH CONNECTED TO THE ANGEL REALMS—THAT WILL NEVER CHANGE. BUT YOU WILL HEAR US MORE CLEARLY SOME DAYS THAN OTHERS.

AS YOU KNOW, YOUR HUMAN LIFE IS AFFECTED BY EMOTIONS, DISTRACTIONS, ILLNESS—SUCH AS YOUR CURRENT SYMPTOMS—THAT KEEP YOU MORE EARTH-TETHERED ON THOSE DAYS.

OTHER DAYS YOUR ENERGY AND LIGHT SOAR UPWARD AND SPREAD OUTWARD WITH EASY CLARITY ABOUNDING. THE MELDING HAPPENS WITH US READILY THEN. A TRUE CONNECTION IS ACHIEVED. IT'S THE NATURAL WAY OF THINGS. ALL IS WELL.

April 12, 2021 – "It's so depressing with this COVID-19 pandemic going on and on. Everything is affected and everyone around the world is feeling the strain, Angel Sandalphon. I'm sorry I bring this subject up so much, and seem to ask the same questions over and over. How should I be looking at this mess?"

THERE IS ALWAYS STRIFE GOING ON IN YOUR WORLD. BUT YOU MUST TURN YOUR ATTENTION TO AND ABSORB ALL THE BLESSINGS AVAILABLE TO YOU.

WE UNDERSTAND THAT THINGS LOOK BLEAK FROM YOUR HUMAN PERSPECTIVE. THE INFORMATION YOU RECEIVE ON A REGULAR BASIS IS FLAWED AND NARROW, AS ARE THE SOURCES OF THE INFORMATION. AND THOSE UNTRUTHS ARE GIVING YOU A POOR FOCUS.

YOU MUST PERCEIVE THE TRUTH WITHIN YOURSELF; THE REAL TRUTH THAT RESONATES DEEPLY. CREATE YOUR INNER PEACE BY IDENTIFYING WHAT DISTURBS YOU. THEN IMMEDIATELY RE-ARRANGE YOUR THOUGHTS TO WHAT PLEASES YOU. IT IS WITHIN YOUR ABILITY TO DO SO WITH PURPOSE. KEEP YOUR THOUGHTS THERE. AGAIN AND AGAIN.

THIS WILL HELP YOU TO BE OPEN TO, AND AVAILABLE FOR THE GOOD LIFE. THERE IS A MULTITUDE OF REASONS TO FOCUS ON AND BEHOLD ALL THE JOY AND

BEAUTY AVAILABLE TO YOU. SEEK THOSE THINGS THAT LIGHT YOU UP SUPREMELY.

"Well, I do want to be open and available for the good life, and the good life only. So I'd better work on rearranging my thoughts.

"I'm sure you know I've been praying to God a lot lately, and I know you have been delivering my prayers to Him. I want to say thank you, thank you so much, Angel Sandalphon. Goodnight."

IT IS THE PLEASURE OF OUR DIVINITY. GOODNIGHT TO YOU, OUR CHILD.

Chapter Eleven
Archangel Azrael
Helper of God

Archangel Azrael's name means 'Helper of God.' He is widely known as the Angel of Death. But instead of a scary Grim Reaper type of being, he is actually the Angel of Comfort, guiding souls through their dying process with a loving gentleness. He is there to help them pass away as smoothly and easily as possible.

Then he assists those newly-departed souls as they adjust to their transition, providing comfort and peace as he accompanies them home to God.

Archangel Azrael also comforts the deceased's grieving loved ones, surrounding them with his love, energy, and emotional support, when he is called upon.

He bolsters grief counselors and spiritual teachers, helping them best serve their clients, yet shielding them from absorbing their grief and pain.

People can also ask Archangel Azrael to help them during important life transitions. He will soothe the raw, emotional endings and calm the jittery new beginnings of relationships, careers, schooling, re-locations, etc.

Archangel Azrael projects a creamy off-white color.

November 21, 2015 – "Welcome Angels. Who is here to speak to me tonight?"

WE ARE ALL HERE WITH YOU FOR COMMUNICATIONS, AND THIS IS AZRAEL AT THIS TIME.

"Oh ok, welcome Angel Azrael. I'm not familiar with you. You've never come through before. Do you have a message for me?"

YOUR MOTHER IS GOING HOME SOON.

"Oh no. Are you the … Angel of Death?"

THAT IS MY AREA OF FOCUS.

"Well, I'm not too surprised, really. We've noticed that Mom's been growing thinner and weaker as she approaches her 96th birthday in a few months. But she's still pretty healthy, pain and disease free, and feeling good. So, you're freaking me out right now."

SHE GROWS CLOSER TO HER POINT OF DEPARTURE.

"How soon? I know you can't give me the exact date, Angel Azrael. As I've already discovered about Archangels, your timelines and mine don't always match up."

VERY SOON. BUT, BE AT PEACE, AS SHE WILL BE. ALLOW YOURSELF TO BE REMINDED OF YOUR MANY SIGNIFICANT INTERACTIONS AND MUCH TIME SPENT TOGETHER THROUGHOUT ALL THE YEARS OF YOUR LIVES.

"Thank you for letting me know. I do like to be as prepared as possible with everything. But this is so hard. Could you give me an approximate date?"

IT WILL BE IN THE NEXT MONTH.

"Are you saying next month, as in December?"

YES.

"Oh no. That's so soon. Angel Azrael, will you and the other Angels please start being with my mother now?"

YES, WE ARE WITH HER ALREADY.

December 20, 2015 – "Oh hello, Angel Azrael. My heart just started pounding when I heard your name. And I'm not surprised you've come through to me again. As you know, on Thanksgiving day, five days after you first spoke to me, Mom lost her balance and fell at her assisted-living care home. She broke her shoulder. At this point, she is too weak for surgery and spends most of her time in bed now."

YES, THE TIME IS NEAR FOR YOUR MOTHER'S JOURNEY HOME WITH US.

"Thank you. I know her shoulder hurts, she's tired, and sleeps a lot now. I think she is really ready to go. But this is terrible for all of us who love her. Will you personally be with her when she passes?"

YES. AND SHE WILL BE LIFTED UP, SURROUNDED BY LOVE, AND REPOSITIONED TO HER RIGHTFUL PLACE.

"Will Grandma Mary, Grandpa Morris, Uncle Bob, and Dad be there to welcome her?"

YES, SHE WILL BE WELCOMED BACK BY HER ORIGINAL EARTH FAMILY AND BY MANY OTHERS AS WELL.

"It's so comforting to hear that she'll be free of pain and among her other loving family members."

A few days later, Mom confided to my sister, Mel, that she could look upward from her bed and see and talk with her favorite cousins. Those cousins had passed away a long time ago.

The next day, Mom greeted me with more energy than I'd seen in her for quite a while. Her fun personality was back, jokes and all. I began to hope that she was recovering.

"Look at that," she said suddenly, pointing to the ceiling. "Bob is painting me the most gorgeous picture!"

She was giddy with excitement that her brother, Bob, a professional artist, was creating something just for her. As she glanced upward, there was a look of pure joy on her face. Uncle Bob had passed away years before.

Squinting, I looked up, trying so hard to see through that white painted ceiling. I wanted a glimpse of what Mom was seeing. But of course, my eyes couldn't see through the veil between worlds, the veil that had now thinned and was lifting for Mom. It wasn't my time.

I knew Mom wasn't hallucinating. She was still alert, still a part of the things there in the room with me, still cognizant of everything going on around her. But now she could participate in the happenings of both worlds at the same time.

After a few minutes, Mom re-focused her attention on me and we happily chatted for another hour.

The next time I dropped in to see her two days later, Mom told me about someone who had been visiting her, who sat by her bed at all hours.

"The lady is really pretty. She's tall, thin, and young. She has long brown hair and bright eyes."

"Who is she, Mom? What's her name?"

"She told me her name is Katherine. She seems so sweet. I don't want to be rude to her, but sometimes I have to tell her that I'm tired and I need to sleep. So, I fall asleep and wake up later, and she's still sitting there."

"That's amazing, Mom. What does this Katherine do for you?"

"She just sits there smiling at me."

"Well, what does she say to you?"

"Not very much. She's usually pretty quiet."

My sister and I had always visited Mom four or five days a week. Mom's description of the lady didn't fit anyone we knew who'd cared for her in that small, wonderful care home for the past two years.

So, I checked with the hospice staff who had been providing extra care for Mom recently. Not only was there no one named Katherine assigned to Mom, but there was no one that they presently employed who matched her description, either.

The tall, thin, young lady's presence at Mom's bedside was now a comforting mystery. I became convinced that Katherine was an Angel, one of Mom's Divine Best Friends, who was staying by her side, as Archangel Azrael had assured me.

Mom passed away, peacefully, the morning of December 30th, within the month time frame, as Archangel Azrael had said.

And Uncle Bob's daughter, my cousin Maxene, pointed out that Uncle Bob had also passed away on December 30th, exactly eleven years before.

December 30, 2015   "Thank you for coming through to me tonight, Angel Azrael, especially since Mom passed away this morning, as you know. I am really glad you're here, and I appreciate how you came through and prepared me ahead of time. And thank you for how you took care of Mom, sending Katherine and all. But I hope I don't hear from you again for a very, very long time, if ever. Please don't take offense. I'm sure you understand."

YOUR FEELINGS ARE UNDERSTANDABLE. YOUR GRIEF IS PALPABLE WITH THE FRESH PAIN FROM MOURNING YOUR MOTHER'S DEPARTURE.

BUT AS YOUR TEARS FORM, NOW AND IN THE MONTHS AND YEARS TO COME, DRAW UPON THE STRENGTH OF KNOWING YOUR MOTHER WILL NEVER BE COMPLETELY GONE FROM YOUR REALITY. THAT BOND IS FOREVER FORGED IN THE LOVE BETWEEN YOUR SOULS.

A week or so later, I was tearfully opening condolence cards alone in my kitchen. When I got to the last card I gasped, "It's Katherine!"

On the cover was a drawing of a tall, thin, stunningly beautiful young woman, with long dark hair caught up in a bun at the base of her neck.

She was in profile, wearing a glittering white robe. More glitter illuminated the beams of sunlight she stood in front of, representing her halo. One of her hands cupped the other, held in front of her heart.

I gripped the card, staring at it for a long time, as the tears flowed. The people who had sent the card had no idea about Katherine—only a few family members had even heard the story.

I silently thanked Archangel Azrael and Angel Katherine, for being by Mom's side during her transition, and for this loving message sent to me just when I needed it.

I knew Mom was fine; she was with God, the Archangels, and her loving family members. And her journey over the last six weeks of her life had taught me how to not fear the dying process. What a precious gift.

I've kept the card in a prominent spot on my altar over the years. It still takes my breath away whenever I gaze upon the likeness of Mom's Angel Katherine.

(You can view the color photo at www.debraschildhouse.com.)

Chapter Twelve
Archangel Chamuel
Eyes of God

*A*rchangel Chamuel's name means 'Eyes of God' or 'He Who Sees God.' That's because he has all-seeing, omniscient vision, and he sees every connection, in every realm, between everything and everyone.

He uses his Divine vision to make sure humans are at peace by helping them find what they're looking for. That's his main mission, bringing universal peace to all, even in chaotic, unstable times.

His eyes can see the solution to everyone's problems, and the location of everything and anything that is missing in our lives. In that way he can ease anxiety and assist in bringing personal and global unity and calm.

Archangel Chamuel projects the color light fluorescent green, and he is just waiting to help us find our lost keys, wallets, cell phones, or even our life's purpose, a better job, a different place to live, or true love in a new relationship. Nothing is too mundane or overly complex for his attention.

For the four years that Howard and I lived in the active adult community in Peoria, it was required that we use our identification key cards in order to access the doors to the mail room, pool areas, fitness centers, etc. The cards were the all-important gateway to admittance, so whenever someone's card went missing, they would try hard to find it. Usually they gave up looking pretty quickly, though, and had to purchase a new card. I think the replacement cost was under forty bucks, but it was still a nuisance.

One afternoon Howard realized his key card was missing. After looking in all the obvious places around the house, garage, car, and driveway, we admitted defeat. We'd have to bite the bullet and buy another card.

"Wait a minute," I said, my eyes shifting upward. "I know someone who can help us. Angel Chamuel, with your all-seeing vision, would you please show us where Howard's key card is? It's lost and we really need it. Thank you."

Howard smiled, then turned and walked into the den. He grabbed his book, sat down in his favorite recliner, and pulled back the lever to raise the foot of the chair.

I continued looking around the house for the card, and a few minutes later, I walked by the den. My eyes immediately detected something under Howard's recliner. With his nose in his book, he was oblivious to what was lying under his feet.

Grinning, I bent down and snatched up the key card, which had apparently slipped out of Howard's pocket at some point and fallen into the space between the seat and the arm of the chair. When the chair had been in its normal position, it was impossible to see underneath where the card had landed.

"Well, thank you, Angel Chamuel," I laughed, holding the card up for Howard to see.

"Oh good, you found it," Howard said, reaching for the card. He put it back in his pocket.

Over the years Archangel Chamuel has found many missing objects for me. They haven't always shown up that quickly, but eventually all my lost items, except one, were recovered.

That one thing, still lost after a year and a half, was a white candle that smelled like a pomelo (a type of large grapefruit) in a pretty, lidded glass jar. Jill had given it to me as a gift, and I adored the citrusy aroma.

I guess that candle, which had disappeared when we moved from the adult community to our home in the White Mountains, was somehow meant to stay lost.

Or was it? I'm now writing this paragraph in August of 2022, two months after writing the above one. I had to go back and amend this portion of the chapter. You'll never guess what happened today!

Howard was looking high and low around the house, the garage, and the outdoor shed for his waterproof shoe covers. He was packing for an upcoming Alaskan adventure he was going on with Jill. It had been a while since I'd seen those shoe covers, so I didn't expect him to find them.

"Why don't you just ask Angel Chamuel to help you? You know he's found lots of things for us before."

"You ask him. He likes you better," Howard quipped.

"Okay," I said, looking up towards the kitchen ceiling. "Angel Chamuel, would you please help Howard find his shoe covers for this trip? He really needs them … it's rainy there this time of year."

"Thank you," Howard added, eyes skyward.

"So now, honey, you need to be open to any ideas that come to you."

"Well, I'm already thinking I should look inside our big suitcases in the garage," Howard said, as he headed toward the back door. "That's the last time I used those shoe covers on our trip to the British Isles."

"Sounds like a good idea. We haven't used those suitcases since we moved here."

Ten minutes later Howard was back in the kitchen, holding something in a plastic bag. He had that cute twinkle in his eye.

"Oh, you found the shoe covers in one of the suitcases? That's great."

"Nope, but I found something you're going to be happy about," he said opening the bag. He pulled out an item completely wrapped in a blue micro-fiber cloth.

"Is that what I think it is? My pomelo candle? I can't believe it!" I screeched. "I remember wrapping it to protect it during the move. But how'd it get in the suitcase?"

Howard shrugged. "I don't know, but I'm still missing my shoe covers."

Examining the candle, I saw that the wax had melted and shifted to one side of the jar. It was a bit lopsided now, and not so pretty, but it still smelled heavenly.

"Thank you, Angel Chamuel, for directing Howard to the suitcases. We hadn't had a reason to look inside them until now. I really appreciate how you came through for me again. Now, could you please find those silly shoe covers?"

They haven't turned up yet, but if Howard's shoe covers make an appearance before I finish writing this book, I'll happily amend this chapter once more!

August 28, 2016 – "Angel Chamuel, what is actually happening to me when I am communicating with you in these journals? I mean, how is it that I'm even able to connect with you in the first place?"

AS YOU RELAX AND FOCUS, AND BREATHE DEEPLY, YOU WRITE DOWN YOUR QUESTIONS AND COMMENTS AND SOON YOU ENTER INTO A STATE OF MIND THAT DOESN'T COME NATURALLY TO YOU OR OTHER HUMANS.

THAT'S WHEN YOU ARE ABLE TO GAIN ACCESS TO OUR MESSAGES AND ANSWERS, AND OPEN YOURSELF UP TO YOUR TRUE AND FULL POTENTIAL TO MELD WITH US. YOU ARE ACTUALLY ESCAPING THE BONDS AND LIMITATIONS OF HUMAN THINKING FOR AWHILE.

"Well that's amazing. I'm sure everyone would benefit from that kind of escape from time to time. In fact, now I want to do so even more often."

July 2, 2017- "Good evening, Angel Chamuel. Do you have a message for me tonight?"

REMEMBER TO KEEP YOUR ZEST FOR LIFE BY FINDING MORE HUMOR IN THINGS. YOU MUST LAUGH MORE AND MORE. MUCH MORE. IT IS NEEDED. BE FUNNY AND FUNNIER STILL. SEEK FUNNY PEOPLE TO LAUGH WITH. FIND NEW COMEDY FROM A DIFFERENT SENSE OF HUMOR. CREATE YOUR OWN FORMS OF FUNNY. IT IS TIME TO WORK ON THIS. LAUGHTER IS LOVE OF LIFE.

"Thank you. It's funny you're saying that. I just read an article that stated children laugh an average of three hundred times per day, while adults laugh less than fifteen times per day.

"It went on to say that laughter is good for the body, aiding circula tion and releasing endorphins that feel good. It can even lower blood pressure and contribute to healing.

"I want to laugh more and I'll look for opportunities to do so. But things just don't seem as funny as when I was younger, Angel Chamuel."

JUST START WITH ONE GIGGLE AIMED AT ONE FUNNY THOUGHT OR JOKE. THEN REPEAT. AND AGAIN. AND SOON YOU'LL NOTICE MORE FUNNY THINGS AND THE HUMOR WILL SPREAD WITHIN YOU AND BUBBLE OUTWARD. YOU WILL FEEL YOURSELF RELAXING. LAUGHTER SOOTHES THE SHARP EDGES OF LIFE. SEEK ITS COMFORTS OFTEN.

"Okay, that sounds good. So could you please tell me a joke to laugh at tonight?"

YES, TWO DOGS WERE SLEEPING COMFORTABLY AT HOME IN FRONT OF A CRACKLING FIREPLACE. OUTSIDE A WINTER STORM GUSTED LOUDLY. ONE DOG WOKE UP AND SCRATCHED HIMSELF, STRETCHED, AND LOOKED OUT THE WINDOW AT THE DANCING SNOWFLAKES. THEN HE SAID TO HIS FRIEND, 'HEY, DO YOU KNOW WHAT THE FASTEST TYPE OF WIND IS?' THE OTHER DOG OPENED ONE EYE AND SHOOK HIS HEAD. THE FIRST DOG LAUGHED AND SAID, 'IT'S A HURRYCANE!'

"Hahaha Angel Chamuel. That was a pretty corny joke. But you did make me giggle. I can't believe it. Who knew Angels told jokes?"

December 3, 2017 – "Angel Chamuel, thank you for coming through to speak with me tonight. My main question is, would you please explain why I returned to this earthly life? What was I supposed to accomplish here? I know you have the ability to see my soul's purpose this time around. What is it, exactly?"

YOU CAME BACK HERE TO THE EARTHLY PLANE TO FULFILL YOUR NEED TO IMMERSE IN AND SHARE THE KIND OF WISDOM THAT HELPS OTHERS IN THEIR OWN LIFE EXPERIENCES. YOU ARE WORKING TOWARD THAT QUEST AS YOU SPEAK AND WRITE FROM YOUR OWN HEART, DEAR ONE.

THE TIMING OF THESE SPECIFICS IS EXACT. THESE OCCURRENCES FOR YOU ARE TIMED PERFECTLY, TO THE MILLISECOND, IN ORDER TO ARRIVE AT THE DESIRED OUTCOME.

"Whose desired outcome?"

IT IS THE DESIRED OUTCOME—THE WAY IT IS SUPPOSED TO BE—FOR THE WILL OF GOD. IN SUCH INSTANCES, THERE IS NO GOOD OR BAD TIMING, ONLY ACCURATE TIMING.

"Well, I have to say that for some other things in life, it doesn't always feel like my timing is accurate. Why is that? Timing is so important in this life. So, how can I know for sure when to act on things?

"I've heard and read about folks asking for and receiving downloads of special information from spirit sources. Suddenly they have all kinds of new understanding. At least that's what they claim. Could I have that, Angel Chamuel? Could you please just cram some important information into my brain?"

OH NO, IT IS NOT EVER NECESSARY TO CRAM SUCH SPECIFIED KNOWLEDGE INTO YOUR BRAIN. WE WILL JUST LET IT TRICKLE IN SLOWLY AND NATURALLY, AND IT WILL REMAIN WHERE YOU CAN ACCESS IT WHEN NECESSARY.

WE KNOW YOU ARE IMPATIENT FOR MORE AND MORE UNDERSTANDING. IT WILL COME. MEANWHILE, REST ASSURED THAT THE TIMING WITH REGARD TO YOUR LIFE'S MOST IMPORTANT SITUATIONS HAS ALWAYS BEEN AND WILL ALWAYS BE ACCURATE. THINK BACK AND YOU'LL REMEMBER IT AS SO. DO YOU FEEL THIS TRUTH DEEP INSIDE YOUR BEING?

"Um, honestly, not right now. But I'll keep trying to do so, Angel Chamuel. Sometimes I can't tell what I'm feeling inside my being. It can be a lot of work to figure out. So, you're saying the download is definitely not happening for me?"

YOU HAVE EXPERIENCED SOME OF THESE SO-CALLED DOWNLOADS ALREADY IN YOUR LIFE. MORE WILL BE AVAILABLE WHEN NECESSARY. THEY HAVE BEEN MORE

SUBTLE IN YOUR CASE FOR GOOD REASON. MAYBE FOR
OTHERS, A BARRAGE OF KNOWLEDGE WAS NECESSARY.
BUT FOR YOU THE SLOWER APPROACH IS WORKING
WELL.

"Oh okay, darn it. I'm sorry if I push things too much, but you know how I am. In the meantime, thank you, Angel Chamuel, for sharing what you see ahead for me. Goodnight for now."

YOUR APOLOGY IS NOT NECESSARY. WISHING FOR
MORE INFORMATION IS A COHERENT REQUEST. BUT YOU
ARE DOING VERY WELL ON YOUR TIMELINE. GOODNIGHT
TO YOU, DEAR ONE.

Chapter Thirteen
Archangel Raziel
Secrets of God

Archangel Raziel's name means 'Secrets of God.' He sits so close to God's throne, he is privy to all God's words and secrets. He is the keeper of the universal truth, and knows the spiritual journeys of all the souls on earth.

Regarded as the wizard and alchemist of the Archangels, he is often depicted wearing a brown hooded robe, holding a staff in one hand and carrying a book in the other. His greyish brown beard matches his long hair.

Archangel Raziel's persona is like Merlin the Magician, an old, gentle, wise man always happy to impart cosmic knowledge.

He projects the rainbow colors, like a prism, as he assists us with our spiritual development, strengthening our connection to God. He can unlock mysteries for each of us to hear and ponder, clarifying important aspects of our past, present, and future.

November 6, 2018 – "Good evening, Angels. I'm chatting to you from The Hassayampa Inn in Prescott, Arizona. As you know, Howard and I drove up here to spend a few days seeing the sights around the area. The drive took less than two hours from our home in Peoria, and it's the first time since my back injury, four months ago, that I've been able to physically tolerate a road trip.

"So, who is here to chat with me tonight?"

IT IS ANGEL RAZIEL WHO SPEAKS WITH YOU NOW.

"Welcome, Angel Raziel. You've never come through to me before. Do you have a message?"

I HAVE BEEN WITH YOU BEFORE, BUT TONIGHT I ANNOUNCE MYSELF TO YOU AND BRING THIS MESSAGE. PREPARE FOR SOME SELF-DISCOVERY AS IT PERTAINS TO YOUR INDIVIDUAL PATH.

"Okay, but in what way, may I ask?"

IT IS IMPORTANT TO SEE YOURSELF IN A POSITIVE, LOVING, LIGHT. WE NOTE YOU HAVE BEEN OFFERING OTHERS ADVICE, HELPING THEM SEE WITH THE CLARITY AND INSIGHT YOU HAVE LEARNED. YOU HAVE BEEN A VERY CARING SOUL.

YET YOU DOUBT YOUR OWN WORTHINESS IN THE PRESENCE OF OTHERS LATELY. WE FEEL THIS. YOU MUST EMBRACE YOUR RIGHTFUL AND WELL-EARNED PLACE, AGAIN, IN ALL THAT YOU DO AND ALL ARENAS YOU ARE IN.

"Thank you, Angel Raziel. It's so true what you say. Because I'm still healing, and still going to physical therapy appointments, I don't feel whole. I don't feel worthy; I require special attention, which makes me uneasy, especially in front of friends. I walk slow and so carefully now, afraid I'll trip and fall and reinjure my back. It's hard to get comfortable in any type of chair as I need a pillow, placed just right behind my lower back, in order to sit for any length of time.

"I don't laugh as easily as others do, as I used to do, before I was confronted with my own vulnerability. I seem to have lost my sense of humor and confidence in my ability to be light and fun and easy to be with. I feel awkward, heavy, and somber. I also feel old, disabled, and always very afraid. Then I feel sorry for myself. It isn't pretty."

YOU HAVE BEEN THROUGH A TIME OF GREAT SUFFERING, BUT YOU MUST REMEMBER YOUR VALUE TO US AND OTHERS. YOU WILL AGAIN BE WHOLE, LIGHT, FUN, AND EASY WITH YOUR FRIENDS AND FAMILY. EVEN

NOW, YOU ARE WORTHY AND YOU ARE ENOUGH, JUST AS YOU ARE.

YOU HAVE GROWN IN YOUR SUFFERING. YOU ARE NOT THE SAME AS YOU WERE BEFORE…WHICH IS AS PLANNED AND SUPPOSED TO BE. YET YOU ARE HERE— STRONGER, MORE COMPASSIONATE OF OTHERS' PAIN, AND CLOSER TO YOUR TRUE SELF THAN EVER BEFORE. PLEASE LOVE THAT ABOUT YOURSELF.

"Aww, thank you for those touching words, Angel Raziel. I will try; I will remind myself of what you've said."

The next morning, Howard and I drove to Jerome, Arizona, an old mining town, turned artsy and fun for tourists, about an hour's drive from Prescott.

I wasn't able to climb steps or hills very well yet, so Howard kept parking and re-parking the car along the sloped streets for my easiest access. Taking our time, we made our way around the unique shops, galleries, and historic buildings.

A few minutes before noon, we slowly climbed the stairs into The Haunted Hamburger restaurant. Once a miners' boarding house, it was now a popular place to eat despite, or because of, its reputation for being regularly visited by ghosts.

We were seated in a back room lined with huge windows overlooking the Verde Valley. We stared at the spectacular views that stretched fifty miles to the San Francisco Peaks in Flagstaff.

"While you were reading last night, I had a quick chat with the Angels," I told Howard, as we waited for our burgers.

"Yeah, I noticed you writing in your journal."

"A new Archangel came through. He said he was Angel Raziel. I'm familiar with his name, but I don't know much about him, yet. I'll have to do some research. But he was very encouraging, as they always are."

"I'm glad. I know this trip isn't easy; it's taken you out of your comfort zone right now. But you're a real trooper."

We were nearly finished with lunch, sipping our iced teas and talking, when Howard's eyes suddenly grew wide as he looked at me.

"What?" I asked. "What is it?"

"Whoa. Deb, this is the weirdest thing I've ever seen."

"What is? What are you talking about?" I couldn't help giggling at the serious look on his face.

He grabbed his cell phone to take some photos of me. "You've got a … it looks like a … there's a prism on your face. It's in your hair."

"What's in my hair?" Now alarmed, I patted around my head.

"Look at these."

The photos clearly showed a streak of radiant rainbow colors nestled in my bangs. Another part of the prism dipped sideways down my nose, above my upper lip, over my teeth, and continued down my chin. A blob of yellow, green, blue, and purple shone brightly under my left eye. (You can view the color photo at www.debraschildhouse.com.)

"Wha … how is this possible?"

Howard looked up at the window we were sitting in front of. Then he glanced around at the other windows nearby. "It must be the sun's rays coming through all this glass creating the prism, but the rainbow is only shining on you. There's nothing on me, nor on anyone else sitting in front of these windows. It's almost like it's coming from inside you."

Howard called out to our waiter who was walking by.

"Look at my wife," he said pointing at my face.

"Wow, that's cool," the waiter said.

"Does this happen to people often when the sun shines through these windows?" Howard asked.

"No, I've never seen it happen before."

"Well, how long have you worked here?" I asked.

"Five years."

Howard and I just looked at each other.

The rainbow continued to shine on me for about ten more minutes. We just laughed and shook our heads in amazement. And then, just as quickly as it had appeared, my personal prism faded away—even though the sun was still shining brightly through the window.

I didn't realize, since I wasn't familiar with Archangel Raziel yet, that his projected color is the entire rainbow. I had just been talking about him, and in response he sent this incredible sign.

And it happened right before Howard's eyes. In fact, just like with the Angel cloud in our backyard in Tucson, I would never have noticed if Howard hadn't pointed it out.

The Archangels seemed to make sure that Howard saw these signs, and the only conclusion I can draw is that they wanted him to experience, along with me, what's possible when you invite these heavenly beings into your life.

There was one more awesome sign from the Archangels that day. After lunch, Howard and I walked into a gem and rock shop where I was immediately drawn to a fairly large cream-colored stone tinged with hints of blue, sitting by itself on a dusty shelf. I carefully picked it up, my palms tingling with its energy.

"It's called Angelite," the clerk called out, noticing my interest. "It's a crystal that promotes spiritual communication with your higher self and with Angels. It also helps heal grief and physical and emotional pain."

I couldn't help but smile. "I'll take it!"

Back in the hotel room that night, I asked the Angels what the prism on my face had meant. Archangel Raziel came through instantly.

IT WAS A SIGN OF BEAUTY, LIKE OUR LOVE FOR YOU. YOU ARE NEVER ALONE, EVEN IN YOUR SUFFERING. PLEASE HAVE FAITH RENEWED NOW.

THINGS IN YOUR BODY THAT ARE NOT YET HEALED AND FEELING NORMAL WILL CONTINUE TO HEAL AND TURN AROUND. YOU MAY EVEN START TO FORGET ALL THE FEELINGS OF PAIN AND ALL THE MISTRUST YOU NOW HARBOR ABOUT YOUR OWN BODY AND ITS INNATE ABILITY TO HEAL.

YOU MUST REALIZE THAT YOU WERE NEVER ALONE IN YOUR PAIN AND FEAR. WE WERE THERE, EVEN WHEN YOU THOUGHT WE HAD ABANDONED YOU.

THIS IS THE KIND OF LEARNING THAT REQUIRES FAITH AND TRUST. WE BESEECH YOU TO REALIZE THE DIVINE SPARK THAT LIVES INSIDE YOU. GO WITHIN TO FIND YOUR PEACE. IT IS SOMETHING YOU REALIZE FROM DEEP INSIDE. SHOWER IN IT AND LET IT GROW AND

SPREAD THROUGH YOUR BEING, LIGHTING YOU UP FROM WITHIN.

"Like the rainbow did on my face today?"

UNQUESTIONABLY. WE APPRECIATE YOUR YEARNINGS AND STRUGGLES AND WISH TO HELP YOU REALIZE YOUR TRUE NATURE AND DIVINE POWER.

THE AMOUNT OF LOVE WE FEEL FOR YOU, IF YOU REALLY KNEW, WOULD CHANGE YOUR ENTIRE WORLD TO ONE OF BLAZING POSITIVITY.

"Thank you so much, Angel Raziel. I am humbled by your love, and I'm so grateful for you and all the other Archangels in my life. Goodnight."

Chapter Fourteen
Archangel Jophiel
Beauty of God

Archangel Jophiel's name means 'Beauty of God.' She is the Angel of beauty, and has a distinct feminine energy. She projects the colors hot pink and canary yellow.

Her earthly mission is to bring beauty and thus, joy, to human lives. Physical, visual, emotional, and all other facets of beauty and happiness are important aspects of the Divine. So, Archangel Jophiel can help us see the beauty in ourselves and others, inspire us to think beautiful thoughts, and enhance our creativity so we can create beautiful art, music, writings, etc. She brings us vitality and soul-stirring power to escape from the bonds of ugly negativity.

On the practical side, she is an expert in Feng Shui, and loves to help humans improve their homes. She brings in the right energies, giving us ideas on how to reduce clutter and add light and warm coziness for an aesthetically appealing environment.

She can help us in our quest to find the perfect dress, purse, or shoes for a particular occasion, as well as the right color scarf, or which shades of make-up look best for our complexions. Or ask her to help you decide on the best paint colors for your walls or the right carpet or flooring when you re-decorate.

There is nothing that is too trivial to ask her. You cannot pester her; she loves helping us with these kinds of things. Whenever I ask her to accompany me on a shopping trip, I always have the best luck finding exactly what I'm looking for.

Because she is all about the importance of self-care, she knows how a bit of pampering keeps us properly energized and at our best for all of life's demands.

Archangel Jophiel can help us wake every day with a fresh perspective on life, clear away dark thoughts, and help bring back our appreciation for the beauty of simplicity. She can open our eyes to all the gorgeous things there are around us that we ignore every day. With her help, we can find the joy of living again, even when it's been lost to us for a long time.

The first time Archangel Jophiel came through to me during an Angel chat was right after I'd painted my toenails bubble-gum pink. I sat in a recliner with my pen and journal, my elevated toes drying and stretched by rubber separators.

January 3, 2017 – "Hello. I think I heard you say you're Archangel Jophiel? If so, that's awesome. You've never visited me before. Welcome, and thanks for being here. I've read about your mission of beauty, so I'm wondering…is it my freshly painted pink toenails that attracted you tonight?

"And why am I suddenly picking up the scent of a strawberry-flavored candle? Am I smelling you? I haven't smelled Angels before. It's lovely."

YES, YOU ARE PERCEIVING MY ENERGIES IN AN OLFACTORY WAY. HERE'S A GLORIOUS BEAUTY IDEA— WANT TO CREATE A PERFECTLY FLAWLESS FACE? COVER ANY OF YOUR PERCEIVED FACIAL IMPERFECTIONS BY LIGHTING YOURSELF UP WITH A BRIGHT SMILE. NO MORE IMPERFECTIONS.

"Aww, thank you Angel Jophiel. You're so right. A big smile can work wonders. But if you wouldn't mind, I'd love to hear some of your actual make-up tips. You know how much I love that stuff."

USE COLORS FOR YOUR FACE THAT CONTAIN WARM ROSE, GOLDEN PINK, OR CORAL TONES AS OPPOSED TO COOL BLUE-BASED PINK OR MAUVE SHADES. WARMER COLORS BRING OUT THE BEST IN YOU.

"Okay, that sounds good. I do prefer those warmer shades of foundation, blusher, and lipstick on my skin. Angel Jophiel, I know each Archangel projects a color or colors. Are your colors really hot pink and hot yellow?"

A VIVID ROSE PINK AND SUNNY YELLOW.

"Because you facilitate joy as the Angel of Beauty, here's a question. Are a steady stream of positive thoughts really important for humans to strive for? Do negative thoughts really adversely affect the quality of our lives and even our health, like I always read about? Sometimes I wonder if it's all just hype and exaggeration."

YES TO BOTH QUESTIONS. THOUGHTS ARE FOCUSED ENERGY WITHIN AND OUTWARD. THEY ARE SO IMPORTANT FOR THEY CONVEY MEANINGFUL, SITUATIONAL MESSAGES TO THE SUBCONSCIOUS MIND IN AN ABBREVIATED, YET POWERFUL MANNER.

HOW THOSE MESSAGES ARE PERCEIVED CREATES MINUTE BUT PROFOUND CHANGES THROUGHOUT BODY AND SOUL, SOMETIMES VERY QUICKLY, THAT WILL CAUSE EITHER POSITIVE OR NEGATIVE CONSEQUENCES. THE HUMAN BEING IS PRIMED FOR QUICK RESPONSE UPON RECEIVING SUCH MESSAGES.

"So, negative thoughts can really make us ill for example?"

OH YES—BELIEVE IT. NEGATIVE THOUGHTS ACT UPON YOU AS IF BEING TRULY DIRECTED THROUGH ACTUAL EXPERIENCES. THE BODY, DOWN TO THE CELLS, CANNOT DETECT THE DIFFERENCE. THE CELLS CONSTANTLY EVALUATE YOUR ENVIRONMENT LOOKING FOR CHANGES OR DANGERS. IF THEY PERCEIVE SUCH, THEY WILL CREATE MUTATION PROCESSES TO HELP YOU ACCLIMATE.

SO WHEN YOU ARE DEALING WITH A BIG PROBLEM OR CRISIS, YOUR BODY WILL BE REACTIVE. IT BECOMES EXTREMELY DIFFICULT TO KEEP POSITIVE THOUGHTS FIRING INTO YOUR PSYCHE AND SOUL DURING SUCH A TIME. BUT THAT IS WHEN IT IS MOST IMPORTANT TO DO SO TO PREVENT ANY STRESS-RELATED ILLNESSES AND ANY DAMAGE OVERALL.

"Sorry, Angel Jophiel. But how the heck can we keep positive thoughts during a crisis?"

YOU CAN TRY THIS TO HELP DURING A STRESSFUL TIME—CHOOSE A SOFT COLOR IN YOUR MIND'S EYE, LIKE MUTED BLUE, OR LILAC FOR EXAMPLE. PICTURE THAT COLOR SPREADING THROUGH THE BACKGROUND OF YOUR MIND. THAT SETS THE STAGE.

THEN PLANT THE TINIEST POSITIVE THOUGHTS, LIKE IMAGINING SEEDS OF HOPE THAT ARE TAKING ROOT AND BEGINNING TO GROW. SEE THEM AS A BRIGHT GREEN. KEEP STOKING YOUR POSITIVE ENERGY INTO PRAYERS, THOUGHTS, HOPES, VISIONS, DREAMS, AND MEMORIES. LET THEM GROW LARGER, WILDLY UNFETTERED, IF ONLY FOR A FEW MINUTES. REPEAT. AND REPEAT AGAIN THROUGHOUT THE DAY AND NIGHT AS YOU NEED TO, TO MAINTAIN THIS FLOW.

AND AS KINDLING IGNITES FROM A FEEBLE FLAME TO A ROBUST FIRE, YOUR HIGH VOLTAGE THOUGHTS WILL LIGHT UP YOUR REALITY WITH POSSIBILITIES FOR TRUE CALMING AND HEALING AND IMPROVEMENTS OF ALL KINDS. THIS WORKS EVEN IF YOU DON'T FEEL LIKE DOING IT.

"Thank you, Angel Jophiel. That's such an interesting concept. I've always heard about the power of positivity, but I was a bit dubious. It's not our natural inclination to think like that, creating such hopeful thoughts during a crisis. But now that I understand its purpose and the power that's available to us, I would love to try and master that ability."

February 19, 2017 – "Good evening, Angels. Who is here to chat tonight?"

BE OPEN TO THE IDEA OF LETTING YOUR HAIR GROW LONGER.

"Well, good evening Angel Jophiel. Thank you for coming through to me tonight. I've actually been thinking about letting my hair grow back since I recently had three inches lopped off the bottom and I've been struggling with the new shorter length."

FRESHLY CUT LAYERS WILL SUIT YOU AND FIX THAT PROBLEM. ESPECIALLY LAYERS CUT IN AROUND YOUR FACE.

"I wondered if that's what I needed because my hair has been laying too flat around my head.

"So, as you know, Howard and I are going to be moving from Tucson to Peoria, outside of Phoenix, very soon. I want to say a big thank you to you and Angel Chamuel for helping us find the right home.

"I had asked you both for assistance because Angel Chamuel helps with finding things and you help analyze the important details. It's such a daunting task. But I know we'll be happy in the house we finally chose. Way to go Angel Jophiel and Angel Chamuel!"

YOU ARE WELCOME, DEAR DEBRA.

"And now I just wish I could touch you so I could give you a big hug."

HOLD OUT YOUR HANDS WITH PALMS TOGETHER RIGHT NOW.

"Okay, hold on, I have to put down my pen."

GET READY NOW.

"Hey! I held my hands together like you said, and I just felt a warm pulsing sensation in my palms like a heartbeat! Over and over it beat. That was so cool. Was that really you, Angel Jophiel?"

IT WAS OUR LOVE FOR YOU.

"Aww, now you really have brought me joy. Thank you.

"If I may ask you a question now on another topic? You know, sometimes I struggle with being judgmental instead of compassionate with people, especially strangers. It's usually after reading an article about some senseless violence that people committed, or after hearing on the news about dangerous or reckless things they did.

"I'm trying to catch myself and stop this. It doesn't make me feel very good. I guess that many of these people are drug addicted or mentally ill. Why is it so easy to judge others or feel smugly superior to them?"

EGO BEARS DOWN HARD ON THE HUMAN MIND WHICH FEARS THE PHYSICAL DANGERS FROM OTHERS. THE IMPORTANT SENSE OF SECURITY IS ERODED CAUSING ANGER AND UNEASE. AND EGO RESENTS THOSE WHO REJECT THE ACCEPTED NORMS OF SOCIETAL BEHAVIOR, THEREBY CAUSING PROBLEMS FOR OTHERS AND MAKING THEIR OWN RULES.

BUT YOU CAN RESET YOUR AUTOMATIC EGO-FUELED FEELINGS AND STEER CLEAR OF JUDGMENTAL OR CONDEMNING THOUGHTS BY SEEING THESE PEOPLE AS BEING ON THEIR OWN LIFE JOURNEYS TO LEARNING THEIR UNIQUE LESSONS. THEY ARE WORKING THROUGH THEIR OWN LONG PROCESSES, WHICH HAVE NOTHING TO DO WITH YOU UNLESS YOUR PHYSICAL SAFETY IS AT RISK. IN THAT CASE, TAKING PROTECTIVE STEPS WOULD BE ADVISABLE.

APART FROM THAT, JUDGING OTHERS THROUGH THE WINDOW OF SOCIETY'S NARROW FOCUS ONLY HARDENS YOU TO THE WORLD. ALLOW YOUR NATURAL COMPASSION FOR OTHERS TO SHINE THROUGH YOUR BEING. IT WILL BE NOTED AND DEEPLY APPRECIATED ON THE HIGHEST LEVELS.

May 28, 2017 – "Hi Angel Jophiel. I have a question for you tonight, please. I know it's okay if I ask you to protect and watch over my loved ones, and if I ask you to send an Angel blessing to someone. And I love being able to do that.

"But if I ask you to help someone take better care of themselves, or guide someone in finding love or forgiveness in their heart, and they don't know I've asked you, does that violate their free will?"

NO, IT DOESN'T. THEIR FREE WILL REMAINS INTACT BECAUSE THEY MAY OR MAY NOT CHOOSE TO ACCEPT OUR OFFERED MESSAGES, SIGNS, VISIONS, DREAMS, WHISPERED ADVICE, AND MORE. IT IS UP TO THEM COMPLETELY.

"Thank you. That's good to know. And as always, I am totally open to all your messages and advice, Angel Jophiel. So, would you please tell me what you'd like me to know tonight?"

YES. WHENEVER YOU FEEL YOU NEED SOME HELP, EVEN IF YOU DON'T KNOW WHY OR WHAT KIND, JUST REMEMBER THIS. LET US GUIDE YOU ON YOUR PATH TOWARD THE BEAUTY OF FORGIVING YOURSELF FOR THINGS YOU DID AND FELT IN YOUR PAST. SOMETIMES THESE THINGS CAUSE DISQUIET THAT HITS OUT OF THE BLUE.

YOUR PAST DEEDS WERE TRIVIAL THINGS COMPOSED OF YOUTHFUL ARROGANCES, INEXPERIENCE, MISPLACED BLAME, AND PERCEIVED SLIGHTS.

YOU HAVE GROWN SO MUCH AS YOU HAVE TRAVELED ON YOUR LIFE'S PASSAGEWAYS. BE PROUD OF ALL YOU HAVE LEARNED AND ARE ACCOMPLISHING WITH CONTINUED GENTLE SELF-EXAMINATION.

WHILE YOU ARE ON THIS ROAD THAT IS SOLELY YOURS, KNOW THAT IT IS NOT A FOOT RACE, BUT A FOOT PACE OF YOUR OWN UNIQUE TIMING. LISTEN TO YOUR INNER WISDOM. YOU CAN HEAR THIS WHEN YOU SEEK QUIET.

AND YOU WILL KNOW WHAT TO DO IN MANY CIRCUMSTANCES. WHY? BECAUSE YOU ARE YOUR OWN TEACHER. THIS IS VITALLY IMPORTANT TO REALIZE AND REMEMBER.

"I'm my own teacher? I have never even considered that. Now that's really a 'wow' moment. I've sought out many others for their advice and knowledge and truth about many subjects throughout my lifetime. I've read so many books, heard so many lectures, etc., always hoping to be introduced to that one teacher who can tell me what I need to know."

YOU MUST TRUST YOUR OWN COUNSEL. YOUR INNER WISDOM DWELLS IN UNIVERSAL TRUTH AND UNDERSTANDING. YOU CANNOT GET THAT FROM OUTSIDE OF YOURSELF. WE MUST REPEAT...PLEASE REMEMBER THIS, OUR DEAR DEBRA. YOU ARE YOUR OWN TEACHER. TRUST THIS AS GOSPEL.

"Thank you, Angel Jophiel. I will trust my own inner wisdom more, I promise. It feels good to know it's all in there, somewhere inside me. Now I just need to figure out how to access it, and not just sometimes, but whenever I need to, and then how to trust it. So much work, yet such good things to think about. Well, goodnight Angel Jophiel. I'm sending love to you and all the other Archangels!"

Chapter Fifteen
Archangel Jebediah
My Essence Angel

January 30, 2017 – "Good evening, Angels. Who is here to chat with me tonight?"

IT'S ARCHANGEL JEBEDIAH.

"Oh? Hello Angel Jebediah. Or did I hear your name as Angel Jedediah? I'm not sure if it's a 'b' or a 'd.' I've never heard from you before."

EITHER WAY WILL WORK; EITHER NAME IS FINE.

"Well, it's nice to meet you. Thank you for coming through. But I'd like to call you by your true name. Please tell me again, what is it?"

JEBEDIAH.

"Okay. Got it. Do you bring a message for me tonight Angel Jebediah?"

KEEP YOUR GOALS AND DREAMS ENERGIZED BY USING THE POSITIVE THOUGHTS THAT ARE WAITING FOR YOU IN YOUR MIND. THOSE THOUGHTS WILL IGNITE INTO THE GROWTH THAT'S POSSIBLE WHEN YOU HAVE SUCH FOCUS.

"That sounds good. I appreciate the reminder about how powerful our positive thoughts can be. Thank you Angel Jebediah."

There wasn't much more to our chat that night, and when it ended about fifteen minutes later, I used a search engine online to look for some information about Archangel Jebediah.

I only found one source with any mention of him at all. The article said that Jebediah was actually a character in a story somebody had created. Apparently he was a fictional high-ranking Archangel who was very tall with a pale complexion, blue eyes and long wavy blonde hair. He also wore a white tunic.

From then on I was suspicious of Jebediah and figured that whoever he was, he wasn't a real Archangel. I didn't know why he came through to me, but as time went on, he began coming through more and more—almost every time I chatted with the Archangels.

Who was he and what did he want? He seemed supportive and loving, and was never negative, disapproving, or creepy. So I wasn't worried that he was a dark entity. But I didn't, for some reason, trust his intentions. In my mind, he had to be a 'wanna-be' Archangel.

Every time he finished delivering messages to me, I'd give him the third degree, asking who he really was and why he had come through to me.

May 17, 2017 - "Angel Jebediah, if you're really one of God's Archangels in heaven, why is there no information about you on the internet? I realize there must be too many Archangels to ever be listed on a human-created Angelic roll-call, but I have to admit, I'd feel better if you were on it."

THERE IS NO NEED TO BE CONCERNED, DEBRA. YOU WILL SOON SEE HOW WE HAVE A SPECIAL CONNECTION. THAT BOND IS CONSECRATED AND IS NOT PRIVY TO EVERYONE WHO PROVIDES INFORMATION IN BOOKS OR ON THE INTERNET.

"I'm sorry. I don't mean to dismiss you, but I'm having trouble believing you. If you don't mind, I'd rather the other Archangels, whom I've grown to know and trust for six years, come through to chat with me."

WE WILL ALL CONTINUE TO CONNECT WITH YOU AND PROVIDE OUR GUIDANCE, ASSISTANCE, AND LOVE.

"Oh, okay Angel Jebediah. Thanks."

But my disappointment whenever Archangel Jebediah came through to chat continued for nearly two years. I'd have a conversation with him, accept his loving messages, and then ask him to please send in another Archangel (a real one) for me to talk to.

January 28, 2019 - "Archangel Jebediah, what do you specialize in—you know, what is your mission to help humanity and what do you look like? The only information about you on the internet says you are a character in some writer's imagination, and you are tall with blue eyes and long blonde hair. Oh, and you wear a white tunic. Is any of that true?"

I LOOK LIKE ONE WHO IS OF THE LIGHT OF GOD AND I EXHIBIT THE COLORS GOLD AND LAVENDER. MY FOCUS IS TO PARTICIPATE IN A PARTICULAR SOUL'S DEVELOPMENT AND PROTECTION.

"Thank you for letting me know that. I am really trying to be open to your presence in my life. And I appreciate how patient you are being."

March 12, 2019 – "Hello and welcome, Archangels. Who is here to chat with me this evening?"

THIS IS ARCHANGEL CHAMUEL WITH A MESSAGE TONIGHT ABOUT ARCHANGEL JEBEDIAH.

"Oh? That's interesting, Angel Chamuel. Please continue."

ARCHANGEL JEBEDIAH WILL BE AVAILABLE FOR COMMUNICATION WITH YOU ON AN EVEN MORE REGULAR BASIS GOING FORWARD.

"Really? He'll be coming through more regularly? Why, Angel Chamuel? He comes through a lot already. I appreciate his messages, but I'm not sure about him. I know I've asked you this before and you've said he is, but I have to ask again. Is he really an Archangel?"

YES HE IS SO. AND ARCHANGEL JEBEDIAH IS ALSO YOUR ESSENCE ANGEL.

"My Essence Angel? What does that mean? I've never heard of that, Angel Chamuel."

ARCHANGEL JEBEDIAH HOLDS THE ESSENCE OF YOUR SOUL, PAST AND PRESENT.

"Just my soul and no one else's? Why?"

YES. IT IS HIS ASSIGNMENT.

"Does everyone have an Essence Archangel like him?"

YES. EVERY HUMAN SOUL DOES.

"And he is all mine?"

YES.

"Well, I have never read about Essence Angels in all my research. I'm very sorry, Angel Chamuel. I haven't been very welcoming to him. I didn't understand. Why haven't I heard about Essence Angels?"

ARCHANGEL JEBEDIAH UNDERSTANDS AND HAS ONLY LOVE FOR YOU, AS WE ALL DO. THE TRUTH ABOUT ESSENCE ANGELS OFTEN REMAINS AN OBSCURE CONCEPT FOR MOST. BUT IT IS SOMETHING YOU WILL LEARN MORE ABOUT.

"Well, thank you for finally confirming all of this for me, Angel Chamuel. I'm embarrassed now; I've been such an ingrate. I promise I will completely embrace his presence from now on."

March 20, 2019 – "Archangel Jebediah, I'm glad you're here tonight. I've been waiting for you to come through. I am so sorry I doubted you for so long. I just didn't know. I had never heard of you or Essence Angels. I have to stop putting so much trust in books and articles on Angelology and trust my own experiences, instead. It's like Angel Jophiel told me—I need to embrace being my own teacher.

"And now if it's okay with you, I'd like to get to know you. Please tell me about yourself. I didn't even know humans had Essence Angels. You should have told me. Oh, never mind...I probably wouldn't have believed you. Thank you for being mine, though."

DEAREST ONE, IT IS AN HONOR TO BE YOUR ESSENCE ANGEL. I HAVE BEEN ASSIGNED TO YOU FOR A LONG TIME.

"Well, how do you think our relationship is going so far?"

FINE, OF COURSE. BUT IT WASN'T SUPPOSED TO BE TOO DIFFICULT.

"Ha-ha! You have a sense of humor like the other Archangels. Perfect. I love it when you all make me laugh.

"I'm glad you don't think I've been too much of a pain in the neck, Angel Jebediah. I'm feeling so much love and gratitude toward you now for always being there for me. I am truly humbled by your devotion to my soul and to my well-being. I'm so sorry I've been less than gracious."

THERE IS NO NEED TO APOLOGIZE. I KNOW YOUR SOUL. I KNOW THE REAL YOU. AND YOU ARE STILL LEARNING MUCH, WHICH WE UNDERSTAND DEEPLY.

FROM THE OTHER REALM, I REACHED OUT TO YOU BECAUSE YOU WERE READY, DUE TO THE FORCE WITH WHICH YOUR ENERGY SWIRLED WITH WONDERMENT.

I REMAIN PART OF THE ALLIANCE OF ARCHANGELS. WE REPRESENT WHAT IS TRULY NEEDED AT ANY GIVEN POINT IN TIME IN YOUR REALITY AND PROVIDE BUILDING BLOCKS SO HUMAN SOULS MAY PURSUE SPECIFIC ENDEAVORS TOWARD THEIR HIGHEST PATH. YOUR SPECIFIC SOUL IS AND HAS BEEN MY AREA OF SUPREME INTEREST.

"Do you work for God?"

GOD IS THE ONE ABSOLUTE LIFE FORCE AND CREATOR OF US ALL. YES. WE WORK FOR GOD AND WITH GOD.

"I know you love me and my soul too, of course. I do believe that. But how can I actually access that love when I need it?"

LOOK UP TOWARD THE HEAVENS AND FEEL IT NOW—THAT ENERGY GOING THROUGH YOU—THAT IS OUR DEEP LOVE COMING IN WAVES FOR YOU. PLEASE REMEMBER THAT EXACT FEELING WHENEVER YOU NEED A REMINDER OF OUR ABSOLUTE LOVE.

"Oh wow…I did look up and I felt that tingle, Angel Jebediah. I love how it feels when it's penetrating into the middle of my chest. Just amazing. Thank you!"

YOU ARE STRONG, YET, LIKE EVERY SOUL, YOU HAVE SCARS FROM YOUR LIFE EXPERIENCES. THOSE SCARS WILL SOFTEN AND LIFT TO THE POINT THAT YOU WILL NOTICE THE HEALING. AND THEN YOU WILL LEARN TO LOVE YOURSELF COMPLETELY, AS WE DO LOVE YOU.

"That sounds so wonderful. Is there a special way I should approach my life path going forward, Angel Jebediah?"

APPROACH IT WITH THE SAME ZEAL YOU CAME HERE WITH. RECALL IT. CAPTURE IT. FEEL IT. UTILIZE IT.

"Okay. I will try to hold on to that feeling. So if I may ask, what else, besides protecting my soul, do you do all day?"

PLANT KNOWLEDGE WHERE POSSIBLE IN THIS REALM, FILL THE CREATED HOLLOWS WITH MIND-FULNESS, BESTOW DISCERNMENT THAT CAN BE FELT AND APPRECIATED, AND BOLSTER STRENGTH AND PERSEVERANCE IN DIFFICULT SITUATIONS.

"That sounds like a lot of important work. I didn't realize all the ways you've been assisting me. You've been in the background all my life making things better for me, haven't you?"

DEBRA, YOU HAVE BEEN HELPING YOURSELF AS WELL. YOU HAVE BEEN OPEN TO MY NURTURANCE EVEN WITHOUT REALIZING IT IN THIS LIFETIME.

BECAUSE YOU HAVE BEEN SEEKING TO LEARN A MORE SPIRITUAL WAY TO DEAL WITH THE TYPICAL SITUATIONS OF EVERYDAY LIFE, YOU HAVE ATTAINED MY ASSISTANCE IN FORESEEING AND AVOIDING SOME OF THE PITFALLS. AND YOU ALSO HAVE BETTER PASSAGE, NOW, TO THE GLORIES OF YOUR LIFE.

"Thank you, Angel Jebediah. Of course you've got me all teary-eyed now. I'm wondering though, will the other Archangels still come through to chat with me and be with me or am I now just strictly your assignment?"

THEY ARE ALL WITH YOU, AND WILL ALWAYS BE. AND MANY MORE ANGELS ARE HERE TOO, ALL AROUND YOU. BE OF GOOD PEACE NOW, CHILD OF GOD. WE BEINGS OF LIGHT AND LOVE ARE HERE TO SECURE YOUR RIGHTFUL POTENTIAL IN THIS LIFETIME, AS WE HAVE IN MANY LIFETIMES BEFORE. WE LIVE TO INCLUDE YOU WITHIN THE LIGHT OF GOD—TO KNOW HIS ADORATION. OUR LOVE FOR YOU RUNS DEEP.

"Please know how grateful I am to you and the other Angels. Now that I have been so lovingly touched by all of you, I can't imagine life without you. But why must we first formally invite you into our lives? Wouldn't it be great if you saw our human needs and problems and automatically came through to help us all, even those who don't know about you?"

LET US REMIND YOU OF THE CONCEPT OF FREE WILL. WE CANNOT MATERIALIZE UNBIDDEN AND PUT FORTH UNDUE INFLUENCE, BECAUSE HUMAN CHOICES DICTATE THEIR SUCCESSES AND FAILURES. THOSE SUCCESSES AND FAILURES PROVIDE THE LESSONS THOSE SOULS COMMITTED TO LEARN IN THIS EARTHLY LIFE. THAT MUST NOT BE INTERFERED WITH IN ANY WAY. IT IS PARAMOUNT.

April 28, 2020 – "Good evening Angel Jebediah. Thank you for coming through to me tonight. I know you see humanity suffering now with the COVID-19 pandemic and all the fears and division of people and all. It's getting harder and harder to think positively and try to see the good things when so many people are scared and worried. Please give me your insight."

AS TIME PASSES, THINGS WILL BECOME CLEARER TO ALL, MOVING AWAY FROM DARKNESS. THERE ARE REASONS FOR THE STRUGGLES. WE DO FEEL THE FEARS AND WORRIES THAT ARE DIMMING SO MUCH LIGHT AND SO MANY LIVES NOW.

WE SAY, IN THE MEANTIME, YOU MUST USE ALL THE OLD RELIABLE WAYS THAT YOU ALREADY KNOW OF TO KEEP YOUR JOY LEVELS HIGH. CONTINUE TO SEEK OUT THE VAST AMOUNT OF GOOD THAT IS ALWAYS AROUND AND AVAILABLE WHEN YOU LOOK FOR IT.

YOU MAY NEED TO LEARN NEW WAYS TO RETRIEVE THE PEACE INSIDE OF YOURSELF NOW. NEVER LINGER AMONG THE DARK THOUGHTS; WHEN YOUR MIND GOES THERE, PUT YOUR ENERGIES INTO FINDING BEAUTY AND HUMOR. AND LOVE, MOST IMPORTANTLY.

SOON YOU WILL PREPARE FOR A NEW EXPANSION AND BLOSSOMING WITHIN YOURSELF. THERE WILL

BE MORE TO EXPLAIN ABOUT THIS LATER, BUT THE COMING CHANGES WILL BE PLEASING AND TASTE SWEET. REMEMBER, LIFE SHOULD BE PLAYED WITH A PERFECT BLENDING OF REVERENCE, GRATITUDE, AND LAUGHTER.

June 17, 2021 – "Hi Angel Jebediah. I'm so happy you've come through tonight. What would you like me to know?"

THIS MESSAGE COMES TO YOU ALONG WITH THE TRUEST LOVE FROM US AS ALWAYS, DEAR ONE. OUR HOPE IS THAT YOU FOREVER REMAIN CLOSE TO GOD IN YOUR HEART AND THOUGHTS, AND LOVE HIM AS WE LOVE YOU, WITH EVERY PART OF THE MAKE UP OF YOUR BEING.

"Aww, I will and I do very much. Thank you Angel Jebediah. Why do you all love me so much?"

WE LOVE YOU BECAUSE WE KNOW HOW YOU WERE CREATED.

"How was I created?"

WITH FIBERS AND FILAMENTS OF LIGHT AND ADORATION FROM THE ONE.

"But everyone was made like that, right?"

EVERY SINGLE SOUL WHO IS OR HAS EVER LIVED ON THE EARTH WAS, YES. YOU WERE ALL RIGHTFULLY CREATED WITHIN THE LOVING VENERATION OF GOD.

"Well, it's so good to hear that. It makes us hapless humans sound so important."

THERE WILL BE A DAY THAT DAWNS WITH THE SHARED REALIZATION OF JUST HOW IMPORTANT YOU ALL REALLY ARE.

Chapter Sixteen
How the Archangels
Get Through to Us

Communicating with the Archangels, believe it or not, is actually a natural experience for humans, even though most people have never considered trying to do so. Everyone can practice such communication and have incredible success.

That's because we all possess intuitive gifts by virtue of being human and having a God-given soul. We are truly spiritual beings that have been graced with six senses—not merely the five senses of sight, sound, smell, taste, and touch that we've all heard about and experienced since birth.

R. Buckminster Fuller, an American architect, philosopher, inventor, research professor, and engineer who lived from 1895 to 1983, is quoted as saying, 'Since the initial publication of the chart of the electromagnetic spectrum, humans have learned that what they can touch, smell, see and hear is less than one-millionth of reality.'

Isn't that amazing to contemplate? So, because we normally relate to the world with just those five basic senses, we must awaken and sharpen our long-asleep sixth sense when communicating with Archangels.

The Merriam-Webster dictionary defines the sixth sense as a 'keen intuitive power.'

The Spiritual Science Research Foundation states that the 'sixth sense, or subtle perception ability, is our ability to perceive the subtle-dimension or the unseen world of angels, ghosts, Heaven (Swarga), etc. It also includes our ability to understand the subtle cause and effect relationships behind many events, which are beyond the understanding of the intellect.'

Most of us have experienced a gut feeling that warned us not to do something or go somewhere, or not to trust a certain person, especially a stranger. Conversely, we may have experienced a sudden peaceful calm—a sweet feeling that everything was going to be okay—even as things were falling apart around us.

We may not be able to explain why, but we just know we're receiving these messages from somewhere deep inside. That's our sixth sense, our intuition. It's a type of cosmic energy that is there to protect and help us, if only we are wise enough to listen to it.

For me, that intuitive energy has been the key to perceiving a flow of information from the elusive world of the Archangels, an unseen and otherwise unattainable realm.

Since everyone with a soul has a Divine connection whether realized or not, we must respect that there is a Divine order to everything. So our intentions, when communicating with the Archangels, should always be rooted in love for the highest good and in the best interest for ourselves and others.

If our intentions aren't from a loving heart, but instead they're based on our self-serving egos, the information we receive may be incorrect or unclear. And we need the clearest channels possible to understand what the Archangels want us to know.

Mediums, psychics, and other people who work with cosmic energy and deliver messages from beyond our human domain, understand the need for clear connections. They refer to the intuitive abilities and extra sensory perception that connects us with the spiritual realm as the Clair senses. We all possess some of these Clair senses although they may not be well developed. Clair is the French word for clear.

The Clair senses are clairvoyance (clear seeing), clairaudience (clear hearing), clairsentience (clear physical feeling), clairempathy (clear emotional feeling), claircognizance (clear knowing), clairalience (clear smelling), clairgustance (clear tasting), and clairtangency (clear touching).

Clairvoyance, or clear seeing, is the ability to see hidden things using only the mind's eye, otherwise known as the third eye. Examples include perceiving distinct images, symbols, energy fields, vivid dreams, visions, scenes from the past, present, or future, Angels or flashes of Angel colors, spirit guides, or other beings, and colorful auras around people, plants, and animals.

Clairaudience, or clear hearing, is the ability to hear voices, sounds, words, music, and other noise-based messages using an inner perception otherwise inaudible to the normal range of human hearing. Our ears can only detect sound between 20 Hz (hertz) and 20 kHz (kilohertz), which is a mere fraction of the total sound frequency range. By comparison, a dog can hear frequencies reaching up to 80 kHz. Clairaudient messages can sound like they're being whispered in the ear, coming from inside the head, or echoing at a distance as if from another dimension.

Clairsentience, or clear physical feeling, is the ability to physically feel an inner response to a situation. It's that gut feeling I mentioned previously, that is likely to be an important message or warning that shouldn't be ignored. The physical sensations of tingling, pressure, sinking in the pit of the stomach, radiating heat, and shivering chills can often be felt when absorbing the emotions and energies of others, whether one purposely tries to or not.

Clairempathy, or clear emotional feeling, is closely related to clairsentience. This is the ability to pick up on other people's emotions and feel them as your own. Sometimes it's a burden because it can be overwhelming to automatically perceive and experience the fear, dread, anger, sadness, worry, happiness, excitement, or pain of others.

Claircognizance, or clear knowing, is the ability to be one hundred percent certain about something you can't possibly prove. It's a sudden inner knowledge of truth, even if it defies logic and explanation. There is just no doubt about it; it's like knowing your own name. There can be premonitions about places, events, and situations in the past, present, or future, and knowing what the outcome was or will be. Also included is receiving flashes of insight and instinctively knowing personal things about people, as well as having the ability to detect when someone is lying. And finally, having the desire to finish other people's sentences because you know what they're going to say.

Clairalience, or clear smelling, is the ability to smell odors that don't come from a physical source. The sense of smell is heightened to perceive smells from the spiritual realm. For example, the scent of a familiar perfume or the overwhelming odor of cigar smoke may be detected from loved ones who have passed away and are trying to communicate from another realm. Scents from Angels or spirit guides can also be discerned.

Clairgustance, or clear tasting, is the ability to taste something without actually putting the substance into the mouth. It's a way to psychically taste information. For example, the mouth suddenly fills with the deliciousness of a departed loved one's famous spaghetti sauce or infamous burned cookies.

Clairtangency, or clear touching, is the ability to touch an object or hold it in hand and receive information about that object's history or about the person who owned it. The vibrational energy that surrounds the item can be read as a message. For instance, a piece of jewelry that belonged to someone, even if they've been dead a long time, can give information about their likes, dislikes, relationships, personality, career, and other details from when they were alive. And if the object belongs to a person who is still alive, particulars about their present, past, and future may be perceived.

Everyone's experiences communicating with the Archangels is unique, and it'll be through your own intuitive senses that these fascinating connections will happen. You already have all of these tools necessary, deep within you, to facilitate your relationship with your Divine Best Friends.

It's clairaudience, clear hearing, that is the main way the Archangels communicate with me. I 'hear' their words as I write in my journals. And I know it's not my own familiar inner voice, but a voice from somewhere else that I'm hearing.

Sometimes, however, it's through claircognizance, clear knowing, that I am certain of what they're going to say before I even finish a sentence. And other times, it's through clairvoyance, clear seeing, that the Archangel's words light up in my mind's eye before I hear them and write them.

I experienced clairalience, clear smelling, the first time I ever communicated with Archangel Jophiel. The delightful aroma of a strawberry scented candle surrounded me when her energies came through.

And whenever the Angels send me energy, I experience clairsentience, a comforting tingling sensation in my solar plexus area.

And speaking of using energy, frequencies, and vibrations in communication, the act of writing both sides of the conversations by hand, the way I do in my Angel journals, is the ideal avenue.

Euclid, the ancient Greek mathematician, is widely quoted as saying, 'Handwriting is a spiritual designing, even though it appears by means of a material instrument.'

Inside our brains are specific cells called the Reticular Activating System (RAS). These cells are a bridge between our conscious and subconscious minds. The RAS filters all our outer worldly input, grabbing and directing our attention toward only what we want to focus on. So, when we are writing with a pencil or pen, we're triggering the RAS to do its job, totally deepening our concentration.

And, according to a study from Indiana University published in 2010, high-tech magnetic resonance imaging has shown that writing by hand increases neural activity in certain sections of the brain, much like meditation. A greater connection is formed with the emotional regions of the brain when writing by hand.

I've tried chatting with the Archangels while sitting in front of my computer monitor, my fingers expectantly resting on the keyboard. But it just didn't work as well for me. I didn't feel as deep a connection, and the messages didn't flow as clearly as when I'm curled up with a journal, pen firmly in hand.

With practice you'll discover your own personal and distinctive ways to receive Angelic messages. And your Divine Best Friends will know the intuitive senses that are your strongest. Those will be the ones they'll use as the best avenues to blend their powerful energies with yours for the clearest communications possible.

Chapter Seventeen
Using Spiritual Awakening
Tools for Deeper Focus and
Receptivity

The use of spiritual awakening tools such as altars, candles, fruits, flowers, crystals, music, and incense can enhance your Angelic communications and bring a greater focus and clarity when receiving Divine messages.

On the other hand, I have found that using these tools is not always necessary in order for such communication. I have received an abundance of clear, meaningful messages from the Archangels while relaxing in sparse European hotel rooms, rocking along the waves on cruise ships, enduring turbulence on overseas flights, and riding over bumpy highways on road trips, using only a pen and a spiral notebook.

As Divine Beings, the Archangels are always ready, willing, and able to meld their energies with ours and chat for as long as we want. They truly don't care what time it is, where we are located, how we're dressed, or what we are surrounded by. As long as we let them know we want to talk, they will be with us immediately.

But it's difficult for most of us to detach from our everyday worlds, totally relax, and quiet and open our minds to the possibility of receiving

Divine messages. Therefore, any problems we may have with unclear communications will always be on our end because we are presently in our limited human bodies.

That's why using tools can really help us get into a receptive state for easier communications, especially if we are new to these experiences. You may remember from Chapter One that I was initially instructed by email to set up an altar with an apple, a flower, and a candle, in preparation for the Archangels' first visit.

When we make special accommodations like those, we're setting up our expectations that something unusual, unique, or unexpected could happen. Our frame of mind expands to an almost childlike state of anticipation. We're more receptive, our vibrations rise, and that's when amazing things are possible.

An altar is a sacred place of honor, providing a deeply personal and private respite from our responsibilities and workaday lives. It can be made as simply or elaborately as imagination dictates.

A side table, desktop, mantel, dresser top, or section of countertop can be softened with a pretty scarf, table runner, or other piece of fabric. A special dish or two, decorative boxes, trays, or small shelving can be added to create multiple levels or tiers, if desired.

Then the altar can be adorned with whichever things feel right or have meaning to you, from potted plants, herbs, pinecones, bells, shells, rocks, feathers and acorns, to coins, bundles of sage, or symbolic pieces of jewelry.

Adding images or figurines of Angels, religious icons, photos of deceased loved ones, animals, pets, etc., works well in creating uniqueness and significance. Favorite art pieces, handmade crafts, pottery, and precious gifts bring beauty and charm.

The altar should be set up in an area that can be easily converted to a quiet, private space, for when youngsters are asleep and the household is calm. The altar can be mobile, if necessary, able to be rolled up and put away during busy hours, and then re-positioned for later use.

The burning of candles, an ancient art, has been utilized and revered for centuries. Because lit candles look so beautiful and help with concentration and mood setting, the advent of modern electric lights never diminished their popularity.

When you light a candle that you've chosen specifically for Angel communication, it not only traditionally symbolizes all four elements— fire, earth, air, and water—but I believe it signals a deep intention to yourself and to the Archangels that you are making time and space for them. Watching the flickering flame of my altar candle always helps me reach a deep inner calm.

You can take candle lighting a step further, if you'd like, by choosing a particular color of candle or combination of candles to set the tone. A white candle is universal, and means purity and honesty, and is perfect for any situation. Blue candles signify spirituality and sincerity. Purple candles mean truth and protection. Green candles can help with healing. Pink candles signify love, beauty, and relationships. Orange candles are for protection. Yellow candles invite positivity, creativity, and high energy. Brown candles are used for practical matters.

Fresh fruits can be added to your altar to signify abundance of all kinds, including gratitude, happiness, and love. I had been instructed to place an apple on my altar that first night. Apples are said to mean peace. Strawberries signify patience, while oranges and pears signal kindness. Bananas indicate joy, and cherries express goodness. Lemons mean generosity and pineapples show faithfulness.

All I know is, after it sat on my altar for five days and nights while the Archangels were visiting me the first time, that apple was the most scrumptious one I'd ever tasted.

Flowers can add sensual delight to your altar providing beauty, aromas, and other positive aspects of nature. Studies have shown that fresh flowers reduce stress and invoke feelings of positivity, happiness, and serenity. As with candles, the colors of the flowers provide meaning. I was instructed to place a white flower in a vase on my altar that first time. White flowers symbolize purity and infinity.

Yellow flowers are for friendship. Blue flowers indicate joy, harmony, and peace. Green flowers mean hope and the balance between mind and body. Orange flowers are associated with success, pink ones indicate love and caring, red flowers invite romantic love and passion, and purple flowers signify spirituality, wisdom, and protection.

Crystals, stones, and gems are beautiful and can be therapeutic additions to any altar. In her book, *Crystal Healing for Women*, Mariah K. Lyons says,

'Crystals help to unlock many ancient secrets of healing and the wisdom held within the earth. They are often called the "wisdom keepers of earth" as they literally store information in the form of vibration within their molecular structure. They have much information to share with us, information that has been held within the earth for millions of years.

'Ultimately, our true sacred altar resides within—but physical altars activate the sacred in our everyday life and help to consistently bring us back to center.'

Interestingly, each Archangel is associated with a specific crystal, stone, or gem. So, having a few of those on your altar may help promote vibrational melding to make Angelic communications easier and clearer.

On my altar I keep two small glass bowls filled with stones and crystals of various shapes, colors, and textures. I'll often choose one that attracts me at the time, and hold it in my left hand while chatting with the Archangels and writing (with my right hand) in my journal. Sometimes it's just the spark of vibrational energy I need to kick off some great conversations. It's certainly worth a try.

Here are the Archangels' stones and their qualities:

Archangel Azrael – yellow calcite – helps heal emotional wounds, increases inner power

Archangel Chamuel – green fluorite – aids mental clarity, absorbs and neutralizes negative energies in the home or body, cleanses the aura

Archangel Gabriel – citrine – strengthens willpower and the determination to succeed, attracts abundance

Archangel Jophiel – pink tourmaline – infuses love, kindness, and compassion

Archangel Metatron – watermelon tourmaline – encourages self-nurturing, opens the heart center, balances female and male energies

Archangel Michael – sugilite – protects from disharmony from others, creates hope and optimism, encourages expression of inner truth

Archangel Raphael – emerald, malachite – promotes spiritual and physical healing, fuels inspiration and patience, helps foster gratitude

Archangel Raziel clear quartz – amplifies the energy of any other gemstone it touches, encourages spiritual connections, aids concentration

Archangel Sandalphon – turquoise – believed to be the bridge between earth and heaven, promotes spiritual attunement and communication with the physical and spiritual worlds

Archangel Uriel – amber – contains warm and healing energy, brings feelings of new life, alleviates stress, promotes calm and peace, bestows wisdom

Some other stones and gems to consider, and how they assist us:

Aventurine – increases intuition and promotes a positive attitude.

Carnelian – motivates us and fosters our feelings of self-worth.

Sodalite – stimulates physical endurance, promotes peace and harmony, and helps writers and public speakers to communicate more clearly. Yes, I have one of these stones!

Rose Quartz – the love stone that attracts romance, marriage, and fertility.

Tiger Eye – a healing stone for emotional issues, relieves doubt and uncertainty, and gives clarity.

Incense burning can be a beneficial tool to use on your altar as well. It's been used for centuries for spiritual and religious purposes.

The most popular incense is made with cinnamon, frankincense, musk, myrrh, or sandalwood. There are sticks, coils, cones, and powders created to deliver all the benefits of those aromatherapies. Burning incense is said to be effective in:

Driving any negative energies

Purifying the area

Effecting a calm and peaceful environment

Encouraging creativity

Strengthening relationships with the Divine

Bringing out joy and gratitude

Aiding in intent, focus, and vision

Manifesting abundance and love

Relieving tension headaches

Boosting immunity

Improving circulation

Having music playing near our altars can calm and relax us, leading to a uniquely focused mindset far from our typical daily thought processes. Music can block out unwanted thoughts and raise our spirits to a surprisingly intense degree.

According to the *Smithsonian Music* website, 'Music and spirituality are intricately related, with spirituality often being the inspiration for the creation of music, and music so often creating the desired atmosphere for a spiritual occasion.'

Of course the music has to be just right for each individual. For me, it has to be instrumental, as I've found that vocals distract me from my inner focus. What's more, the music must be played at a moderate to low volume (so I can clearly hear the Archangels speaking) and the tempo needs to be steady and consistent as opposed to frenzied.

For this purpose, I enjoy classical music from the Baroque era, especially works by composers such as J.S. Bach, George F. Handel, and Archangelo Corelli (of course).

But there are many options out there, especially on the internet, where numerous audios are available with titles like *'The Best Spiritual Music for Relaxation'* and *'Angelic Healing Music.'*

Sometimes though, I find that I need total silence in order to focus and clearly hear my Divine Best Friends. On those occasions, any kind of music strikes me as annoying instead of relaxing, so I simply embrace the quiet.

With practice and experience, you'll discover which of these tools may help you to temporarily shift from your earthly human role to your true spiritual self, ready to savor your own Angelic conversations.

Chapter Eighteen
You're Ready to Chat with
Your Divine Best Friends

Since you're now ready to chat with the Archangels, you'll want to go to your quiet, serene place. Wait until your household members have gone to bed or have otherwise settled down, so you won't be interrupted.

The idea is to temporarily escape your everyday world and its issues, problems, stresses, demands, etc., so you can inwardly focus for a while. Turn off/mute your cell phone, and put it, along with your beloved pets, in another room.

If you can still hear outside activity that may disturb your focus, you can turn on soft music or plug in a white noise sound machine. I find that the consistent tones of my machine block out distractions and help me concentrate when I need it to.

If you feel so inclined, you may light the candles and/or incense on your altar, if you've set one up.

Have your pen and notebook beside you as you settle yourself comfortably. Take some deep breaths, preferably in through your nose and out through your mouth. Relax your muscles. You can position yourself in whatever ways feel right to you.

I usually slouch. Sometimes I prop my wet toenails up to dry, cross my legs, or hang my right foot over my left knee. I probably should sit up straight, but I am more comfortable sprawling. Luckily, I don't need to have perfect posture in order to enjoy a successful flow of Angelic energy and incoming information.

During my first attempt at communicating with the Archangels, I found it wasn't necessary for me to pray to God for protection, ground myself, meditate, center myself, chant intentions, perform rituals, or do anything else in order to safely chat with them.

But this is a personal practice. So if you feel so inclined, you may certainly ask God for his protection to shield you from any dark energies or entities who might try to enter your space, at least until you feel more comfortable.

Fortunately, you will be calling in the bright and loving light of Divine Beings, which is something dark entities wish to avoid at all costs.

If you are concerned with how long a communication session with the Archangels takes and don't have hours to devote to this endeavor, don't worry. Angelic chats do not have to take a lot of time. Many nights my concerns have been addressed, my questions answered, and any confusion cleared up in under fifteen minutes. Other nights, I've been shocked to see that an hour went by while I was totally absorbed in our conversation.

How often should you practice chatting with the Archangels? At first, until you receive clearer communications, every day or every few days works well. After that, whenever you wish. Your Divine Best Friends are always available to you. Some weeks I'll chat with them once or twice. Other weeks it'll be every night. Sometimes three weeks goes by before I return to my Angel journal. The fluctuations of your life will determine that for you.

To be clear, this kind of Angelic communication is not 'automatic writing,' which is a practice where writers voluntarily open themselves up to allowing outside forces, spirits, or entities—dark or light—to guide and physically control the writing process. Those writers' hands are actually directed on the keyboard or with pen and paper to write what the entities want written.

This is quite the opposite. While chatting with the Archangels, you are always in complete control of your own thoughts and awareness, as well as of your hands as they write. Personally, I am not comfortable with the idea of giving that kind of control over to others, no matter what kind of beings they might be, good or malevolent.

The next step in this process is to feel yourself becoming excited. Why? Because it's important to energize your vibration like an expectant child who knows something very special is about to happen. Tapping into that child-like state is the best way to expand all kinds of possibilities.

So, feel your excitement level rising, as it should be. This is not like any other communication you've ever experienced. You are actually joining energies with Divine Beings. When you allow the building of that lovely elation each time, that joy and anticipation, you'll never feel like it's becoming routine or that you're just going through the motions. That would only be a waste of time because it could never lead to the raising and melding of vibrations necessary for successful Angelic chats.

Next, open your heart with love. This takes some practice because our hearts can be very closed off for our own protection in this world. Think of a person or pet that you adore and let that feeling lift you. I simply imagine my heart space lighting up with a warm, golden glow, filling me up, and flowing outward and upward.

Because of how the Archangels honor and respect our free will, if you haven't already, you must now give the Archangels your permission to come into your life for your highest good.

You can call out to them by saying something like, "Dear Archangels, I give you my permission to come into my life, assist me, enlighten me, and be my Divine Best Friends. Thank you."

You only need to do that one time. After that, before each chat you can just say something like,

"Good evening, dear Archangels. Welcome into my space for a chat."

If you'd like, you may ask who has come through to chat with you. Eventually you may receive a name. Also, you may call in the Archangels specifically by name, especially once you've established a relationship with them. The Archangel you've called will often be available at that moment. I call in Archangel Raphael, for example, when there is a health concern I need help with.

Sometimes more than one Archangel will come through in the same chat session. If that happens, they will let you know. They may then take turns answering your questions.

Do not be concerned if the name or names you're receiving are not ones you're familiar with. And it's okay if you can't find the names listed online or in a book of well-known Archangels. As you will recall from Chapter Fifteen, I made that mistake, over and over, with a very loving, patient, and persistent Archangel Jebediah.

However, it isn't necessary to have the Archangels identify themselves. If you're having trouble hearing their names, or don't feel it's crucial to know their names, especially at first, that is completely fine. You can simply refer to them as Archangels, secure in the knowledge that the support, love, and counsel they're providing is what's most important. Later you can, if you wish, develop a deeper relationship with them and discover their names and personalities.

Grab your journal and write the date and day of the week, too, if you'd like. There's no doubt you'll appreciate having your Angel chats recorded in chronological order and dated like a diary.

It's been so illuminating for me to look back over my Angel journals and see which problems I was struggling with during certain times and how the Archangels advised me regarding those issues. They provided many heads-up alerts about what would be happening in my life, and now I can see how accurate they were.

The Archangels can impart very important information that may make no sense at the time. Looking back, though, maybe years later, you will see it made perfect sense. That is why noting the date each time you journal will provide amazing insights.

Sometimes the Archangels would tell me what to expect outright. Other times their vague hints were obviously meant to keep me calm and thinking. In hindsight, I realize that their ability to see the big picture shaped their gentle and loving guidance in my life.

So, you've given them permission and called the Archangels into your space. Now you can start writing and speaking those written words at the same time, asking questions, describing your general problems, or requesting their help with something specific.

Sample questions you may ask to start your Angelic chat session are:

"What messages do you have for me?

"Is there some information you want me to know?"

"I'm feeling hurt about the disagreement I had with George. Why did he say those things? How should I look at the situation?"

"What do I need to learn right now in order to grow in my spiritual awareness? What are my strengths? What weaknesses do I need to work on?"

The possibilities for questions are endless. Ask anything you want. The Archangels are your Divine Best Friends. They know your heart better than anyone, including yourself. They have known the real you— your soul—since you were first created with a loving spark from God.

So don't worry. They don't get offended or shocked by your thoughts or words. They don't judge you or ever get angry, annoyed, or impatient by your heartfelt questions. They simply love you.

Yes, they know you intimately. So don't try to fool them or yourself by pretending to feel something you don't. If you are filled with spite, jealousy, or pettiness, admit it. Be yourself totally, even if you're embarrassed, knowing that you have serious things to work on. We all do. Be honest so they can help you. Ask the real questions you have, not the questions you think they want to hear.

But always ask for their guidance and answers in a positive way and for the highest good for yourself and others. Never ask for help with negative things such as revenge or manipulation of others. The Archangels will only ignore such requests.

Also, remember to take a couple of deep breaths every few minutes or so while you are writing. The Archangels will meld and blend with your energy via your breathing, your openness, and simply the act of writing. Then the messages will become clear and a two-way dialogue can begin.

You may receive long, detailed downloads of information. And you may understand them immediately. What an awesome experience that will be. But it's unlikely, especially at first.

The Archangels know what each of us can and cannot grasp at any given time, so they usually keep their messages practical and straight forward, at least they do for me. And I must admit, I appreciate the plain talk.

At first the messages you receive and write down may seem strange, more like gibberish than coherent sentences. But pretty soon they will make sense. That's because you will be able to tap into your precious sixth sense, which I detailed in Chapter Sixteen, to clearly know (clair-cognizance), clearly hear (clairaudience), clearly see (clairvoyance), or use a combination of those and the other 'clairs' to be able to truly connect with the Archangels. It will come naturally as part of your human make-up. And as with most things in life, practice dramatically sharpens your abilities.

It's gratifying to know that because of your God-given soul and sixth sense, it'll never be necessary for you to obtain another person's spiritual attunement or purchase a session from a spiritual practitioner of any kind in order for you to connect with the Archangels. You already have everything you need within you, to do so.

This is why I don't do Archangel readings for others. I have done a few in the past, but there was something missing; that same strong connection wasn't there as I was trying to make sense of messages meant for someone else. You don't need a third party. You simply need to develop and deepen your own relationship with your Divine Best Friends.

So now that you've asked your first question, breathe deeply a few times. Then begin writing the first things to pop into your mind. Don't evaluate what words you are writing or change them to make sense. They may make no sense at all, similar to my first attempts. Just record them without judgment. Don't worry about misspellings, poor grammar, or punctuation.

You may begin to write the words in all lower-case letters or all capitals or a combination of the two. Just write how it comfortably and naturally flows for you.

Write all the words that are loudly marching or softly meandering through your head. There will be pauses, sometimes for long minutes, when you aren't receiving anything. That's okay; it's building a rhythm, and the words will flow again. In the meantime, take more breaths. Our soul-to-Archangel connection happens within the breathing.

Relax any muscles that might have tightened up, especially around your neck, and write down a fresh question, or something about your day, or about whom you love. Just keep writing anything until you begin again to notice words or phrases coming through to you.

You may wonder if you're just making these words up in your imagination. And maybe those first words or sentences are really from your own mind. But pretty quickly the Archangels will be blending energies with you and only their words will come through. I know it's hard to believe at first. How is it possible that such communication is really happening? It is. Believe it.

In fact, the sooner you trust that you're receiving Angelic messages, the sooner your connection will grow clearer and the sooner you will be able to take comfort in their words. The messages are loving and will leave you feeling stronger and less alone, no matter what challenges you're facing.

So, how can you know that you're talking to Archangels and receiving messages from them instead of hearing your own thoughts or hearing from some unbidden beings who may not have your best interests at heart?

Well, the Archangels only send you messages that are caring, helpful, supportive, insightful, encouraging, and with an eye to your soul's development. They have no egos so they are only concerned with what's best for you.

No matter what issues or problems you present to them, no matter what dumb or egregious things you've done, your Divine Best Friends are in your corner to gently help you understand yourself better. Their lessons, filled with gentle wisdom, are carried out with love and kindness.

If you ever receive words that are blaming, shaming, angry, bullying, punishing, petty, demanding, or fear-inducing, you are not chatting with your Divine Best Friends.

Break off communication immediately by firmly saying, "You are not an Archangel in Heaven whom I have called in. Whoever you are, you do not have my permission to interact with me. Leave my space immediately and don't ever return!"

Because the Universal Law of free will applies to all beings, they will have no choice but to leave. Fortunately, since it is specifically the Archangels that you are calling into your space, the chances of any other beings intruding are very slight. In twelve years of calling in the Archangels, it has never happened to me.

Another way to know you're really communicating with Archangels is in the way they speak, which is often very different than we do. They've been around since the beginning of time, so they're bound to use different words and phrases than you hear in our present-day lexicon. They once told me to 'float above the fray' which is not a phrase I would ever use to describe getting bogged down by my problems.

Sometimes their answers come in rhyming form. For instance, Archangel Sandalphon once answered one of my questions by saying, YOU CAN ACHIEVE GREAT THINGS BY ALLOWING THE BEST OF YOURSELF TO PERMEATE THE REST OF YOURSELF.

My poetry skills are so lacking, I rarely even attempt a 'roses are red' rhyme, so I know the above poem didn't come from me.

The Archangels may also use pet names when addressing you. They often call me 'dear one' and 'our child' when they aren't calling me by name.

Don't be surprised if you experience strong emotions while receiving Angelic messages. You may cry or feel remorseful, frustrated, angry, or exquisitely joyful. I've experienced them all and I cry (mostly happy tears) so often when I'm chatting with the Archangels, I keep a box of tissues within reach.

Conversely, because the Angels have a sense of humor, they have made me laugh out loud more times than I can count. They truly are funny, which wasn't something I expected from Divine Beings. I guess I imagined they would be proper and somber all the time.

Physical sensations may also occur while chatting with the Archangels. You may grow overly warm and sweaty or begin to shiver with icy chills. You may even feel a buzzing or tingling in your head or chest or soft sweeping pats on your chin, head, arms, or shoulders. Flashes of color might come and go at the corners of your eyes.

Whenever such things happen to me, I ask the Archangels if they are, indeed, creating those sensations. They always acknowledge that yes, they are, as part of their communications with me. I love that because it's more clarification that they are right there with me. I am truly being touched by Angels!

It's important to remember that the Archangels look at the big picture of our lives. They possess present, past, and future knowledge we can't even imagine. Therefore, just write whatever you are receiving as you receive it, even if you can't imagine how it relates to your life. It will become clear someday.

If you are having trouble receiving messages, or the messages aren't clear, start breathing deeply again. That should always be the first thing you try.

If that doesn't help, ask the Archangels to please speak louder or slow down. That is something that's helped me many times. Sometimes you may have to request that another Archangel come in to talk to you. You may be able to perceive a different one more clearly, for some reason, at that time.

Take short breaks if your chat session is going on too long or you're getting sleepy. Yawning can be good though, because it's an easy way to get in those nice deep breaths to help foster clearer communications. But sometimes during a chat my eyelids will get so heavy, I'm soon jerking awake with pen still in hand, not realizing I've fallen asleep.

When you feel that the session has reached a good ending place, thank the Archangels for chatting with you. Write and speak your appreciation to them with true gratitude that flutters inside your heart.

At this point, you have asked the Archangels for loving signs or for answers to questions important to you. You have put your concerns and problems in their hands. Now you must trust and believe that they have heard and will acknowledge and answer in their way.

Give yourself a few minutes to absorb insights, impressions, emotions, or information you received. Slowly and gently come back to your normal state of being.

Congratulations! You have just completed your first chat with your Divine Best Friends. Was it amazing right off the bat with clear, profound messages? Was it a total bust, with little information, if any? Or was it somewhere in between?

However it went, consider it the first step in the process. If you didn't get the results you hoped for, try again the next day. And the one after that.

But rest assured, your first chat session with Divine Beings was just the start of what will become the most valuable, profound, comforting, and loving relationship that has ever been or will ever be in your human existence. And there is no exaggeration in that statement, I promise.

Now it's time to be observant. The Archangels will often send signs in your dreams and in your environment that carry messages pertaining to what was discussed in your chat sessions. So be aware; keep your eyes open.

Sometimes the messages are more subtle than other times. Last year, a week before Saint Patrick's Day, I asked Archangel Jebediah to send me a specific sign; I wanted a green heart. Every day I looked around my home, my yard, my neighborhood, in magazines, in videos, but I didn't see a green heart anywhere. This went on for several days. I even told Howard that I was disappointed that I hadn't received my sign yet.

We went to lunch at one of our favorite restaurants the next day, enjoying the warmth from the crackling fireplace next to our table.

While Howard was scanning the menu, I happened to look behind him. I could see into the next dining room, and noticed a rather spindly philodendron growing out of a white clay pot.

"Well, there it is!" I blurted out, happily pointing toward the plant. My hubby turned in his seat to see, then smiled back at me. He got up and strolled over to the plant to take a photo. One of the leaves, shining like a vibrant green beacon, stood out in all its perfect heart-shaped glory. (You can view the color photo at www.debraschildhouse.com.)

So here is a quick review of the steps to take for your best Angelic communications:

Go to your quiet place, without distractions.

Light candles and/or incense on your altar if you have one.

Relax and get comfortable.

Have your pen and notebook/journal with you.

Date your page entry.

Breathe deeply a few times.

Feel your excitement and anticipation building.

Open your loving heart by picturing a golden light growing within your chest.

Give permission for the Archangels to come into your life if you haven't already.

Call out to the Archangels; welcome them into your space.

Breathe deeply a few more times.

Verbalize your questions and concerns at the same time as you write them. Make sure your questions are aimed toward the highest good for yourself and others.

Be open to your own sixth sense abilities via the 'clairs' as you are writing.

Continue taking deep breaths every few minutes as you write, especially if the communication becomes less clear.

Write what you are receiving exactly the way you're receiving it, without edits, even if it's gibberish.

There will be a rhythm to the flow of words you receive that may stop for a while and then restart.

Take a short break if you begin yawning and getting sleepy.

Ask. Trust. Believe. The Archangels hear you and will acknowledge you in their way.

If you feel ready to end the chat session, thank the Archangels, feeling gratitude in your heart.

Take a few minutes to absorb your feelings and return to your normal world.

Be observant. Keep your eyes open for signs and other amazing things to happen in your dreams and in your everyday environment.

Practice chatting with the Archangels often to improve the clarity of your communications.

Bask in the deep love you receive from your Divine Best Friends. Enjoy the incredible things that will be happening in your life.

Chapter Nineteen
Fine Tuning Your
Angelic Connection

If only communicating with the Archangels was as easy as picking up your phone and punching in the right number to hear their voices, like we do with our human best friends. And how glorious it would be to text with Divine Beings, clearly receiving their written guidance during chaotic or frightening times.

But, since few things of value are ever that easy, we'll just have to harness our own inner antennas, believe that it's in our power to do so, and allow the Angelic connections to happen.

Sure, there are obstacles that may hamper your success, but there are also ways to overcome them and fine-tune your communications.

You may be used to maintaining a high level of independence in your life. That might make it more difficult to admit vulnerability and ask for help from anyone, let alone from Divine Beings. If that's the case, please remember that God created the Archangels specifically to help humanity. That is their number one job.

Our Father knew how challenging things could get for all of us on earth, so he designed this loving 'lifeline' for us to be able to tap into if, and when, we searched for such Angelic assistance.

Maybe your religious beliefs are creating a roadblock. You may have studied a form of theological instruction that frowns upon humans developing personal and independent relationships with Divine Beings instead of going through approved prayer channels.

That is something you'll have to examine within your own heart. But you can certainly design your Angelic relationship to be more comfortable, if desired, by praying to God and inviting Jesus, Buddha, Allah, or any other religious figures to join you in the chat sessions. When you believe and make peace with the idea that the Archangels love you deeply and would like a relationship with you, you'll be ready and able to build it.

Another impediment to a successful connection with the Archangels could be that you are a more practical person who tends to see situations and issues in black and white. I'm thinking of my hubby, an accountant and business problem-solver for over forty years, as I write this. Maybe, like Howard, you're not accustomed to going deep within or examining your spiritual side to look for answers. You might feel uncomfortable chatting with Divine Beings you cannot see, and you're just skeptical of the whole concept.

That's perfectly reasonable. Howard had to see the indisputable signs from the Archangels with his own eyes in order to believe. Being a skeptic can be healthy. Those feelings of doubt can protect us from jumping into dangerous or foolish situations. It's wise to take all the time necessary to analyze, evaluate, and educate ourselves, so we can be perfectly comfortable in any new endeavors, spiritual or otherwise.

Whatever resistance you may be feeling to developing your relationship with the Archangels, just know that they are very patient. They will wait as long as you need them to, because they want you to feel ready, secure, and excited about the idea.

And speaking of their patience, when I first began chatting with them, I asked some of the same questions over and over. I guess I was hoping to receive different answers than the ones they'd already given me. Or maybe it was to make sure they really meant what they had said, like a test.

It could also be that I wasn't confident that I'd heard them clearly. Whatever the reason, I did and sometimes still do this. It's a good thing they possess Divine forbearance, or I'd have driven them nuts by now.

One night I asked them why I felt compelled to keep asking these particular questions again and again. Archangel Michael came through with this answer:

YOU WANT A GUARANTEE…A MORE DEFINITIVE ASSURANCE. THAT'S BECAUSE SOMETIMES OUR ANSWERS CAN SEEM AMBIGUOUS, WISPY, AND FLEETING. VERY SORRY, DEAR ONE, BUT THAT IS THE BEST WE CAN DO FOR YOU WITH THE ORIENTATION AT HAND FOR THAT PARTICULAR INTERVAL.

INVARIABLY, WE CAN SEE MORE THAN ONE ANSWER TO YOUR QUESTIONS. THAT IS BECAUSE YOU HAVE FREE WILL, AND WITH THAT POWER COMES YOUR ABILITY TO CHANGE THE OUTCOME IF YOU SO DECIDE.

NATURALLY, IF YOU EFFECT THIS CHANGE, THE ACCURACY OF OUR ANSWERS WILL CHANGE TOO, AS WELL AS WHAT WE SEE FOR YOU ON THE HORIZON. PLEASE TRUST THAT OUR CURRENT ANSWERS ARE ALWAYS REFLECTIVE OF THE BEST INFORMATION WE HAVE FOR THAT TIME FRAME.

And speaking of time, when you ask the Archangels questions that involve units of time, please understand that their answers may not always be accurate. That's because their timeline doesn't match our earthly one. We think in terms of present, past, and future, in linear time. They see multi-dimensionally, which allows for change.

So if you want to know how many days, weeks, months, or years something will take, or what day or month, exactly, something will happen, their answers may be off by quite a bit. Other times, for some reason, they'll hit the bullseye with accurate timing.

You'll never know until it happens, so I have learned to give the Archangels a wide berth when asking a time-sensitive question. I try not to ask for a specific day or date, but ask, instead, if something will happen within a few weeks or a month's time.

There will be times when you need to ask your Divine Best Friends tougher questions that could really impact your life, such as, 'should I get a divorce?' or 'should I make the change to a new job or a different career path?'

For such serious questions, direct answers would be helpful and welcome. However, you may not receive a quick yes or no. The Archangels will not always spoon feed you the answers. Instead, they may guide you, encouraging you to think it through, expending time and effort to figure things out for yourself.

They may even turn the tables and ask you a few questions to promote new insights and help you to understand yourself better. That way, you can make your own best decisions. For better or worse, they cannot make those decisions for you.

You may be asked to rethink your 'same old way' of looking at a situation. That's a good indication that there are smarter approaches you can take, and making changes could lead to more positive outcomes.

Ultimately, any requests to Archangels for help may not be fulfilled for days, weeks, months, or even years in the future. And some requests may never be granted, especially if what we are asking for is not in harmony with our highest good or in alignment with our spiritual paths.

Those declined requests are especially important, though. When we truthfully examine why we might have been denied, and can learn some hard truths about ourselves, it strengthens our self-awareness and promotes our soul's growth.

Our Divine Best Friends sometimes impart very important information that, at the time, may make no sense to you, or even seem contradictory to a situation. I cannot emphasize this enough. Do not dismiss their words outright when they do not jibe with your human understanding of an issue. The Archangels are always, always right.

Please remember the painful lesson I learned, described in Chapter Nine, when the Angels told me that my husband needed steroids to help reduce the inflammation in his right eye. The doctors told me no, that there were no effective treatments for Howard's condition. And instead of believing what my Divine Best Friends said, and doing my own research at that time, I ignored their wisdom and believed in the medical rhetoric and narrow mind-set of the doctors.

Sadly, when I finally did the research for myself, I found out that steroids could well have saved some of the sight in Howard's affected eye. But that medicine had to be administered within a small window of time after the initial incidence of vision loss. And by that time, Howard had permanently lost most of the sight in that eye.

I am not suggesting here that we should only listen to the Archangels and never consult doctors and specialists when we have medical issues. We should, indeed, consult doctors; they can play valuable diagnostic and clinical roles.

And the Archangels play other important roles such as explaining the big picture view of what is wrong, and helping in the healing process. It seems that the best course of action would entail combining information from both sources, whenever possible, to make the most sound decisions.

So if we can just relax and allow ourselves to receive the words from the Archangels and whole-heartedly believe and trust what they are telling us, we will benefit greatly regarding medical issues as well as everything else. We must believe in ourselves and our ability to truly connect with them. I would say that's the single most difficult aspect to communicating with the Archangels—believing we really can.

Without a doubt, though, it is possible to mishear the Archangels during a chat session. And unfortunately, when there are miscommunications, the fault always lies at the human end of the transmission line. We're the ones who are affected by many factors that impede or distort our clear connection.

Some chat sessions don't seem to work well because our energy level is low, impacting our ability to meld with our Divine Best Friends. Maybe we're mentally tired or physically exhausted. We could be depressed, upset, frustrated, or angry about something. Or we could be physically ill with pain, fever, respiratory symptoms, or stomach issues. Whatever it is, it'll affect our concentration and our ability to clearly receive.

There will also be times when, no matter what or how hard we try, we cannot seem to connect with the Archangels at all. The line is dead and nothing comes through. It happens; don't get discouraged.

Sometimes that particular day or time is just not ideal for communicating for reasons we may never understand. When that happens, I've found it helpful to wait a few minutes and try again. I start taking more deep breaths than usual to see if that provides the necessary spark. As the Archangels have explained to me, it's easier for them to meld their energies with ours through our deep breathing. But, if the connection is still not clear, I accept it and try again the next day or night.

That usually makes all the difference. I'm often surprised at how gratifying the 're-try' experience is and how I can now distinctly receive what the Archangels are sending me.

A fascinating discovery I made early on in the process was that I couldn't always distinctly remember what the Archangels had answered and what I had just written down, even immediately after closing my journal for the night. I would have a general sense of how the conversation had flowed and how some of the questions had been answered.

But I often couldn't recall details or specific words they'd shared. So I'd re-open my journal and turn to those pages right away. And there I'd be, eagerly reading their brilliant insights, as if for the first time.

I'm not certain why this happens. Maybe there's something that temporarily affects the memory during the co-melding process between human and Divine energies. Or maybe it's just a phenomenon unique to me.

Either way, now I always read over what I captured during the chat session, relishing the new content before closing the journal for the night.

So how often have the Archangels' predictions about my life been accurate? As I critically examine all of the journals I've kept since February of 2011, I estimate that I have been able to correctly receive their accurate predictions seventy to eighty percent of the time.

Again, it is not an exact science when humans are communicating with Divine Beings. We have to allow for our mortal limitations. However, in my opinion, those are pretty good odds. And, along with their foresight came vital guidance to help me understand what was going on and how to react in the best way possible.

Practice makes a huge difference in so many aspects of our lives, and communicating with the Archangels is no different. As I've explained before, the more you chat with these Angelic Beings, the easier and more satisfying it will be. Even if it's a short session, it will power up your frequency antenna, fine-tune your connection, and strengthen your bond.

That's the real key to this heavenly castle— bolstering your relationship with your Divine Best Friends. Just like with human relationships, spending time and putting in the effort leads to closer ties and ultimately brings huge rewards.

Deepening this sacred relationship can be done in other ways in addition to chatting in your journal. One way is to just imagine that the Archangels are present with you anytime and anywhere. Picture them in the car with you or sitting at the kitchen table while you're cooking or cleaning.

I just know they're smiling at me as I dance around the house to oldies tunes. I imagine the color of their robes, the glow of their wings, and the love in their kind faces.

One of my favorite ways to enjoy my Divine Best Friends is to take a walk with them. Being outside, strolling in the sun or shadows, feeling the crisp or humid winds, deeply inhaling the fragrant bushes and trees, are all natural forms of meditation. It's so relaxing and invigorating at the same time.

I fill my heart with waves of love and golden light and send them outward and upward. Then I call out to a specific Archangel, or to all of them, if I want to. I picture them joining me on my walk, closing in around me. I feel very safe in this blessed company.

If I need to discuss a problem with them, express my gratitude, or there's something on my mind, I just say it. Sometimes I whisper, and other times I speak loudly. If emotions get the best of me, I'll cry a bit. Having these loving Beings join me in my outdoor sanctuary allows me to turn a typical stroll into a blissful connection filled with possibilities.

As I walk, thoughts come into my mind. I don't hear the Archangels in quite the same clairaudient way I do when I'm writing in a chat session. But I do receive information and ideas from them, and most of all, feelings of comfort and peace.

After taking a walk with your Divine Best Friends, I guarantee you will feel better about anything and everything going on in your life, and more importantly, you will have enjoyed another way to fine-tune and deepen your precious connection with them.

Chapter Twenty
Divine Insight for Us All

In this chapter, I've compiled what I believe to be the most awe-inspiring and loving advice, lessons, suggestions, and even some poetry that the Archangels have shared with me over the past twelve years.

There were many treasures to choose from, so I included a few from each Archangel that especially touched my heart. I hope you will find them to be as insightful, comforting, and uplifting as I do.

I like to call these Divine sentiments 'Archangelisms.' Some of these exquisite nuggets have already been presented in previous chapters, taken from chat sessions. Others I rediscovered as I pored over the pages of my many Angel journals.

So here they are—Archangelisms—from our Divine Best Friends with love:

From Archangel Michael

WE ARE HERE FOR YOU FROM GOD. CAN YOU FEEL YOUR HEART'S LONGING? CAN YOU HEAR YOUR HEART CALLING TO YOU? ANSWER IT. IT WANTS LOVE, UNDERSTANDING, AND ACCEPTANCE BY YOU, FOR YOU. HEAR THE ENTREATIES AND LONGINGS OF YOUR HEART, YEARNING FOR YOUR UNDERSTANDING, ACCEPTANCE, AND ABOVE ALL, LOVE.

ACCEPT YOURSELF WITH LOVE, ALWAYS, AND WITH SINCERE APPRECIATION FOR YOUR SOUL'S ETERNAL WISDOM. DO YOU KNOW WHAT ELSE IS WISE? LEAVING BEHIND ANY OF YOUR UNHEALTHFUL OR UNFAVORABLE TRAITS THAT ARE BEING CATERED TO, SO YOU MAY FULFILL THE AUTHENTIC NEEDS OF YOUR OWN SOUL.

BECOME AN AGENT FOR YOURSELF AND OTHERS WITH A CALM, CLEAR MESSAGE OF LOVE. GOD'S LOVE ERASES FEAR. LET THAT LOVE BE SO LARGE AND SO JOYFUL, YOU CANNOT CONTAIN IT. LET IT BE YOUR TRUTH AND YOUR ESSENCE. AS YOU SPEAK TO OTHERS, REMIND THEM OF THE LOVE THAT GOD HAS FOR THEM.

IT MAY NOT DOUSE THEIR WORRIES IMMEDIATELY. THEY MAY BE DUBIOUS OR DOUBT THAT YOU KNOW THE TRUTH. BUT THE WORDS WILL BE ABSORBED ON A DEEPER LEVEL, LIKE A BLESSING. AND THE EFFECT WILL BE FELT IN WAYS THEY MAY NOT REALIZE UNTIL LATER.

IT IS BEST TO AVOID WORRISOME NEWS AND FRIGHTE-NING VIEWS. THE HEADLINES OF THE DAY ARE HANDED

DOWN AMID OPINION AND SPECULATION FACTS ARE OFTEN IGNORED FOR DRAMATICS.

DO NOT ALLOW THIS DISTRACTION TO BE EVEN A SMALL PART OF YOUR DAILY REALITY. INSTEAD, BRING YOUR FOCUS BACK TO YOUR INNER PATH AND RECOGNIZE THE LOVE, LIGHT, AND POSSIBILITIES YOU HAVE AROUND YOU. WITH YOUR CONCENTRATION THERE, YOU CAN CREATE MUCH POSITIVE, TANGIBLE CHANGE.

WE ARE PLEASED THAT YOU DO NOT ALLOW YOURSELF TO COMPLY WITH OTHERS' EXPECTATIONS OF YOU. CONTINUE TO BE BRAVE AND ACT AND SPEAK AS YOUR SOUL IS DICTATING NOW, WITHOUT RUDENESS OR RANCOR, OF COURSE.

IF OTHERS DO NOT APPRECIATE THAT, YOU MAY NEED TO DISTANCE YOURSELF IN ORDER TO HONOR YOURSELF. THAT WILL BE DETERMINED BY THEIR CONDUCT AS YOU PERSIST IN RESPECTFUL DEBATE, HONORING YOUR OWN HEART AND HOW IT SPEAKS YOUR TRUTH.

OUR LOVE WILL BE WAITING FOR YOU WHENEVER NEEDED. JUST LISTEN…WITHIN YOUR STILLNESS…AND WE WILL BE THERE, ALWAYS.

From Archangel Uriel

THE PRIME REASON FOR UNHAPPINESS AND DIS-SATISFACTION IN LIFE IS THAT PEOPLE WANT MUCH MORE THAN THEY NEED. THEY SPEND MANY PRECIOUS YEARS YEARNING, CHASING, AND ACQUIRING. THEIR UNHAPPINESS REMAINS, BUT THEY OFTEN DON'T COME TO SEE THE TRUTH UNTIL THEY ARE AT THE END OF THEIR TIME HERE.

THE TRUTH IS, THE ANSWER IS ALWAYS LOVE. THAT MAY SOUND AS SIMPLE OR DIFFICULT AS THESE CHOICES WILL BE.

FUN IS NECESSARY FOR SPIRITUAL GROWTH TOO. ONE OF THE PURPOSES HERE IS TO EMBRACE YOUR LABORS OF LOVE. THOSE ARE LIFE'S WORKS THAT BRING YOU SUCH JOY THAT YOU DO NOT MIND THE EFFORT OR STRUGGLE ATTACHED TO THEM. THE FUN GENERATED FROM SUCH ENDEAVORS REACHES DOWN TO INVIGORATE THE SOUL.

PLAY RELEASES CREATIVITY, WHICH PROMOTES JOY. JOY INVITES LOVE. LOVE IS THE ULTIMATE SPIRITUAL WORK.

WE UNDERSTAND YOUR NEED TO KNOW AND TO TRY AND PREPARE, WHERE AND WHEN YOU CAN, FOR THE UNEXPECTED. BUT PLEASE RESPECT THE FACT THAT IT ISN'T NECESSARY OR EVEN POSSIBLE FOR YOU TO BE TOLD EVERYTHING YOU WANT TO KNOW, RIGHT NOW OR ANYTIME.

AWAITING THE OUTCOME IS PART OF THE LIVING OF LIFE. THINGS WILL HAPPEN IN THE WAY THEY ARE SUPPOSED TO, REST ASSURED.

WE WILL GIVE YOU THE ANSWERS WHEN WE CAN
ABOUT THE THINGS WE CAN, AND IN THE MEANTIME,
FIRE UP YOUR FAITH AND PATIENCE. LET YOURSELF
RELAX IN YOUR LIFE'S FLOWING.

From Archangel Metatron

FAITH AND BELIEF,
WILL GIVE YOUR HEART RELIEF,
FROM DEEP QUESTIONS AND PAIN,
YOU CANNOT ASCERTAIN,
AND WE MAY NOT YET EXPLAIN.

WE ARE HERE TO SERVE AS YOUR ANCHORS TO THE REAL WORLD. WHICH WORLD IS THE REAL ONE? YOUR EARTHLY WORLD IS TRULY THE ILLUSION. IT SEEMS SO REAL WHILE YOU'RE THERE, WE KNOW, BECAUSE IT'S SUPPOSED TO BE THAT WAY. IT FOSTERS THE LESSONS, ALWAYS MORE LESSONS, FOR YOU TO LEARN.

ALWAYS PROTECT THE FLEDGING FIRE OF HOPE AND JOY IN YOUR HEART FOR THE GOODNESS TO COME. AND COME IT WILL. THE DIVINE LIVES IN YOU—THAT SPARK IS THE TRUE REALITY THAT WILL BRING SOME MORE HEAVEN TO YOUR EARTHLY EXPERIENCE, AS YOU KNOW IT HAS BEFORE.

WHEN YOU CLEARLY FEEL IN YOUR HEART THAT IT IS THE RIGHT TIME TO PROCEED WITH SOMETHING, DO NOT HESITATE. DO NOT FALTER. YOU WILL HAVE ARRIVED AT THE RIGHT TIME TO GO FULL STEAM AHEAD.

BE NOT AFRAID, CHILD, AS THY MAKER SEES THE BIG PICTURE, ALWAYS. GOOD THINGS CAN GROW ONLY WITHIN A GARDEN YOU HAVE FEARLESSLY AND LOVINGLY PLANTED. CREATE THAT GARDEN NOW. AND PLEASE TREAT YOURSELF AS IF YOU LOVED YOURSELF MORE THAN YOU DO—AS MUCH AS WE LOVE YOU.

ASCENDING IS A NATURAL OCCURRENCE WHEN HUMAN SOULS ARE READY. IT IS AN ELEMENTAL PROCESS. TIMING IS WHAT IS IMPORTANT FOR EACH SOUL.

IMAGINE A NEW REALITY FOR YOURSELF. PICTURE IT IN DETAILS; THE BLUES AND PINKS OF LIFE, THE SIGHTS AND SOUNDS AND SMELLS...REMAIN STRONG IN FAITH AND BELIEVE THIS: IF YOU DON'T CONSCIOUSLY CREATE YOUR OWN REALITY, YOU WILL CREATE IT UNCONSCIOUSLY.

From Archangel Gabriel

BE OPEN AND CHILDLIKE IN YOUR DISCOVERIES OF LIFE'S SECRETS. THERE IS MUCH TO UNCOVER, EVEN IN YOUR ADULTHOOD, AND TO BE IN AWE OF. IT REQUIRES A SENSE OF WONDER FOR SUCH FULFILLMENT TO OCCUR.

WHENEVER YOU PRAY YOU SEND A LOVING LIGHT MESSAGE TO THE DIVINE. SO PRAY AND RECEIVE A BLESSING.

SPEAK AND THINK KINDLY TO AND ABOUT YOU. IT IS NECESSARY TO FORGIVE YOURSELF FOR THINGS YOU MAY HAVE DONE IN THE PAST, EVEN WHEN YOU MAY NOT FEEL PROUD OF SUCH CHOICES OR ACTIONS. YOU ARE BEING REMINDED OF THIS FOR YOU ARE A CHILD OF GOD'S GLORY. AND GOD'S LOVE FOR YOU IS OF THE HIGHEST IMPORTANCE.

ALSO, IT IS WISE TO SPEND SOME TIME RELEGATING OLD PROBLEMS TO THE GARBAGE HEAP. THEY SERVE YOU NOT. BE RID OF THEM. PUSH THEM INTO NON-RELEVANCE, SO AS TO APPROACH LIFE IN A FRESHLY BETTER WAY.

TAKE CARE NOT TO PROJECT YOUR FEARS AND FEELINGS ONTO OTHERS, INCLUDING YOUR FAMILY MEMBERS. LET THEM FEEL THEIR OWN FEELINGS AND SEE THINGS FROM

THEIR OWN EXPERIENCE. SUPPORT THEM, INSTEAD OF
TELLING THEM HOW TO FEEL AND WHY TO FEEL IT.

RESIST THE URGE TO TRESPASS SO FREELY UPON THE
GROUND OF THE LIVES OF YOUR LOVED ONES.

From Archangel Raphael

BECAUSE YOU ARE PART OF THE WHOLE, YOU REPRESENT A PIECE OF LOVE FROM ABOVE.

NOT A DAY GOES BY THAT WE DON'T SEE HOW HAPPY THOSE BECOME WHEN THEY REALIZE THEY CAN COMMUNICATE WITH GOD. AND THEY REALLY ALWAYS CAN. PRAYERS ARE ALWAYS HEARD, ALWAYS. AND THEY NOT ONLY HAVE A POSITIVE EFFECT ON THE PERSON PRAYING, BUT THERE IS A SWEET RIPPLE OF CHANGE THAT HAPPENS IN THE HEAVENLY REALMS TOO.

TRY TO REMEMBER THAT PAIN CAN PROMOTE GROWTH AS A CRACK IN AN EGGSHELL PROMOTES NEW LIFE IN THE HATCHING.

REACH TO THE HEAVENS AS WE CAST OUR LOVING HEALING LIGHT ON YOUR HEAD.

HOW PEACEFUL IS THE NIGHT OF AN UNTROUBLED SOUL.

DEAR CHILD, THERE IS MUCH WISDOM THAT COMES FROM SUFFERING. IT CONNECTS YOU TO MORE SPECIFIC AREAS THAT YOU ARE HERE TO EXPERIENCE AND

LEARN ABOUT IT IS NOT MEANT TO BE EASY, YET IT IS SO NECESSARY. AND MOST IMPORTANTLY, IT IS CRUCIAL AS IT WILL BE BENEFICIAL LATER ON AS YOUR SOUL EXPANDS.

From Archangel Sandalphon

YOU CAN ACHIEVE GREAT THINGS BY ALLOWING THE BEST OF YOURSELF TO PERMEATE THE REST OF YOURSELF.

ALWAYS BE THE KINDEST YOU CAN CONCEIVE OF TO THOSE IN YOUR LIFE, AS THEY ARE TRYING TO GET THROUGH TRIALS. BE TO THEM AS YOU WOULD APPRECIATE THEIR FAVOR.

BE THE ONE YOU'D LIKE TO KNOW,
IN ORDER FOR THE PROPER FLOW,
PUT YOUR SWEET MARK ONTO OTHERS,
FOR THEY ARE ALL TRULY SISTERS AND BROTHERS.

WE COULD NEVER GIVE UP ON HUMAN SOULS BECAUSE WE SEE THE TRUTH IN YOUR EXISTENCE. WE SEE PAST EVERYTHING ELSE. YOU ALL POSSESS THE LUMINOSITY FROM GOD, THE SHINING SHARDS OF THE DIVINE DEEP WITHIN, WHICH MESH SO BEAUTIFULLY WITH THE FABRIC OF CREATION AS A WHOLE. AS DESIGNED.

MANY PEOPLE LONG FOR A SPECIAL FORM OF LOVE THAT WILL FULFILL AND HEAL EVERY CORNER OF THEIR EXISTENCE, AND WILL SHINE LIGHT IN ALL THE DARKNESS OF THEIR BEING. THAT KIND OF TRUE LOVE IS FOUND—SO DEEP DOWN INSIDE, LIKE A DEPTHLESS WELL BRINGS UP

THE PRECIOUS WATER OF LIFE—IN A CONNECTIVENESS WITH THE MAIN SOURCE OF ALL TRUE LIGHT AND LOVE. THAT IS GOD.

THAT IS THE LOVE THAT FULFILLS AND HEALS ALL DARK CORNERS AND BEYOND FOR US ALL. AND YOU ALREADY HAVE GOD'S LOVE. EVERY HUMAN SOUL DOES. NEVER FORGET THAT IT'S THERE FOR YOU ALWAYS.

From Archangel Chamuel

AS YOU RELAX AND FOCUS, AND BREATHE DEEPLY, YOU WRITE DOWN YOUR QUESTIONS AND COMMENTS AND SOON YOU ENTER INTO A STATE OF MIND THAT DOESN'T COME NATURALLY TO YOU OR OTHER HUMANS.

THAT'S WHEN YOU ARE ABLE TO GAIN ACCESS TO OUR MESSAGES AND ANSWERS, AND OPEN YOURSELF UP TO YOUR TRUE AND FULL POTENTIAL TO MELD WITH US. YOU ARE ACTUALLY ESCAPING THE BONDS AND LIMITATIONS OF HUMAN THINKING FOR AWHILE.

REMEMBER TO KEEP YOUR ZEST FOR LIFE BY FINDING MORE HUMOR IN THINGS. YOU MUST LAUGH MORE AND MORE. MUCH MORE. IT IS NEEDED. BE FUNNY AND FUNNIER STILL. SEEK FUNNY PEOPLE TO LAUGH WITH. FIND NEW COMEDY FROM A DIFFERENT SENSE OF HUMOR. CREATE YOUR OWN FORMS OF FUNNY. IT IS TIME TO WORK ON THIS. LAUGHTER IS LOVE OF LIFE.

From Archangel Raziel

LAMENT AGAIN AND AGAIN TO YOUR OWN ILL AND THINGS WILL GO POORLY. BUT FIND REASONS TO REJOICE AND YOU CAN ASCEND TO THE THRONE OF HEAVEN'S LOVE, HERE OR ABOVE.

WE BESEECH YOU TO REALIZE THE DIVINE SPARK THAT LIVES INSIDE YOU. GO WITHIN TO FIND YOUR PEACE. IT IS SOMETHING YOU REALIZE FROM DEEP INSIDE. SHOWER IN IT AND LET IT GROW AND SPREAD THROUGH YOUR BEING, LIGHTING YOU UP FROM WITHIN.

THE AMOUNT OF LOVE WE FEEL FOR YOU, IF YOU REALLY KNEW, WOULD CHANGE YOUR ENTIRE WORLD TO ONE OF BLAZING POSITIVITY.

From Archangel Jophiel

HERE'S A GLORIOUS BEAUTY IDEA—WANT TO CREATE A PERFECTLY FLAWLESS FACE? COVER ANY OF YOUR PERCEIVED FACIAL IMPERFECTIONS BY LIGHTING YOURSELF UP WITH A BRIGHT SMILE. NO MORE IMPERFECTIONS.

THOUGHTS ARE FOCUSED ENERGY WITHIN AND OUTWARD. THEY ARE SO IMPORTANT FOR THEY CONVEY MEANINGFUL, SITUATIONAL MESSAGES TO THE SUBCONSCIOUS MIND IN AN ABBREVIATED, YET POWERFUL MANNER.

HOW THOSE MESSAGES ARE PERCEIVED CREATES MINUTE BUT PROFOUND CHANGES THROUGHOUT BODY AND SOUL, SOMETIMES VERY QUICKLY, THAT WILL CAUSE EITHER POSITIVE OR NEGATIVE CONSEQUENCES. THE HUMAN BEING IS PRIMED FOR QUICK RESPONSE UPON RECEIVING SUCH MESSAGES.

SO WHEN YOU ARE DEALING WITH A BIG PROBLEM OR CRISIS, YOUR BODY WILL BE REACTIVE. IT BECOMES EXTREMELY DIFFICULT TO KEEP POSITIVE THOUGHTS FIRING INTO YOUR PSYCHE AND SOUL DURING SUCH A TIME. BUT THAT IS WHEN IT IS MOST IMPORTANT TO DO SO TO PREVENT ANY STRESS-RELATED ILLNESSES AND ANY DAMAGE OVERALL.

JUDGING OTHERS THROUGH THE WINDOW OF SOCIETY'S NARROW FOCUS ONLY HARDENS YOU TO THE WORLD. ALLOW YOUR NATURAL COMPASSION FOR OTHERS TO SHINE THROUGH YOUR BEING. IT WILL BE NOTED AND DEEPLY APPRECIATED ON THE HIGHEST LEVELS.

From Archangel Jebediah

KEEP YOUR GOALS AND DREAMS ENERGIZED BY USING THE POSITIVE THOUGHTS THAT ARE WAITING FOR YOU IN YOUR MIND. THOSE THOUGHTS WILL IGNITE INTO THE GROWTH THAT'S POSSIBLE WHEN YOU HAVE SUCH FOCUS.

DO NOT PERMIT YOUR PEACE OF MIND TO BE STOLEN FROM YOU. LET THE TRIALS OF LIFE WASH OVER YOU, THEN RETREAT, AS AN OCEAN WAVE. RELEASE THE FEAR AND TREPIDATION IN YOUR HEART.

WHEN A DOOR TO YOUR HEART HAS CLOSED, THE ROUTE THROUGH WHICH LOVE FLOWS IS SHUT DOWN IN BOTH DIRECTIONS. LOVE NEEDS TO BE AVAILABLE TO YOU AND FROM YOU. THAT'S ALL THAT REALLY COUNTS.

OUR HOPE IS THAT YOU FOREVER REMAIN CLOSE TO GOD IN YOUR HEART AND THOUGHTS, AND LOVE HIM AS WE LOVE YOU, WITH EVERY PART OF THE MAKE UP OF YOUR BEING.

WE LOVE YOU BECAUSE WE KNOW HOW YOU WERE CREATED. WITH FIBERS AND FILAMENTS OF LIGHT AND ADORATION FROM THE ONE.

EVERY SINGLE SOUL WHO IS OR HAS EVER LIVED ON THE EARTH WAS RIGHTFULLY CREATED WITHIN THE LOVING VENERATION OF GOD.

THERE WILL BE A DAY THAT WILL DAWN WITH THE SHARED REALIZATION OF JUST HOW IMPORTANT YOU ALL REALLY ARE.

REMEMBER, LIFE SHOULD BE PLAYED WITH A PERFECT BLENDING OF REVERENCE, GRATITUDE, AND LAUGHTER.

Chapter Twenty-One
Archangel Help Guide
Whom To Call Upon and When

As you've come to know, each Archangel possesses expertise designed to help us in a specific area or areas of our human experience. If we put an open call out for help to any or all Archangels, we will certainly be covering our bases.

However, it can be a much more profound and intimate experience if we call upon one particular Angel when we're struggling with an issue they specialize in. It strengthens our bond with that Archangel, as well.

I created this chapter for you to use as a quick guide. So please turn to it often to determine which Archangel is best suited to help you in a particular situation.

Archangel Michael

Protection, Safety, Physical and Emotional Freedom, Truth, Justice, Travel

Call upon Archangel Michael:

If you are feeling fearful or under attack, even a psychic attack, or you're worried for your safety and need protection for your body, mind, or soul.

If you'd like for family members, pets, friends, and neighbors to be protected physically, mentally, or emotionally.

If your property and possessions require protection from people, wildlife, or the elements.

If you're tired of being held back from accomplishing your goals by fears, low self-esteem, ego, old karma, physical addictions, or anything else that is keeping you in bondage.

If you are seeking the absolute truth in any situation, even when it's hard to hear, such as in relationships and business dealings, or acknowledging the truth about yourself.

If you or your loved ones are having legal issues with landlords, police, lawyers, judges, lawsuits, etc., and you need the truth to shine through so that justice can be served.

If you or loved ones are traveling by foot, car, bus, plane, train, or ship, near or far, and want the trip to go safely and smoothly from start to finish.

Archangel Uriel

*Wisdom, Knowledge, Studies, Inspiration,
Motivation, Writing, Weather*

Call upon Archangel Uriel:

If you need an infusion of wisdom to help you figure out the best solutions to problems, and what to do during dark and confusing times.

If you are a seeker of higher thinking and need help with studying and understanding difficult principles.

If you desire to learn and remember new things or need a spark in order to come up with fresh ideas and concepts, either alone or when brainstorming with others.

If you need a gentle kick in the pants to inspire or motivate you to quit procrastinating and do something you've been putting off.

If you are a writer, teacher, or a student of any kind and you crave better focus and a higher level of comprehension and creativity.

If you are worried about the weather and concerned with bodily or property damage from rain, snow, ice storms, high winds, severe lightning, or any other dangerous weather-related situation.

Archangel Metatron

*Ascension, Akashic Records, Clarity for Record
Keepers, Negative Energy Clearance, Vibrational
Raising, Spiritual Growth, New Beginnings*

Call upon Archangel Metatron:

If you yearn for understanding and guidance around the ascension process, and how to work your way up to the Heavenly realms.

If you want information and insight regarding your soul's past, present, or future, as well as help tapping into your soul's extensive wisdom, from the Keeper of the Akashic Records, himself.

If you're a bookkeeper, accountant, historian, writer, court reporter, or any other kind of record keeper, and you require accuracy and clarity.

If you need your negative energies and old, limited thinking and beliefs cleared away. The Cube of sacred geometry will rotate, sending you positive thoughts to raise and balance your vibrational energy. The Cube will also rid your mind of distractions so you can more easily focus.

If you would like guidance in seeking higher spiritual understanding and support for your inner growth.

If you need help comforting sensitive children or adults (or yourself) while adjusting to new situations.

If you crave the compassion and loving advice of a Divine Being who used to be human and remembers the struggles, stress, emotions, and pain that can plague all of us.

Archangel Gabriel

Communication, Messages, Dream Interpretation, Parenting

Call upon Archangel Gabriel:

If you need assistance in calmly and clearly communicating your views, and choosing the right words while in conversations with others.

If you want guidance in getting your messages across to others and standing up for yourself, yet still wish to show the kind of positivity that could lead to mutual understanding.

If you wish for better clarity and explicitness when writing emails, letters, articles, books, poetry, plays, lyrics, movies, etc.

If you would like to have your strange or unusual dreams, recurring dreams, or nightmares analyzed, interpreted, and explained.

If you desire help and support in all aspects of parenting from adopting, conceiving, pregnancy, childbirth, and child rearing, to how best to parent adult children.

Archangel Raphael

Healing, Health, Illness, Injuries, Recovery, Relationships, Depression

Call upon Archangel Raphel:

If you are in need of healing, whether it be physical, mental, emotional, or spiritual.

If you require advice regarding diet, exercise, nutrition, sleep issues, relaxation techniques, therapeutic protocols, etc.

If you are ill or suffered an injury and need support for as long as it takes to heal.

If you are about to have a medical procedure or surgery and you're worried about your doctor or surgeon's expertise, and your recovery.

If you are a doctor, nurse, therapist, caregiver, spiritual healer, massage therapist, etc., and you would appreciate assistance with your patients or clients.

If you would like guidance on how to help your marriage or other close relationships be healthier.

If you are struggling with anxiety, depression, addiction, exhaustion, pain, stress, helplessness, or hopelessness, and you crave support and healing.

Archangel Sandalphon

Delivers Prayers to God, Music

Call upon Archangel Sandalphon:

If you don't know how best to pray to God, what words to use, or what things to pray for.

If you aren't sure that your prayers are really being received by God.

If you want deeper concentration when you pray, for a greater connection to God.

If you crave the compassion and loving advice of the other Divine Being who, like Archangel Metatron, used to be human.

If you are playing music or singing praises to glorify God, alone or in a house of worship, and you yearn for a more uplifting experience, a true communication with God.

If you are a musician, composer, singer, or any way connected to music and you wish for heavenly inspired creativity, originality, productivity, finesse, and artistry.

If you would like ideas for adding music, in any way that you choose, to energize your prayers to God.

Archangel Azrael

Dying, Death, Grief, Life's Transitions, Endings

Call upon Archangel Azrael:

If you or a loved one are in the dying process and would appreciate a loving guide to not only ease any fears, but also to help with the transition and accompaniment to heaven.

If you are grieving the death of a loved one, human or animal, and need comfort, support, and consolation to help assuage your suffering.

If you are a grief counselor, spiritual teacher, or a friend who is helping others through their grieving process, and you need to be shielded from absorbing their pain and sorrow.

If you need help going through any of life's transitions, beginnings or endings, new schools, graduation, new jobs, job loss, moving, retirement, loss of friendships, death of family members or friends, or the breaking up of a partnership or marriage, and you feel alone, anxious, fearful, stagnant, or stressed out.

Archangel Chamuel

Peace, Problem Solving, Finding What You Need or Lost

Call upon Archangel Chamuel:

If you are craving peace in your hectic, stormy, over-committed and too-busy life.

If you are shocked and fearful about the chaotic craziness of the world around you and you dream of global calm and unity.

If you are puzzling over a problem and need a brilliant solution.

If you feel like there is something truly missing in your life and you'd like to explore and find what that could be.

If you want to find more favorable options relating to your current situation—a better relationship, true love, or a new job, home, community, car, lifestyle, or hobby.

If you need help finding something, anything you've lost, from important to trivial, whether it be your faith, nerve, marbles, sense of humor, passion, motivation, memory, mojo, appetite, opportunity, or your keys, cell phone, or wallet.

Archangel Raziel

Spiritual Development, Cosmic Knowledge, Strengthens Connection to the Divine

Call upon Archangel Raziel:

If you crave to know your true path and purpose in this lifetime and are seeking guidance to fulfill that purpose.

If you need to heal and move on from painful traumas and memories from the past, even from past lives, which is necessary for soul development.

If you want a deeper understanding of spirituality and the laws of the universe by being connected to Divine wisdom.

If you're looking to boost your psychic abilities and your sixth sense to strengthen your connection to the Archangels.

If you desire guidance in working on your spiritual development toward a stronger connection to God.

Archangel Jophiel

Beauty and Joy

Call upon Archangel Jophiel:

If you would like to see with 'new eyes' to appreciate the beauty in art, nature, landscapes, the sky, your neighborhood, the world, other people, and yourself.

If you need inspiration to think beautiful thoughts, enhancing your creativity and vitality.

If you need help with shopping to find the perfect coat or deciding which outfits, shoes, or accessories enhance your own natural beauty.

If you aren't sure which colors work best for you in makeup, clothing, fabrics, etc., and want help finding out.

If you want to feel happier in your home, create better Feng Shui energy, reduce clutter, and add the right lighting and décor.

If you would love to recapture the wonder, appreciation, and joy of living again.

Chapter Twenty-Two
An Angelic Promise Kept

In March of 2023 I was finishing Chapter Twenty-One, the final chapter of this manuscript, after three years of gratifying work. I felt satisfied that my writing was complete. So I certainly wasn't planning that there would be a Chapter Twenty-Two.

However, something unexpected happened. It was something so perfect in its Divine timing that there was no question that it had to be included. In fact, I'm sure the Archangels knew it would be the best and most loving way to end this Angelic book.

Chapter Twenty-Two brings my story full circle, re-visiting a conversation and fulfilling a promise that began in Chapter Two. That was February 24th of 2011, the second night of the Archangels' first visit with me. It was also the very first time I tried chatting with them and was actually able to hear their answers to my questions.

You may remember, dear readers, that our initial communications began rather awkwardly. I had attempted to speak out loud to the Archangels, asking questions and hoping to hear their answers using my ears as I normally would. When that didn't work, I tried writing down my questions in a spiral notebook, finally saying the sentences aloud as I wrote them.

After a couple of futile attempts, I heard a voice that sounded different from my own thoughts. It was quiet, yet discernable, seeming to come from deep within my right ear. As I scribbled what I was hearing, I worried because those words were far beyond my ability to comprehend.

I decided to ask the Archangels to please speak more plainly to me, because I wasn't good at deciphering deep esoteric concepts. It worked. Their words, from then on, were more down-to-earth, perfectly matching my ability to understand them.

I had asked some light-hearted questions about Jill and David, delighting in the answers I was receiving about my children. But then it was time for me to throw out some heavier questions about things that were concerning me.

So I asked, "Those new body scanners at the airport. I've read how harmful they are, due to the radiation they emit. Our airport here in Tucson isn't using them yet, but Sky Harbor airport in Phoenix is using them, and we fly through that airport sometimes.

"I've tried to avoid excess radiation for years, even shunning most dental x-rays. I don't know—maybe you already know that about me? Anyway, I guess this isn't really a question. But I'd hate to get cancer from a security device. I'm scared for my health and for the health of my family, Angels."

I was amazed that I could hear their answer immediately.

NO NEED TO FEAR AROUND THIS, WE ARE HERE AND WE WILL PROTECT YOU AND YOUR FAMILY IF YOU MUST GO THROUGH SUCH MACHINES.

"Angels, you would do that? You would really shield us from radiation?" As I listened for their reply, my tears of relief and gratitude dripped onto the paper, smearing the ink.

YES WE WOULD, AND WE WILL.

That was when it began to dawn on me just how powerful and loving the Archangels were. Yet, I wondered if it could really be that easy. Did I just have to ask and I'd automatically receive their help and protection? That seemed too good to be true.

And wow, what a beautiful promise I'd just received from my Divine Best Friends. I was touched and filled with gratitude that they had pledged to protect me and my family from those machines.

So, did the Archangels keep their promise?

Fast forward twelve years to March 20th, 2023. Jill and I had an action-packed mother-daughter trip planned. We'd be flying to Palm Springs, California from the Phoenix Sky Harbor Airport.

In those prior twelve years, I had managed to avoid the body scanners, that I refer to as radiation machines, at many airports in the United States. The machines had eventually been changed from the initial backscatter x-ray machines to millimeter-wave scanners, supposedly lower in the radiation exposure to passengers.

Nevertheless, I didn't trust the 'it's safe' hype. No amount of radiation was healthy in my book, so whenever Howard and I flew during our many travels, we always 'opted out' when faced with having to enter one of those machines.

But opting out was always an uncomfortable and inconvenient experience. A TSA (Transportation Security Administration) agent, a female one for me, would be called in, taking anywhere from ten to twenty minutes to appear, and then she would have me stand with my feet apart in front of everyone, and proceed to roughly pat me down in every conceivable place, looking for anything considered a security threat. Not fun at all.

This happened a number of times, even though Howard and I had spent one hundred dollars each, agreed to be fingerprinted, and had passed interviews in order to be issued Global Entry cards, good for five years. We were supposed to be able to enjoy expedited screening through security checkpoints, with no need to take off our shoes or light jackets, remove our laptops and liquids, nor go through the machines or pat down procedures. But sometimes things went awry, and we were chosen for extra security checks.

As offensive as the pat downs were, I still considered them preferable to risking any possible long term health effects from the machines. Opting out protocols were simply what I had to endure, sometimes, in order to get on an airplane.

In the back of my mind, I remembered how the Archangels had promised to protect me from those scanners. But I wasn't ready to call in that favor until I had absolutely no choice. And maybe in those early years of our relationship, I wasn't completely convinced, yet, that my Divine Best Friends would truly be there, shielding me when the radiation started flowing.

Jill's fiancé, Ryan, drove Jill and me to Sky Harbor Airport on the morning of our scheduled trip. I sat comfortably in the back seat of Ryan's

SUV. But as we tooled along with the freeway traffic getting closer to the airport, I became filled with dread.

I could see on my cell phone that for some reason, some twist of fate, my airline boarding pass was not TSA Pre Check eligible. Jill's boarding pass was clearly marked TSA Pre Check. That meant she would be able to breeze through security, going through the expedited lane with ease, while I would be directed to the slow, crowded line of passengers taking off their shoes, taking out their liquids, and being funneled into the scanners.

My heart raced and my mouth was dry as a sandbox. I had a sinking feeling that I would finally have to submit to the radiation machine. I didn't want to opt out and delay our arrival at the boarding gate. And I didn't want to be subjected to a pat down while Jill waited for me. She knew how much the scanners upset me, and she was hoping I'd be directed to a line that sent passengers through a harmless metal detection machine, instead.

So, sitting in the backseat, I did what I always do when I'm worried, upset, scared, or stressed out. It was the best thing possible; I began a dialogue, silently, with my Divine Best Friends.

"Dear Archangel Michael (Angel of protection and travel) and Archangel Raphael (Angel of healing), please help me now. I've got a real problem. As you can see, I'm about to arrive at the airport and I have a feeling the time has come for me to go through a scanner.

"I'm sure you know how I feel about that. I've hated and feared being radiated for many years. It's just something that frightens me to my core. I don't know why I react like this, but it doesn't matter now. What matters is it's about to happen and I don't want to freak out or make a big fuss about it.

"Please help me be brave. As I enter the machine, please be with me, surrounding me with your protection, healing, and love. And please give me a sign that you are definitely with me now. Thank you so much."

As a lump swelled in my throat, I was close to tears, but I held them back as Ryan maneuvered the car toward the busy passenger drop-off area.

"Oh look, Ryan. Over there," Jill said, pointing. "There's an open spot right at the curb."

He pulled into the spot easily, immediately hopping out of the car to unload our luggage from the trunk. Jill gathered some papers and her carry-on bag and opened her door to exit.

I began to follow suit, my fingers reaching for the door handle. But something ahead caught my attention. My eyes widened with astonishment at what I saw through the windshield.

A perfect set of huge silvery Angel wings glittered brightly, the graphics expertly applied on the back windows and doors of the large white van parked in front of us!

The Archangels had done it again; they had come through for me, sending me a sign of their love and support that I couldn't possibly miss. I was overcome with emotion and quietly sent them my heart-felt thanks, too rushed to point out the wings to Jill as she and I hugged Ryan, grabbed our suitcases, and wheeled them through the airport doors.

Yes. I had to go through a radiation machine. And it was no stroll through the daffodils for me, I can tell you. But I only hesitated for a few seconds and I was calm throughout the process. No one could tell by looking at me what a big step this was because I acted like everyone else who made their way to and through the scanner.

Inside though, I truly felt safeguarded knowing my Divine Best Friends were with me, surrounding me with the kind of loving armor that radiation could never penetrate.

Jill was waiting for me, and as I joined her, she studied me carefully to see how I was holding up.

"Oh Mom, you look like you're going to cry. I'm so sorry you had to go through the scanner. Are you okay?"

"I'm fine, honey. I'm not feeling emotional because of the scanner. I'm just so grateful to the Archangels. Let's walk to our gate and I'll tell you all about it."

Jill and I enjoyed a fantastic week-long trip driving up the California coast. We spent time in and around the beautiful areas from Palm Springs to Santa Barbara, to San Luis Obispo.

We flew home from the San Luis Obispo airport, where we breezed through security, as both our boarding passes, this time, were clearly stamped with the words TSA Pre Check.

I looked over at the area where passengers were taking off their shoes, pulling out their liquids, and being funneled through a radiation machine. And because of the promise my Divine Best Friends had made to me and kept, I knew that if I ever had to go through a TSA scanner again, I'd have nothing to fear.

Conclusion

April 20, 2023 – "Good evening, dear Angels. I've got some big news, although I'm sure you know already. This is an exciting night for me. I finally, just now, finished writing the manuscript for this book. Welcome in, all of you, to help me celebrate this special occasion.

"As you so well know, I've been working on this manuscript for quite a while. Right now, unedited, it's about sixty-five thousand words and twenty-two chapters.

"At least I think I'm done writing, dear Angels. Since this book is all about you and the sharing of your love and wisdom over the years, I want to know if you feel that I have adequately covered everything you hoped I would. Or should I add more? Also, who is here to chat tonight?"

ANGEL URIEL HERE. HELLO AND CONGRATULATIONS FROM US ALL, DEAR DEBRA. YOU DID IT! YOU WORKED VERY HARD, ESPECIALLY THE LAST YEAR OUT OF THE THREE YEARS SINCE YOU BEGAN TO SIFT THROUGH YOUR JOURNALS TO CREATE THIS BOOK.

AND WE ARE DELIGHTED. WE APPLAUD YOUR WORK EFFORTS GREATLY. TAKE HEART. YOU DID A GRAND JOB AND WE ARE VERY PLEASED AT THE FINAL OUTCOME.

YOU DO NOT NEED TO ADD ANYTHING. YOU HAVE COVERED EVERYTHING WE DESIRED AND MORE. YOU ARE DONE WITH THE WRITING ASPECT OF THIS BOOK.

"Thank you all so much. My heart is very full. And my gratitude is overflowing right now. Obviously, I couldn't have done it without you.

"Angel Uriel, as the Archangel of writers, you've given me motivation, focus, and clarity so many times during this journey, and it means a lot. And even now, you've given me the reassurance that I am, indeed, done with the writing.

"Thank you all, dear Archangels, for sharing your wisdom, compassion, ideas, and insights with me over the years. Not just toward the creation of this book, but in my day-to-day existence. And I look forward to receiving more and more from you until the end of my life, and beyond.

"Thank you all for being so available over these years and eager to help me with any matters, overwhelmingly large or ridiculously trivial.

"And thank you, beloved Archangels, for the incredible amount of support, comfort, and love that you give me and will be giving my dear readers when they, too, invite you, their Divine Best Friends, into their lives."

WE ARE FILLED WITH THE LOVING LIGHT OF GOD. AND WE ARE HONORED TO SHARE IT WITH ALL OF YOU.

Acknowledgments

To Howard—how did I ever get so lucky having you for a husband, life partner, and my biggest fan for half a century? I'm so blessed and grateful for your love and support.

To Jill—my darling daughter, thank you for your love, encouragement, and writing advice. And thank you for allowing me to write snippets from your life into my books. Our close bond lifts my soul daily.

To David—my awesome son, thank you for being so deeply caring and supportive. And funny, too … you've been able to make me laugh like no one else since you were a boy. It's a form of love I'll forever appreciate.

To Mel Fink—my remarkable big sister, thank you for your excitement about this book and your love and moral support whenever I've needed it throughout my life.

To Shelley Holtzman Kipner—my sweet 'little sis.' We bonded over fifty years ago and made it through a mutually dark time in our lives. I want to thank you for your unwavering love and support for my writing as well as for everything else in my life. And thank you for reminding me how Archangel Uriel, Angel of Light and Weather, became my brightest lifeline during a dark desert storm last fall.

To Madeline Friedman—thank you so much for inviting me and a group of lovely people into your home on several occasions so I could teach them how to chat with the Archangels. Their success and excitement was awe-inspiring, confirming to me that everyone can, indeed, connect with their Divine Best Friends.

To Melanie Pelchat—I'm very grateful for our special friendship and our shared Angelic connections. They've been such a source of joy over the years. Thank you for believing in me, in this book, and in the Archangels themselves, who had such fun sprinkling your world with feathers...sending you their loving hellos.

To Melissa Joyce—your pure enthusiasm for this book, even early on in the process, and your gentle, uplifting support through the journey kept me believing I really could write it and do it justice. Your beautiful spirit is a soothing, healing balm, my friend. Thank you so much.

To Jen Rinaldi—we have so many interests in common, the best, of course, being the Archangels! Thank you for your caring support and for being such a terrific listener. And thank you for sharing your deep understanding, as an author, of what writing journeys are all about.

To Mariann Falcetti, Susan Franke, Jan Arnold, Wylie Glad, Tess Durfee, Margie Basney, and Lynn Renard—thank you, awesome ladies, for being my much needed and appreciated cheer leaders, always showing your interest and asking how the writing was going. Your excitement for the subject matter and eagerness to read the book motivated me more than you know.

To Bill Gladstone and Josh Freel with Waterside Productions—thank you for another great collaboration through the publishing process. I know you take special interest in books that help people, and I'm grateful that this book will do so in many ways.

To Kenneth Fraser—thank you for designing my book cover. I really wanted to use the Cloud Angel photo on the cover and you made it happen beautifully!

About the Author

Debra Schildhouse is the author of *Bio-Touch: Healing With The Power In Our Fingertips*. She loves to read, write, listen to classical music, and spend time with her family. Delighted by having regular chats with Archangels since 2011, she wants to teach others to do so, so their lives can be dramatically enriched by the love and support of their Divine Best Friends. Debra is the mother of two grown children, and she lives with Howard, her husband of nearly fifty years, in the White Mountains of Arizona.

Printed in Great Britain
by Amazon

33597135R00136